JUDAISM

Cover art by *Terry Doerzaph*

JUDAISM

By Jay G. Williams

This publication made possible with the assistance
of the Kern Foundation

The Theosophical Publishing House
Wheaton, Ill. U.S.A.
Madras, India/London, England

This is a Quest original, published by the
Theosophical Publishing House,
a department of the
Theosophical Society in America.
Inquiries for permission to reproduce all,
or portions of this book should be addressed to:
Quest Books
306 West Geneva Road
Wheaton, Illinois 60187

Lib. of Congress Cat. in Publication Data

Williams, Jay G   1932-
    Judaism.

        (Quest books)
        Bibliography: p.
        Includes index.
        1. Judaism-History.   I.   Title.
BM155.2.W54   296'.09   80-51551
ISBN 0-8356-0540-X (pbk.)

Printed in the United States of America

CONTENTS

Passover, known in Hebrew as Pesach, is celebrated in the Spring, at the time of the first full moon of the lunar year. Ancient Israel took over motives from both an ancient agricultural festival of unleavened bread (Matsos) and a shepherd's sacrifice of Spring lambs (Pesach) and wove them into the fabric of her own historical memories. Passover commemorates the time when the Angel of the Lord smote the first born of the Egyptians but passed over the houses of Israel, which were marked by the blood of a lamb. (See Exodus 12:1-51)

Today, Jews no longer sacrifice lambs to God, because the temple is destroyed. Instead families meet together to share the traditional Seder meal and to remember once again God's salvation of Israel. Depicted above are the Seder plate and the cup of wine drunk four times during the celebration. A fifth cup of wine and a place at table are reserved for Elijah who will return to herald the Messiah and resolve all disputes in the Law.

INTRODUCTION

The purpose of this volume is simple; it is to introduce the interested reader to the major men and movements of the history of the Jews. How does this history differ from the several other competent accounts already available? What are its essential characteristics?

First, the history itself is intentionally brief. That is, it is written for the person who wishes to gain an overview of a most complicated subject in one or two sittings. Second, unlike most general surveys of Jewish history, it is written by a non-Jewish historian of religion who has no particular apologetic purpose and hence may present the basic material from a somewhat different perspective. There is little attempt to argue for or against Judaism, though the approach is certainly meant to be sympathetic. Third, the aim is to give a thumb-nail sketch of both mainline Rabbinic Judaism and those other, dissident, movements which may have occasionally emerged during Judaism's long history. The Talmud is not forgotten, but neither are the Zohar and Sabbetai Zevi.

Basically, then, this is not a work designed to offer some new thesis or to turn over virgin research soil. What are given are basically the central, generally accepted facts. This is simply an attempt to bring into focus the major events of Jewish history for the person who asks, "What is the history of

Judaism all about?" The aim is not to satisfy such curiosity completely but to lead the reader to a point where more specialized study may be profitable. Selected bibliographies for each chapter are provided to facilitate further exploration.

Accompanying the historical survey is a compendium of documents and extracts designed to illustrate and enlarge upon each chapter of Judaism's history. Some of the items are of an historical nature; others are philosophical and/or theological. Some are by Jews, others express opinion about them. When dealing with intellectual figures an attempt has been made to provide whole sections of a work rather than just snippets. In order to do that the anthology tends to concentrate upon certain questions treated by a wide variety of thinkers rather than upon the whole spectrum of philosophical questioning. This anthology tends to emphasize questions related to the authenticity of revelation as well as Judaism's mystical tradition. It is hoped that this collection will be useful both for teachers offering a course on Judaism and for the individual reader.

Some may object to the fact that our documented history begins, not with Abraham and the Patriarchs, but with exiled Jews returning home from Babylonia in the sixth century B.C. This point of departure has been chosen for two reasons: 1) The Biblical period is so extraordinarily complicated that any attempt to deal with it would extend our history unduly and, 2) until the fall of Jerusalem in 587 the religion of Israel was primarily a national culture, not a world religion. Only after the exile and the return of the Jews to their land is it appropriate to speak of Jews and Judaism. If the reader finds the lack of knowledge about Biblical history too confusing, Chapter 4 of the author's *Understanding the Old Testament* (Barrons, 1971), is recommended for further study.

Our story, which begins about 538 B.C., is divided into four, approximately equal, 500-year time periods. For each, it is a non-Jewish figure (Cyrus, Pompey, Mohammed, and the Spanish king, Ferdinand), who acts as a punctuation mark. This, in itself, is significant for it indicates that our account is about the interaction of a distinct and separate people with those worldly powers which continually have molded Israel's existence.

From the beginning, the ship of Jews seems to have blown perilously between the Scylla of assimilation and the Charybdis of annihilation. Conversely, the "Gentiles" have alternatively been attracted and then repelled by the marvels and mysteries of Judaism. Seldom have the Jews been able to sail for long with an even keel between these twin threats to their existence. Again and again they have come close to disaster. Never, however, has assimilation become so completv that their identity has been destroyed nor annihilation so absolute that the people could not continue. Each tragedy has been succeeded by an hour of glory; each triumph, by the shadow of despair.

This, then, is not just a factual story to be retold for the satisfaction of idle curiosity. The history of the Jews reveals more than a little about sin, suffering, and the capacity of human beings to endure. It is a story to be recognized and understood particularly by Christians, for throughout much of the drama Christianity appears, not as a loving, suffering friend, but as the persecuting enemy. The history of the Jews reveals a side of Christendom which most of us do not like to remember; yet it is a deep shadow which must not be forgotten. Perhaps the Jews have more to teach Christians about the meaning of the cross than all the systematic and dogmatic theologians put together, for in their very lives they have revealed what sin and grace are all about.

There is no need to moralize, however; the facts speak for themselves. Let us then begin our temporal journey by returning to the sixth century B.C. and to that moment of rejoicing when the Jews were, after a period of exile, released from bondage.

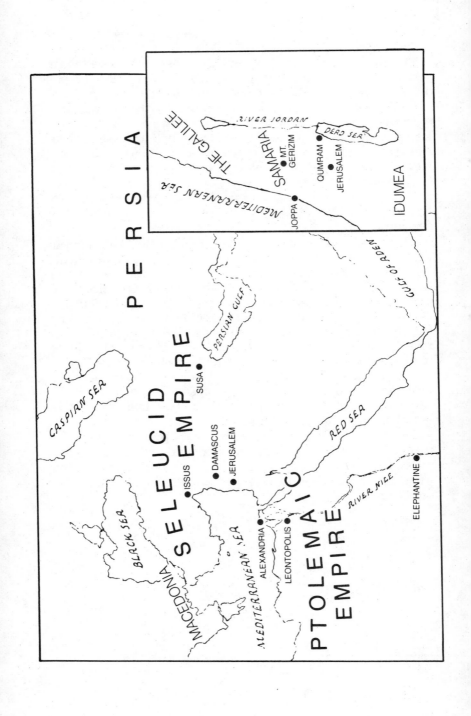

1

FROM CYRUS TO THE
LAST OF THE HASMONEANS
(538 – 63 B.C.)

In the year 538 B.C., a band of eager travelers set out from Babylonia for what the Persians called "the Satrapy Beyond the River," but which Israel knew as the land of their forefathers. These were no ordinary caravaneers setting out in search of merely pleasure or profit; they were members of an exiled community of Judeans returning to their homeland, the district of Judah, after years of forced absence. Since the days of desolation in 587 B.C., when Jerusalem fell and was razed by the Babylonian army, many Judeans had been required to take up residence in the Mesopotamian region. Now, after years of yearning and dreaming, the day of destiny had arrived. At least a few hardy souls, out of the many who lived in Babylonia, were returning home.

Cyrus, the Persian king, fresh from his victories over the crumbling regime of the Babylonian Emperor Nabonidus, proclaimed release for the captives of his enemy. According to Ezra 1:1-11, he supported Jewish endeavors by promising public funds for the rebuilding of their sacred shrine, the Temple of Jerusalem, and by guaranteeing the return of the sacred objects stolen from it before its demise under the forces of Nebuchadrezzar.

In so doing, Cyrus showed no particular love for, nor appreciation of, the heritage of Israel. His action was simply an expression of his general plan of founding his new empire upon a policy of goodwill and ethnic pluralism. The Temple was regarded as but one more public building within his realm for which he was responsible. Doubtless he granted the same sort of privileges to many other national groups which had also been transplanted by the Assyrians and Babylonians in order to cool indigenous revolutionary ardor. His action, however, paved the way for a whole new religious era. The seed which he allowed to be planted in the Holy Land eventually flowered into the religion of Judaism and from Judaism, in turn, fell the seeds from which both Christianity and Islam sprang.

To the untutored eye, this band of travelers probably appeared quite unexceptional. Caravans were as common then as jet flights are today. What the external observer could not see, however, was the unique baggage which these men and women carried—not on donkey-back but in their minds and hearts. The returning Judeans were heirs of an old and luminous tradition which stretched back in the past to the third millennium B.C. Not only had they retained memories of their ancestors from ancient days; they believed that in the history of their forefathers was revealed the very key to the meaning of existence. Israel was the chosen nation, chosen as God's treasure among the nations, chosen to be his light to the Gentiles. The people of Judah were returning home according to his will, to do his will.

This is neither the time nor the place to review in detail the memories of Judah nor to assess to what extent those recollections conformed to historical facts as we now know them. Perhaps it is enough to listen to the words of the great scribe, Ezra, who, upon returning to the homeland in the 5th Century, confessed his faith in the following way:

> And Ezra said: "Thou art the LORD, thou alone; thou hast made heaven, the heaven of heavens, with all their host, the earth and all that is on it, the seas and all that is in them; and thou preservest all of them; and the host of heaven worships thee. Thou art the Lord, the God who didst choose Abram and bring him forth out of Ur of the Chaldeans and give him the name Abraham; and thou didst find his heart faithful before thee, and didst make with him the covenant to give to his descendants the land of the Canaanite, the Hittite, the

Amorite, the Perizzite, the Jebusite, and the Girgashite; and thou hast fulfilled thy promise, for thou art righteous.

And thou didst see the affliction of our fathers in Egypt and hear their cry at the Red Sea, and didst perform signs and wonders against Pharaoh and all his servants and all the people of his land, thou didst get thee a name, as it is to this day. And thou didst divide the sea before them, so that they went through the midst of the sea on dry land; and thou didst cast their pursuers into the depths, as a stone into mighty waters. By a pillar of cloud thou didst lead them in the day, and by a pillar of fire in the night to light for them the way in which they should go. Thou didst come down upon Mount Sinai, and speak with them from heaven and give them right ordinances and true laws, good statutes and commandments, and thou didst make known to them thy holy sabbath and command them commandments and statutes and a law by Moses thy servant. Thou didst give them bread from heaven for their hunger and bring forth water for them from the rock for their thirst, and thou didst tell them to go in to possess the land which thou hadst sworn to give them.

But they and our fathers acted presumptuously and stiffened their neck and did not obey thy commandments; they refused to obey, and were not mindful of the wonders which thou didst perform among them; but they stiffened their neck and appointed a leader to return to their bondage in Egypt. But thou art a God ready to forgive, gracious and merciful, slow to anger and abounding in steadfast love, and didst not forsake them. Even when they had made for themselves a molten calf and said, "This is your God who brought you up out of Egypt," and had committed great blasphemies, thou in thy great mercies didst not forsake them in the wilderness; the pillar of cloud which led them in the way did not depart from them by day, nor the pillar of fire by night which lighted for them the way by which they should go. Thou gavest thy good Spirit to instruct them, and didst not withhold thy manna from their mouth, and gavest them water for their thirst. Forty years didst thou sustain them in the wildernHss, and they lacked nothing; their clothes did not wear out and their feet did not swell. And thou didst give them kingdoms and peoples, and didst allot to them every corner; so they took possession of the land of Sihon, king of Heshbon, and the land of Og, king of Bashan. Thou didst multiply their descendants as the stars of heaven, and thou didst bring them into the land which thou hadst told their fathers to enter and possess. So the descendants went in and possessed the land, and thou didst subdue before them the inhabitants of the land, the Canaanites, and didst give the land into their hands, with their kings and the peoples of the land, that they might do with them as they would. And they captured fortified cities and a rich land, and took possession of houses full of all good things, cisterns hewn out, vineyards, olive orchards and fruit trees in abundance; so they ate, and were filled and became fat, and delighted themselves in thy great goodness.

Nevertheless they were disobedient and rebelled against thee and cast thy law behind their back and killed thy prophets, who had warned them in order to turn them back to thee, and they committed great blasphemies. Therefore thou didst give them into the hand of their enemies, who made them suffer; and in the time of their suffering they cried to thee and thou didst hear them from heaven; and according to thy great mercies thou didst give them saviors who saved them from the hand of their enemies. But after they had rest they did evil again before thee, and thou didst abandon them to the hand of their enemies, so that they had dominion over them; yet when they turned and cried to thee thou didst hear from heaven, and many times thou didst deliver them in order to turn them back to thy law. Yet they acted presumptuously and did not obey thy commandments, but sinned against thy ordinances, by the observance of which a man shall live, and turned a stubborn shoulder and stiffened their neck and would not obey. Many years thou didst bear with them, and didst warn them by thy Spirit through thy prophets; yet they would not give ear. Therefore thou didst give them into the hand of the peoples of the lands. Nevertheless in thy great mercies thou didst not make an end of them or forsake them; for thou art a gracious and merciful God.

Now therefore, our God, the great and mighty and terrible God, who keepest covenant and steadfast love, let not all the hardship seem little to thee that has come upon us, upon our kings, our princes, our priests, our prophets, our fathers, and all thy people, since the time of the kings of Assyria until this day. Yet thou hast been just in all that has come upon us, for thou has dealt faithfully and we have acted wickedly; our kings, our princes, our priests, and our fathers have not kept thy law or heeded thy commandments and thy warnings which thou didst give them. They did not serve thee in their kingdom, and in thy great goodness which thou gavest them, and in the large and rich land which thou didst set before them; and they did not turn from their wicked works. Behold, we are slaves to this day; in the land that thou gavest to our fathers to enjoy its fruit and its good gifts, behold, we are slaves. And its rich yield goes to the kings whom thou hast set over us because of our sins; they have

power also over our bodies and over our cattle at their
pleasure, and we are in great distress.

— Nehemiah 9:6-37

Ezra's words have been quoted at such great length because
they provide a good summary of Biblical history as it was
understood by post-exilic Jews and because they express the
mood of so many people of the time. A number of features of
this confession bear emphasizing:

First, the faith of Judaism which Ezra expresses is an
historical faith which underlines the divinely-sanctioned relation between the people and the promised land. The return to
Judah is not just for convenience or profit; it is a matter of
destiny. The mystery of Israel is wrapped up in her relation to
the land that God promised to Abram and gave into the hand
of Joshua.

Second, although God is conceived to be particularly concerned with the people of Israel, he is also regarded as the
universal lord of heaven and earth. Somehow, Israel's history
is central for the whole of human life. Creation and election are
interrelated. Israel's role among the nations has cosmic
significance.

Third, there is a strong sense that Israel before the exile
went astray, sinned, and brought doom upon her own head.
The exile just endured was no mere accident; it was God's will.
Now the Jews—that is, the people of Judah—are being given
another chance. This time the law must be obeyed so that
things will go better.

Fourth, the return has not brought the paradisaical age of
peace and joy promised by the prophets. Judah is still the
"slave" to external political powers. Ezra is keenly aware that
Judah's future depends upon God, but he also indicates that if,
this time, the people are fastidiously obedient to the Law, God
will express his love to them once more.

The Judaism born out of the ashes of the destroyed Israelite
kingdom, then, is a religion of memories: memories of God's
promises and their subsequent fulfillment, memories of the nation's sins and the resulting punishment and, finally,
memories of those prophetic promises for a great and glorious
day when all those shattered hopes of the past will be fulfilled.
The travelers return to the destroyed land, intent upon obeying the law and filled with hope for a new day.

Because of the lack of historical documentation, our knowledge about their actual experiences in the homeland is very limited. Only occasionally do our sources grant us a glimpse of this struggling Jewish community.

According to the book of Ezra (2:64-65), some 42,360 Jews plus 7,337 servants and 200 male and female Temple singers returned to Judah that year, but most scholars believe these numbers to be greatly exaggerated. No matter what the number, the group surely did include Sheshbazzar, a prince of Judah, Zerubbabel, a descendant of David, and Joshua, the high priest. These men, who became the leaders of the new community, soon began the monumental task of rebuilding.

We do not know how many "people of the land" were there to greet them, but surely there must have been descendants of those left behind by the Babylonians living in the land. It is clear that there was a sizeable community of people located in Samaria who believed themselves to be members of the house of Israel. Many of these, however, were actually the descendants of non-Israelite families who had been exiled in the north by the Assyrians. They had converted to the religion of the area but had also retained many of their old pagan practices. Hence, the Judeans looked down upon them as religious anomalies. Eventually, the descendants of these folk became the Samaritans, a community of believers who revered the Torah but regarded Mount Gerizim and not the Temple of Jerusalem as its central holy place.

When the returnees refused to allow these northern neighbors to participate in the rebuilding of the Temple in Jerusalem, serious tensions emerged and the Jews were obliged to cease their work. Hence, although sacrifices were offered at the site, no Temple was constructed until 520 B.C. In that year, two prophets, Haggai and Zechariah, arose to urge the rebuilding of "God's house." As a result of their preaching, work was reinitiated and in 515 B.C. a somewhat diminutive holy place was completed. The era of the second Temple had begun.

A curtain then falls upon the history of the people and we are told almost nothing about them for the next fifty years. We can be quite sure, however, that little Judah existed as but one district in a much larger satrapy with central offices in Damascus and with regional officials in Samaria. The Jews had returned but were by no means politically free.

Nehemiah and Ezra

When the stage of history is again illumined, certain changes have clearly taken place. In the age of which we have just spoken, a son of David seems to have been at the helm politically. Indeed, Haggai describes Zerubbabel in highly Messianic terms and expresses the belief that he will soon restore the kingdom of old. Now, in the fifth century B.C. the Davidic line has lost its immediate political importance; political control is in the hands of a governor appointed by the Persians.*

Haggai and Zechariah themselves represented the revival of the prophetic office which had, in earlier times, been so important in the history of Israel. When we reach the age of Nehemiah and Ezra in the mid-fifth century, prophecy appears to be a thing of the past. To be sure, men like the authors of Isaiah 55-66, Zechariah 8-14, and Malachi may have proclaimed their messages during the period between Haggai and Nehemiah, but they were, by and large, only pale reflections of the earlier prophets. They do remind us, however, that conditions during the early days of resettlement were hard, cruel, and often desperate. Return had brought poverty, not fulfillment; struggle, but little joy. Judah remained but a tiny bubble in the midst of a vast Persian Sea. The Messiah had not come, the new covenant promised by Jeremiah (Jer. 31:31) had not been enacted; the glory of the Lord seemed peculiarly absent. A great sense of disenchantment pervaded the community as a whole.

It was into such a situation that Nehemiah came in the fifth century. Unfortunately, the books of Ezra and Nehemiah seem to be chronologically confused and are difficult to reconcile historically. Following John Bright *et al* however, it seems safe to say that Nehemiah preceded Ezra and was the first to institute reforms in Judah.†

Nehemiah, a Babylonian Jew, was cup-bearer to King Artaxerxes I in Susa, the capital of the Persian Empire. While

---

*John Bright, *A History of Israel* (Philadelphia: Westminster Press, 1959), pp. 375-386.

†Bright, *History of Israel.*

serving in that important capacity, he met with a delegation from Judah which informed him about the wretched conditions prevailing in the homeland. Concerned about his people, Nehemiah informed the Emperor of the situation and requested that he be allowed to travel to Judah to serve as Governor. His wish was granted and in 445 B.C. he arrived in Jerusalem.

Despite strong opposition from the half-Israelites of Samaria, Nehemiah was able to rebuild the walls of Jerusalem and to institute civil reforms. In particular, he successfully attacked the abuses of the nobility and freed the poor from their economic slavery. After several years of vigorous activity, he returned to the Persian capital.

His sojourn in Susa, however, was only temporary, for again he made the arduous trek back to Palestine, apparently bringing with him Ezra, an Aaronite priest, who continued the reforms and established new patterns of life. Ezra is said to have read the Law before the people and, having convinced them of their sins, instituted much stricter observance of the Sabbath, a Temple tax, and a better organized system of offerings. He also attacked marriages to foreign women and commanded all those involved in mixed marriages to divorce their pagan spouses. Clearly, Ezra believed that the Jews, to survive, had to accentuate their religious and social distinctiveness.

Although comparatively little is said about Ezra in the Bible, the Great Scribe kindled the imagination of Jews in succeeding generations. Around his name clustered a host of imaginative traditions. According to Mishnah, which shall be described in chapter 2, Ezra founded the Great Synagogue, the predecessor of the Sanhedrin, and initiated the tradition of the *sopherim*, the scribes. These "Men of the Book" sought to interpret and clarify the Law, making its requirements clear and exact for the people. Although we have no historical evidence for the existence of the legendary Great Synagogue, there are indications that the *sopherim* did get their start at, or shortly after, this time.

Later writers were also to turn Ezra into a visionary figure who, among other things, recovered the books of the Law which had been burned by the Babylonians, receiving them from an angel during an ecstatic vision (II Ezra 14:37ff).* To what extent he was actually responsible for the final canonization of the first five books of Moses (the *Torah*) we do not know, but many scholars, though obviously doubting the story about angelic revelation, believe that not long after his time, the Torah, that most authoritative part of the Hebrew Scriptures, attained its final form and was canonized.

Conservative scholars, of course, demur, arguing that the Torah had been the sacred possession of Israel since the time of Moses. Surely there is some truth to that assertion, for the "Five Books of Moses"—Genesis, Exodus, Leviticus, Numbers, and Deuteronomy—contain many ancient reminiscences from the times of the Patriarchs and Moses. Nevertheless, it is also clear to those unblinded by dogmatic presuppositions that the traditions of the Torah evolved over the centuries, receiving fresh insights from many successive generations. Not until the fifth century did that process of development and growth finally cease. At that time the living tradition came to be fixed forever on five scrolls and Judaism became the religion of the Book.

Also ascribed to Ezra are the two books of Chronicles, Ezra, and Nehemiah. Few modern scholars uphold his authorship, but it does seem reasonable to believe that these works were written not long after his time and embody much of his spirit. Chronicles, which offers a history of Israel that parallels the books of Kings, emphasizes throughout the importance of the priesthood, the Temple, and the cultus. Even David is seen primarily as the pious planner of the Temple rather than as a military man. In a sense, Chronicles points forward to Ezra himself as the refounder of the purified cult and hence a "new David."

Ezra has often been considered by non-Jewish scholars as the one preeminently responsible for transforming Judaism into a narrow-minded, legalistic faith which rejected the Gentiles with abhorrence. Such, however, is itself a narrow-minded judgment, for in retrospect it seems obvious that it was Ezra,

---

In the Roman Catholic canon II Ezra is named IV Esdras.

through his emphasis upon obedience and good order, who saved Judaism from oblivion. He and Nehemiah gave to the people a sense of pride and purpose which was to override their natural despair and which kept them faithful during the days when national hopes seemed dim. Furthermore, the book of Jonah and much of the post-exilic wisdom literature reveal that Judaism was by no means entirely narrow and legalistic. Indeed, in the centuries following Ezra, Judaism proved itself to be amazingly flexible and open to new influences.

From Ezra to the Maccabees

After Ezra we lose virtually all sight of the Jews for more than one hundred years. Not until the time of the Maccabean revolt in the second century is there any continuous historical account of what was happening in Palestine. There are, however, a few documents deriving from a Jewish community located on the Upper Nile in Egypt which should be mentioned.

Apparently a colony of Jewish mercenary soldiers had existed on the island of Elephantine, near the first cataract of the Nile, since Neo-Babylonian times. They were hired by the Pharaoh to guard the southern border of Egypt. The Elephantine papyri, which come from the fifth century B.C., reveal that though these Jews continued to celebrate the national Jewish festivals and kept in contact with Jerusalem, they were also, by any standards, quite heterodox. Not only did they maintain their own temple for sacrifice when the Law recognized but one temple in Jerusalem; they also worshipped at least three deities, including God's consort!

This startling fact is a very important reminder to us that the history of Judaism ought never to be equated with the history of the Jews in Palestine. Also, the orthodoxy of the Biblical writings may conceal from our eyes much greater theological variety within Judaism than one might surmise. We must constantly remind ourselves that in Babylonia, Egypt, the Greek Islands—indeed, all over the ancient Near East—there were communities of Jews who, after their own fashion, continued to celebrate the traditions of their fathers. Although many of these groups looked to Jerusalem as the center of their world, the fact is that Palestinian Jews were in the minority. Judaism had already become a world religion of great diversity.

During the first half of the fourth century, the Persian Empire which had, on the whole, ruled quite well, began to experience internal decay. Concomitantly, the Greeks, who had withstood Persian military incursions in 480, began to exert their own commercial power in Western Asia. Potsherds and coins found in Judah are characterized by Greek designs and style, a premonition of things to come. By the last half of the fourth century, the tide which had flowed westward from Persia toward Europe had begun to ebb. The Greeks and Macedonians were on the march.

In 333 B.C., Alexander the Great, with a comparatively small army, defeated the Persians at Issus, marched down the Mediterranean littoral and took virtual control of Western Asia. Curiously, there are no contemporary Jewish documents which describe in any detail this monumental shift in power, but it would seem that the Jewish district welcomed the new conquerors gladly. In fact, during the years to follow many Jews, both in Palestine and in other regions of the now defunct Persian Empire, adopted Hellenistic customs and found themselves relatively comfortable with the new culture thrust upon them. Only when their own Jewish institutions and customs were severely threatened did militant resistance to Hellenism arise.

Alexander's own policy was to conquer the Asiatic "barbarians", not simply through military skill but also by cultural conversion. Therefore, he not only occupied the old centers of culture, he also built new cities, complete with gymnasia, theaters, and other public institutions of Hellenic origin. Thus, one of his first actions after occupying Egypt was to found a new city named, appropriately, Alexandria. Before many decades had passed that city was inhabited by a population which was about two-fifths Jewish. This fact alone demonstrates that the Jews of the time were by no means entirely conservative and reactionary for Alexandria was a city built for and reflecting the new age. For a long time to come the Jews of Alexandria were to represent the intellectual avant-garde of Judaism and, indeed, of the ancient world. So many Jews adopted the Greek language as their own and neglected the study of ancient Hebrew (which was a dead language even in Palestine), that it was necessary for a translation of the Hebrew Scriptures into Greek to be made.

An account of how that Greek translation, commonly called the Septuagint (LXX), took place is to be found in "A Letter to Aristeas," a work of doubtful authenticity. According to this letter, Ptolemy II Philadelphus (285-246), the ruler of Egypt, desired a copy of the Hebrew Torah for his great library. When he discovered that none was available in Greek, he commissioned a translation to be made. In response, the High Priest in Jerusalem sent seventy-two scholars, six from each of the twelve tribes of Israel, to Egypt. Closeted together on an island in the Nile, they produced the translation which was to be used among Greek-speaking peoples. Hellenistic Jews read it both in and out of synagogue; eventually, it also became the Old Testament of the Greek-speaking Christian Church.

As apocryphal as the account of Aristeas is, it does point to one important fact. Not only were many Jews enamoured with Hellenistic ideas and customs, many Gentiles were also impressed by the rich traditions of Judaism. The idea that non-Jews would want a translation of Scripture for their library is not far-fetched. Although many were put off by the particularity of the Law, they were also attracted by the beauty and profundity of Biblical literature, by the antiquity of the people of Israel, and by their lofty monotheism. Long before Christianity burst forth from the womb of Israel, Judaism was already attracting proselytes among the so-called pagans.

In Palestine itself, the district of Judah became evermore increasingly hieratic, with the High Priest of Jerusalem serving as chief official for both "church" and state. Historical records from before the exile place little emphasis upon the High Priest or the house of Aaron from which he descended. After the exile, this office assumed much greater importance until the incumbent was considered the supreme leader of Judaism both at home and abroad. Both local residents and Jews of the Diaspora paid a temple tax which greatly strengthened the splendor and the power of Judaism's primary leader.

Since the High Priest served in a political capacity, he frequently had to enter into negotiations with Gentile overlords and rulers. Hence, it is not surprising that the High Priests and their followers were often at the forefront of the movement toward Hellenization. Far from being reactionaries who favored separatism, they entered freely into relations with non-Jews. Religiously, however, they were quite conservative, holding to the pre-eminence of the Torah and resisting the intrusion of novel theological ideas.

The center for the High Priest's power was the Temple. Although originally built as King Solomon's chapel and hence as one temple among many, it had become, through the reforms of King Josiah in the seventh century, the one and only place where Jews could offer sacrifice. Three times a year all male Jews who were of age were expected to celebrate the ancient festivals there. Thus the Temple served as the focus for both cultic and national life.

The fact that many Jews could not go to the Temple frequently, however, meant that there was the need for a more local religious organization to meet personal and social needs. Thus, with the centralization of the Temple, there also arose a new type of organization called, after the Greek, the synagogue.

The origins of the synagogue can be traced back to the Babylonian exile when Jews, cut off from their homeland and its religious institutions, met together to study the traditions of their fathers, to pray, and to plan for return to their land. Out of this kernel grew a new tradition of worship and study which was to continue long after the Temple was no more. It was in this context that a whole new type of religious leader also emerged.

The central Temple was staffed by the sons of Aaron (the priests) and by the Levites, who attended to the paraphenalia of the cultus, the music, etc. The local synagogue, however, needed no priests, for there was no sacrificial cultus to maintain. Instead, learned men trained in the Law (who eventually came to be called Rabbis), predominated. They were not officially ordained nor did they serve as full-time, paid professionals. The Rabbi — which means "my Master" — was a layman whose leadership was basvd upon his learning and his wisdom. After the destruction of the Temple in 70 A.D. Judaism knew no paid professional leadership outside its academies until the late fifteenth century. It is noteworthy that the traditions of prayer and instruction which these laymen established became, in due time, patterns for both Christian and Islamic worship and life.

In many respects, the synagogue tradition, in so far as we can learn about it during these years, was more politically and socially conservative than was the priestly tradition. When political resistance was called for, it usually came from the grass roots, not from the priestly hierarchy. At the same time, the synagogue tradition fostered theological developments which were by no means reactionary. The local teacher of the Law was constantly called upon to deal with hard cases and to make the Law relevant to contemporary conditions. Hence, while the High Priest and his supporters could maintain an attitude of detached orthodoxy, the leaders of the synagogue were challenged to develop new traditions to answer the needs of the time. The Torah was, of course, considered authoritative and beyond reproach by both groups, but beside the written Law, the Rabbis accepted and developed the Oral Law, a body of tradition which expanded upon and elaborated the 613 laws of the Torah.

The Oral Law was a rather fluid tradition embodying both legal judgments (*halakah*) and more anecdotal material (*aggadah*). As we shall see, this Oral Law grew over the years and was refined by successive generations until it eventually came to dwarf, in volume if not in authority, the Mosaic Law itself. In many respects, the course of Judaism ever after can only be understood through reference to this oral tradition which emerged when the Torah itself became fixed. The priestly party might protest, but the Rabbis, armed with their innovative law, had their way.

Too much can be made of the distinction between synagogue and Temple and between rabbi and priest. The synagogues supported the Temple and considered its work vital. Conversely, a synagogue found a place in the very Temple itself. Laymen supported the priesthood and many priests may have favored the Oral Law. Still, there did develop a divergence of opinion between rabbi and priest which eventually issued in the bitter struggle between Pharisee and Sadducee of which we will speak later.

The Prophets

By the third century B.C., if not before, the prophetic tradition had virtually ceased as a living movement. No longer did divinely-called spokesmen for God arise to call the king and the nation into judgment, for there was no Jewish king and the nation was no longer independent. The traditions of the prophets, however, did not die but were edited, sometimes revised, and finally put into fixed form. Just when and how the process occurred we do not know, but sometime before 200 B.C. the prophetic books achieved their final form and were accepted by the Jews—but not by the Samaritans—as canonical.

The books of the prophets are of basically two types. First, there are four scrolls (Joshua, Judges, Samuel, and Kings) which contain a history of Israel from the time of the conquest until the fall of Jerusalem. Although strictly speaking not prophecies, they offer an account of the history essential for understanding the prophets as well as stories about several important prophetic figures like Nathan, Elijah, and Elisha who left behind no writings. No other ancient Near Eastern people have left behind such a well-balanced, continuous history as is contained in these works.

Second, along with these historical books were canonized four scrolls of prophecy: Isaiah, Jeremiah, Ezekiel, and the Twelve. The last is an obviously composite work, for it includes the prophecies of at least twelve different men. Amos, who preached in about 750 B.C., is undoubtedly the oldest of the group, while the book of Malachi, dating between the fourth and fifth centuries B.C., is the latest. The other three scrolls, though each bearing the name of one prophet, are also the work of many hands. Isaiah was composed by at least two or three authors who were decisively separated in time. Jeremiah and Ezekiel, though somewhat more uniform in character, also incorporate sections derived from later periods than their own:

Although each prophet has his own particular emphases and interests, nearly all of the prophets reiterate two common themes: 1) Israel has sinned, and unless repentance occurs, will be punished, and 2) Israel will eventually find favor in God's eyes and can look forward with hope to a glorious future. Doubtless these books were finally chosen because at least one half of their message had come true. Israel had been punished. Jerusalem had fallen in 587 to the Babylonians and many people were forced to endure the horrors of exile from their homeland. The glorious rewards had not yet come, but since the prophets had been correct about the judgment, the Jews regarded the fulfillment of God's promises as only a matter of time. Eventually a Messiah would arise, defeat Israel's enemies, and establish once more the Davidic kingdom. This time, however, God's glory would protect Israel and the whole world would experience the long-awaited age of peace and joy. During their long history, Jews have returned again and again to these promises, looking for signs of the Messiah and sometimes attempting to force God's hand by beginning the great revolution themselves. Particularly during the second and first centuries B.C. Messianic expectations flourished, becoming a major driving force in Jewish life.

Wisdom Literature

Not everyone, however, spent his time looking forward to the day of the Lord and the fulfillment of the glorious prophetic hopes. The fourth century also witnessed a turning away from these prophetic emphases upon history to a different source for knowledge and truth: wisdom. Wisdom literature had, of course, been around for millennia all over the Near East. In Egypt, Mesopotamia, Edom, Greece, and also Israel there had been teachers employing proverbs, epigrams, and dialogues to instruct others about how to live wisely in this world.

The wise man, unlike the prophet, does not appeal to dreams or ecstatic trances, or heavenly messages for his authority. He does not usually forecast historical doom nor does he paint verbal pictures of some glorious future paradise. Instead, with open and reasonable eyes he looks at the world about him and offers advice about how to survive in an era seemingly filled with foolishness, viciousness, and temptation.

Among those books of wisdom probably written during the Persian and early Hellenistic periods are three—Proverbs, Ecclesiastes, and the Wisdom of Jesus ben Sirach (Ecclesiasticus). All three doubtless drew upon the traditional wisdom of Israel and may, therefore, incorporate sections which are very ancient. Each, however, reveals the distinctive stamp of its compiler and hence is more than simply a collection of "familiar quotations."

Of the three, Proverbs is most clearly a composite work. Essentially its message is: work like an ant, be a good son, and, above all, fear God. Much of what is said reflects the wisdom of a father who is attempting to give his son advice. Avoid wanton women, bad companions, and all those tempting lusts which lead men astray. Most of Proverbs scarcely transcends such simple platitudes. Striking, however, is the picture of wisdom painted in chapter 8. Wisdom here is not merely a human capacity or abstract type of knowledge. Rather wisdom is pictured as a beautiful woman who calls men to follow her. She is a power who has been since the foundations of the earth.

> The Lord created me at the beginning of his work,
>> the first of his acts of old.
> Ages ago I was set up,
>> at the first before the beginning of the earth.
>
> Proverbs 8:22-23

Wisdom is an intermediary between God and man who reveals herself in the structure of the universe. Man can know and obey God by following the course which Wisdom has laid out for him. The foolish man is tempted by seductive glances of the harlot. The wise man knows who his true love is. She is *Hokmah* (Wisdom), the primordial lady who has existed since the foundations of the earth were laid.

Ecclesiastes, by way of contrast, is far more existential in character, for the author has little use for personified wisdom. Of what value is wisdom, asks the Preacher (Koheleth), when all men face death and beyond death there is nothing? How can man rest secure in anything when all is flux and vanity? The answers the author gives to these questions are by no means simple-minded or easy to grasp. By juxtaposing seemingly conflicting maxims, he portrays the life of man with all its paradoxes and enigmas. Scholars continue to debate his meaning but to this reader it would appear that for Ecclesiastes true wisdom is to be found, not by trying to avoid the ambiguities of life, but by looking them straight in the face.

The third work, the *Wisdom of Jesus ben Sirach,* is of particular interest because it can be dated rather exactly—in about 180 B.C. According to chapter 50, verse 27, the author was Jesus the son of Sirach, son of Eleazar of Jerusalem. The prologue, however, is by his grandson who, having been educated in Egypt, is translating the work there for the benefit of Greek-speaking people.

Much of the work purveys, for the most part, prudential advice about how to deal with others and live in this world, but like Proverbs, Jesus ben Sirach also sees wisdom as a cosmic power who was from the beginning.

> Wisdom was created before all things
> and prudent understanding from eternity.
> The root of wisdom — to whom is has been revealed?
> Her clever devices — who knows them?
>
> 1:4-6

Therefore, when one follows the precepts of wisdom one is doing more than assuring his own success or popularity. The wise life is one lived in harmony with both the cosmos and God.

One other feature of this wisdom book also bears mentioning. In chapter 44, after offering much advice and counsel, Jesus ben Sirach proposes to praise famous men. It is noteworthy that although he includes in his words of praise such heroes of the faith as Noah, Abraham, Moses, and David, it is Aaron and his sons who receive the most attention. The whole passage ends with a rapturous encomium for Simon ben Onias, the High Priest who served from 219-196 B.C.

In this the author expresses very well the mood of the time. Despite the innumerable synagogues, the Oral Law, and the variety of theological opinion, early Hellenistic Judaism centered its attention and faith in the Temple of Jerusalem and its ruler, the High Priest. It is Simon ben Onias' blessing that Jesus ben Sirach savors above all. In chapter 7 he says,

> With all your soul fear the Lord,
> and honor his priests.

That is the essence of Hellenistic Jewish wisdom for Jesus ben Sirach.

Judaism, the Seleucid Empire, and the Maccabeans

Soon after the death of Alexander the Great in 323 B.C. his empire was torn apart by squabbling among his generals. Ptolemy, Alexander's governor in Egypt, occupied both the Nile valley and the Palestinian strip, while Seleucus I, Nicator, one of Alexander's generals, took the satrapy of Babylonia and, eventually Syria, centering his empire in Antioch on the lower Orontes River. Predictably, Palestine became a bone of contention between the two rival powers. After considerable conflict which lasted much of the third century, Antiochus III, the Seleucid ruler, was able to wrest the Palestinian area from Ptolemaic control in 217.

The people of Judah apparently welcomed the Seleucid troops gladly and Antiochus, in his turn, dealt kindly with them. Jewish slaves were released, taxes were ameliorated, and certain privileges were extended to the sanctuary in Jerusalem. Such friendly relations, however, were not to endure, for both external and internal pressures turned the Syrian ruler from easy-going magnanimity to ruthlessness.

Soon after the victory over the Ptolemaic Empire, the Seleucids became involved in bloody conflict with Rome. In 190 Antiochus was defeated by the Roman legions and had to submit to humiliating terms of peace. This defeat and the continued struggle which followed, decisively changed the attitude of the Seleucid rulers.

In the first place, they became strapped for funds and hence not only raised taxes but eyed rapaciously the many rich Temples which dotted the Empire. Second, the Roman threat produced political paranoia. The Seleucids, who were officially regarded as God-men, became ever more suspicious of any persons, like the Jews, who would not worship the ruling "Son of God," and hence undermined the religious (and political) unity of the Empire. Needless to say, the monotheistic Jews could hardly accept the ascription of divinity to a pagan like Antiochus III.

The whole matter came to a head in 175 when Antiochus IV,Epiphanes, ascended the throne. While Antiochus eyed the Jews with suspicion because of their nonconformity, a large segment of the Jewish population, known as the *Hasidim* (the pious ones) began to react with vigor to the Hellenizing tendencies which encouraged their sons to run naked in the gymnasia in "honor of Apollo." Not only the conservative Hasidim but all Jews were appalled when Antiochus, desperately needing money to support his war machine, looted their Temple in order to obtain the needed funds. Their anger became intense when a certain Jason succeeded in having the High Priest, Onias, removed from office by promising to Antiochus rich gifts and a more vigorous policy of Hellenization, if he were to be High Priest. Unfortunately for Jason, Menelaus, who was not even of a priestly family, offered the king greater sums of money and hence he replaced Jason in the sacred office.

In the meantime, Onias III, the rightful High Priest, had escaped to Egypt where he succeeded in building a rival Jewish Temple in Leontopolis. This Temple, although considered heretical by Palestinian Jews, because it was not located in Jerusalem, continued to exist for two and a half centuries as the sacrificial center for Egyptian Jews.

In 169 B.C., a rumor spread through Judah that Antiochus had been killed in battle. Immediately Jason returned and, with force of arms, compelled Menelaus, the priestly pretender, to flee. Antiochus, however, was not dead and when he discovered what had transpired, decided to solve the Jewish problem once and for all.

He attacked Jerusalem as an enemy city, killing thousands and taking women and children as slaves. He forbade the observance of the Sabbath and the customary offering of sacrifices under penalty of death. In place of the traditional Jewish cultus, he set up in the Temple the statue of the Olympian Zeus and had swine's flesh offered to it.

Antiochus was ruthless, depending upon the fear which his military might engendered to quell resistance, but he greatly underestimated both the depth of the Jewish faith and the vigorous opposition which that small district could offer his imperial armies. Before long, armed rebellion, which was to alter drastically the political fortunes of the Jewish people, broke out.

The incident precipitating the protracted guerrilla war which followed took place in the outlying village of Modein. Mattathias, the father of the Hasmoneans, raised the standard of resistance by killing both a Syrian official and a Jew preparing to offer pagan sacrifice. His cry went up: "Whoever is zealous for Torah and maintains the covenant, let him come after me." Mattathias and his five sons retreated to the hills with their followers and began a hit-and-run war which was to cause the harried Syrians no end of trouble, particularly because the main Seleucid force had to occupy itself with resistance against the Romans.

When Mattathias died the next year, his son Judas, nicknamed *Makkabios* (the Hammer) took over leadership of the resistance. Through a number of crucial victories he was able to drive out the Syrian army, secure Jerusalem, and cleanse the Temple of its pagan abominations in 164. This rededication of the sanctuary, which culminated this stunning and surprising victory, is still commemorated each year on the 25th of Kislev by the celebration of Hanukah.

In 162 Judas, intent on complete freedom from Syrian control, began a fresh campaign, but this time his followers were divided. The Hasidim, essentially interested only in preserving a modicum of religious freedom, were satisfied that the abuses of the Syrians had been removed and wanted no more of war. Hence, with his military power sapped, Judas' campaign floundered. In 160 Judas Maccabeus died in battle and was succeeded by his brother, Jonathan.

Jonathan secured a peace settlement in 157. In reward for his partial submission to Syrian hegemony, he was accorded territory in the north and was appointed, by the Syrians, High Priest. When Jonathan was murdered in 143, still another of the Hasmonean brothers, Simon, succeeded him. Simon extended Judean territory, adding the maritime plain and the seaport of Joppa but, like his brother, met a bloody end in 134.

Simon was then followed by his third son, John Hyrcanus (134-104), who, though by no means universally beloved, proved to be the most durable and successful of the Hasmonean rulers. Not only did he gain from the Syrians virtual independence, he added considerably to Jewish territory by capturing both Samaria to the north and Idumea to the south. Inhabitants of both areas were converted to Judaism at sword point. The boundaries were expanded even further by his son, Aristobulus, who conquered the Galilee, and by Alexander Jannai (103-76) who extended the territory of the Jewish State almost to those boundaries once maintained by David and Solomon. Thus, for a few brief years the Jews recaptured something of their old national glory. The story of how that glory soon faded before the Roman legions must wait, however, while we review other aspects of the age of the Hasmoneans.

Apocalyptic Literature

During the crisis engendered by Antiochus IV in 167 a little tract appeared full of bizarre symbolism and not-so-veiled allusions. That work, the Biblical book of Daniel, purported to be about a hero of the Babylonian exile but, in fact, spoke directly to those suffering under the persecution of the Seleucids.

Through the use of images drawn in part from the writings of Ezekiel and Zechariah, the author recounted for the people their recent history and revealed to them that before long God himself would enter to set the world straight.

Daniel, like most of the other apocalyptic works which followed, is much too complicated to review briefly. In this survey it is perhaps enough to say that it is the first of a whole series of apocalypses to be written by Jews during the Hellenistic and early Roman periods. As an apocalypse it draws aside the curtain of mystery and reveals to the reader, albeit through veiled imagery, some of the secrets of God himself.

Among those apocalyptic writings which were probably written in whole or in part before the take-over by Pompey in 63 B.C. are the following: I Enoch, (see III.A), The Book of Jubilees, and The Testaments of the XII Patriarchs. These were followed, during the Roman period, by such works as: The Psalms of Solomon, The Assumption of Moses, The Ascension of Isaiah, The Life of Adam and Eve, II Enoch, II Ezra, etc. Early Christians also adopted an apocalyptic style producing such a specifically Christian work as the book of Revelation.

Apocalyptic literature is, to say the least, difficult to define, if only because it was written for so many different purposes and in so many different ways. In one sense, it was not new to Judaism at all, for examples of strange visions, peculiar imagery, and descriptions of the last days of the world, can be found in Ezekiel and Zechariah. Nevertheless, there are certain characteristics which distinguish the apocalyptic literature which flourished from about 167 B.C. to 150 A.D. from the prophetic literature of an earlier age. Among these characteristics are the following:

1. Most commonly, the apocalyptic works are pseudonymous, claiming to be writings of some ancient worthy like Adam, Enoch, Noah, Moses, or Ezra. Enoch was a particular favorite because Genesis enigmatically states that "Enoch walked with God; and he was not, for God took him." (Gen. 5:24)

2. There is great concern in apocalypses for the mysteries of creation. While both the prophets and wisdom literature tend to point to these mysteries as understandable only to God, apocalyptic literature attempts an explanation. In the book of Enoch, for instance, Enoch is taken up into heaven where he

learns, among other things, about what makes the sun and moon move and where thunder and lightning come from. The *Book of Secrets of Enoch* (II Enoch), a much later work, devotes considerable attention to the 365¼-day year. In part, then, the apocalypses are pseudo-scientific works which "reveal facts" about the universe and reconcile them with the traditions of Judaism.

3. Angelology and demonology abound. Most Biblical works have little to say about either named angels or demons. The apocalypticists, probably due to the influence of Persian religion, introduce the reader to such angelic worthies as Michael, Raphael, Uriel, and Gabriel as well as to the levels of heaven and hell and their other inhabitants.

So also do some of the heroes in the course of their heavenly travels meet a Messianic figure, often called the Son of Man, who is preparing to intervene in the affairs of man and establish his rule of righteousness. Frequently, though not invariably, the apocalypses speak of the Last Things and maintain that in the very near future the end of the world will occur and God's judgments will be meted out.

4. The apocalyptic writings do not explicitly deny the authority of the Law and the Prophets but sometimes claim that beside the exoteric revelations found in these books, there are also esoteric secrets known to men like Enoch and Moses without which the literal Scriptures cannot be fully understood. Thus we find expressed a claim which was to be reiterated many times by Jewish mystics: that the canon of Scripture tells the truth, but not the whole truth. To be truly enlightened one must also know the secret wisdom preserved by the few.

5. The literature is filled with primordial images so familiar in other examples of world mythology. Sacred trees, holy mountains, and strange beasts dot the visionary landscape. There are frequent references to numerological mysteries and to proto-alchemical lore. It is as though, after fighting pagan mythology for centuries, the Jews finally found a way to incorporate archetypal, mythic images into their theology without doing violence to monotheism. God remains alone supreme, but around him cluster a whole host of principalities and powers, angels and archangels, celestial beings and supercelestial forces. Ranged against the forces of God are the fallen angels, giants, demons, etc.

The interpretation of all these works is difficult for a variety of reasons. First of all, few of them can be dated precisely. Because the historical context is usually unknown, many subtle allusions may be passed over unnoticed. Second, it is very hard to tell whether these writings were widely influential in Jewish circles or whether, even in their own day, they were known only to the few. Third, because it was the Christians who generally preserved these writings it is not easy to tell how much they have been "doctored" by Christian scribes. It may be that some of the ideas which seem to foreshadow Christianity were really added by Christians after the fact.

Nevertheless, the rise of Christianity in the first century A.D. can hardly be understood without thorough acquaintance with such works as I Enoch and II Ezra (see III.A). It is not too much to say that the early Christian interpretation of Jesus was profoundly shaped by the images and attitudes of the Jewish apocalyptic writers. When Jesus says the following, he speaks like a good apocalypticist:

> But in those days, after that tribulation, the sun will be darkened, and the moon will not give its light, and the stars will be falling from heaven, and the powers in the heavens will be shaken. And then they will see the Son of man coming in clouds with great power and glory. And then he will send out the angels, and gather his elect from the four winds, from the ends of the earth to the ends of heaven.
>
> Mark 13:24-27

Whether the apocalypticists formed a special, pre-Christian sect within Judaism is unclear. Surely it is obvious, however, that connections existed between them and that recently-unearthed community at Qumran, near the northern end of the Dead Sea. One of the greatest archaeological discoveries of the twentieth century has been the recovery, from caves near the Dead Sea, of the library of that community.

Some of the Dead Sea Scrolls uncovered are primarily of value for the Biblical scholar, for they contain Biblical texts written at an early time. Other scrolls, like the *Manual of Discipline,* tell of the rules of the monastic order which existed at Qumran and of the practices and beliefs of its members (see IV.B). Clearly, members believed that the Last Days were approaching when the final struggle between the powers of Light and Darkness would take place. Qumran was founded to make straight in the desert a highway for the coming of God. Beside the apocalyptic "War of the Children of Light against the

Children of Darkness," the "Commentary on Habakkuk" found among the scrolls may also be regarded as apocalyptic in idea if not in form.

Perhaps further study and discovery will make clear the relations which existed among the apocalypticists, the Qumran monastics, and the early Christians. At this time, however, we must plead ignorance and conclude with a frustrating but evocative question mark.

Jewish Parties and Sects

The famous Jewish historian, Josephus (b. circa 37 A.D.), identifies three major parties which existed during the Hasmonean period — the Sadducees, the Pharisees, and the Essenes (*see* IV.A). Most modern scholars, for want of more accurate information, accept his identification of these groups as more-or-less authoritative. It should be noted, however, that although Josephus offers us an eye-witness account of the sects which existed in his day, he had his own "axe to grind" and often simplified (distorted) the facts in order to make the Jewish situation understandable and palatable to his Roman readers. He deemphasizes revolutionary ideas, treats Jewish sects as "philosophical schools," and sometimes omits important considerations.

In chapter 8 of Book II of his *Wars of the Jews*, Josephus gives us a relatively lengthy account of the Essenes. He describes them as a pious, communistic sect with stiff rules and regulations for members. According to him, communities of Essenes were to be found in many of the cities of Judah. Not only did they adopt a special mode of dress and particular rules for eating; they also apparently had, beside the Scriptures, works of their own which they highly prized. Strangely enough, neither the New Testament nor later Jewish writings make mention of this group. Many scholars believe that the men of Qumran were, in fact, Essenic, but not all of Josephus' comments are consistent with what we know of Qumran.

Josephus is somewhat less expansive about the Pharisees and the Sadducees (*see* IV.A), but we meet both of these groups in the New Testament and the Talmud. From what we can piece together it would appear that the Saducean party was composed of basically wealthy and aristocratic supporters of the High Priest. Theologically they were conservative, accepting only the Written Law while rejecting the oral traditions of the *sopherim.* Unlike the Essenes, who believed in the immortality of the soul, the Sadducees rejected all doctrines of life after death. To what extent common people were to be found among the ranks of the Sadducees is unknown.

In contrast, the Pharisees, despite their image as the arch-conservatives, were the innovators who, in their interpretation of Scripture, adopted many theological and educational ideas from Hellenistic and Asiatic culture. They affirmed belief in the resurrection of the body, in all sorts of angels, archangels, and demons, and in the Oral Law which they both inherited from earlier interpreters and developed in their own way to answer pressing contemporary issues. They were lay intellectuals who devoted much time to study and to the education of the young. More than any other group, they turned Judaism into a community devoted to the study of the tradition.

Whether or not the Pharisaic party encompassed all the adherents to the Oral Law is a difficult question to answer. The fact that the New Testament makes a distinction between the scribes *(sopherim)* and the Pharisees may indicate that in fact the Pharisees were only one sect within the much larger body of Jews who supported the oral tradition. We do know, at least, that the Pharisees were regarded as lenient in their attitudes toward punishment but were often quite ready to engage in dispute and even revolt.

Membership in these groups, of course, constituted only a small percentage of the entire population. Most of the people were simply Jews, struggling to maintain themselves against overwhelming odds. The *'am ha'aretz* (the people of the land) were poor and uneducated farmers who could have cared less about the refinements of Temple sacrifice or the subtleties of the Law. Neither the aristocratic priesthood nor the intellectual Pharisees helped them much as they strove to pay their taxes, cultivate their fields, and keep their heads above water. Still, if any group won their devotion it was the lay scholars, including the Pharisees, who, despite their judicial scrupulosity, did strive to create an Oral Law sympathetic to the downtrodden and open to liberal interpretation. When disaster befell the Jews again in the first century A.D. it was the Rabbis and not the priests who picked up the pieces.

The Sanhedrin

During the Hasmonean period, the ruler of Judah was both High Priest and, as it were, uncrowned king. Maintaining the judicial system, however, was a series of courts of considerable importance both juridically and politically. On the local level, there were courts of three men. Large cities had also courts of twenty-three officials. The great tribunal of Jerusalem, the Sanhedrin, served as the highest court and also as a sort of parliament for the nation. This body was composed of seventy members plus a president or *Nasi.*

Rabbinic tradition traces the origins of the Sanhedrin back to the seventy elders whom Moses called together (Ex. 24:9, Num. 11:16ff), but there is little evidence of a functioning Sanhedrin before the Hasmonean period. It may be that Ezra's organization of elders was the seed from which the Sanhedrin grew, but even this is uncertain. It should be noted that with the destruction of Jerusalem in 70 A.D., the function of this body changed radically and, in fact, became something quite new.

During the Hasmonean period, however, the Sanhedrin served as a major battle ground between the Sadducees and the Pharisees. Originally an aristocratic organization filled with priests and wealthy land owners, it was naturally controlled by the Sadducees. Gradually, the Pharisees gained ground in its ranks. Then John Hyrcanus, initially an adherent of the Pharisaic party, reconstituted the assembly, filling it with Pharisees. When some of the more vocal Pharisees attacked their patron, however, they were removed from the Sanhedrin and the Sadducees again came to power. Until the end of the reign of Alexander Jannai (76 B.C.) the Pharisees constituted the not always so loyal opposition. Because of their massive support among the people, the Pharisees were by no means a minor stumbling-block for the civil rulers. As a consequence, several Pharisaic leaders were executed and tensions mounted.

On his death bed Alexander Jannai advised his wife and successor, Salome Alexandra, to reconcile herself with the Pharisaic party. This she did and the Pharisees once more gained control of the Sanhedrin. Tradition has it that during her reign they exerted considerable influence over the Temple and its rituals, making changes in liturgical practice which ought to have been under the purview of the priests. While Alexandra's rather weak-willed son, Hyrcanus, served as High Priest, the Pharisees reached the zenith of their power.

With her death in 67 B.C., however, the Sadducees reasserted themselves, backing the more forceful Aristobulus, Hyrcanus' younger brother. Hyrcanus momentarily took over the High Priesthood and the Kingship but Aristobulus was able to wrest both offices from him. Had it not been for Antipater, an Idumean whose people had been forcibly converted to Judaism by John Hyrcanus, Aristobulus would doubtless have become permanent head of the Jewish State. Antipater, however, goaded the peaceful Hyrcanus into open revolution. As a result, both sides appealed to Rome for support. In 63 B.C. Pompey and his legions marched into Judah, not simply to arbitrate the dispute, but to take over the land for Rome. Thus Judah's political independence quickly came to an end and a new bloody era began.

Pentecost, in Hebrew Shevous, comes fifty days after Passover. Although, in origin, a festival of wheat harvest (Exodus 23:16) it became for Israel a time when she remembered the giving of the Law at Mount Sinai. Although of very ancient origin, Shevous is neither as popular today as Passover nor as solemnly observed as Yom Kippur. Traditional houses are, however, decked with greenery and flowers and, in Reform Judaism, confirmation is observed.

In Christianity the celebration is preserved as a time for remembering the coming of the Holy Spirit to the disciples. For Judaism, however, Shevous is best symbolized by the two tablets of the Decalogue which form the core of the whole Law. Although the day itself may not be as popular as some other festivals, the Law remains central for all good Jews.

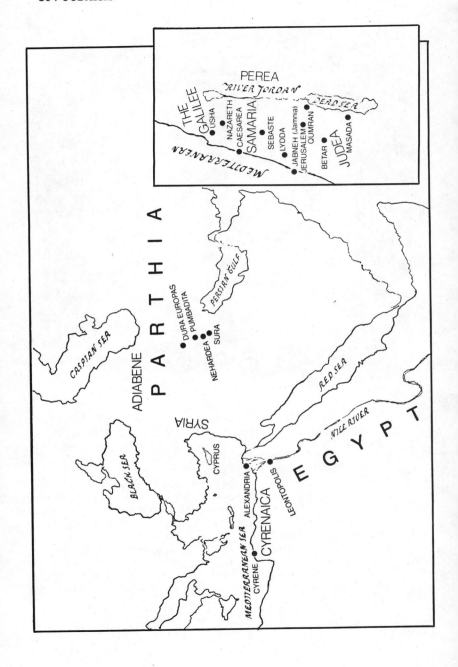

2

FROM POMPEY TO THE CLOSE OF THE TALMUD (63 B.C. - 500 A.D.)

The years following Pompey's occupation of Judah in 63 B.C.were bloody ones for all the parties involved. For Rome, this was an era of civil war — between Pompey and Julius Caesar, Antony and Cassius, Octavian and Antony. In Judah, while Hyrcanus II sat upon the throne, the wily Antipater curried the favor of whomever was in power. Pompey was his benefactor and friend while he lived, but when the Roman general died in 48 B.C., Antipater was quick to turn to Caesar, winning his support by granting him military assistance against Egypt.

Antipater was eventually poisoned but his son, the notorious Herod the Great, inherited his powerful position. No sooner had he begun to build upon the foundations laid by his father, however, than the Parthians, who now controlled a large empire stretching from Iran westward, galloped into Syria and Palestine, sweeping all before them. Herod, fighting desperately, barely escaped with his life. The Parthians set Antigonus upon the throne and carried Hyrcanus, with ears mutilated, into exile.

Herod made his way to Rome and laid his case before the triumvirs. Against all hope, his case was listened to carefully and he was proclaimed King of the Jews. Roman legions were sent with him to drive out the Parthians and, after much bloodshed, Herod ascended the throne. Thus, in 39 B.C., began one of the most glorious and one of the most ignominious chapters in Jewish history.

Herod proved himself to be a surprisingly able and vigorous ruler. He suppressed the bandits who harried the land, developed a splendid harbor city at Caesarea, and greatly expanded and beautified the Temple in Jerusalem. He reduced taxes when famine struck and even sold the plate and furnishings of the palace to help the needy in times of distress. Aiming to gain the support of all factions, he took care to respect the scruples of the Pharisees as much as possible while also offering support to the Essenes.

But the populace hated him. They hated him for being a half-Jew — an Idumean slave, they called him. They despised his love for Greco-Roman culture and his building of baths, *stoae*, and sports arenas. They goaded him and chafed against him, frequently threatening revolution. Herod, to be sure, was no saint. On more than one occasion he stained his hands with innocent blood, even the blood of his own kin. Most tragically, in a fit of paranoic rage, he condemned to death his beloved Mariamne, a beautiful Hasmonean princess whom he had married to legitimize his reign. Only after her death did he realize how much he loved her. As the tensions mounted, Herod became more and more vicious, more and more paranoic. Finally, despised by all and inconsolable for the loss of his wife, he died of intestinal cancer in 4 B.C.

During Herod's reign, a new sect, the zealots, had risen in importance. Their battle cry was simple, dogmatic, and revolutionary: "No God but YHWH, no tax but to the Temple, no friend but the zealot."* Hezekiah was perhaps the first of these vocal supporters of national independence. When he was executed by Herod, his son, Judas of Galilee, organized the zealots and fomented rebellion. His forces were eventually defeated, but his cause and organization lived on. Herod and his successors repeatedly crushed the zealot uprisings only to discover that other determined men had risen to replace the fallen.

---

*Abraham Leon Sacher, *A History of the Jews,* 5th rev. ed. (New York: Alfred A. Knopf, 1967), p. 117.

Herod's death only made matters worse, for his sons quarreled among themselves for power while the land was again wracked with famine and banditry. Eventually the Romans had enough; they exiled the king, Archelaus, to Gaul, and put Judah directly under the control of a Roman procurator. Although the Galilee, Peraea, and an area northeast of the Sea of Galilee remained under the control of two of Herod's sons, Judaea and Samaria lost even the semblance of home rule.

The politics of the land of Palestine in the first century A.D.are so complicated that a whole monograph series could be devoted to the subject. It suffices, perhaps, to say that no matter who the procurator was, he met with intractable resistance from the zealots. Mass slaughter and crucifixion were the order of the day. The voices of temperance and restraint were virtually drowned out by the clamoring for freedom from Roman rule and for the reestablishment of Judah as an independent national state.

Jesus and the Christians

Into this era of eschatological quest for independence was born Jesus of Nazareth. Since this is a survey of Jewish history and not of Christianity, there is no need to review his career or its impact in detail. Indeed, there is so much disagreement about the "historical" Jesus that nearly anything which could be said about him would be disputed by some. The fact is that reputable scholars, using the same materials and examining them with equally well-informed eyes, have seen in him radically different characteristics.

Some, pointing to his proclamation of the Kingdom of God and of the last days of the world, argue for his close connection with Qumran and the apocalypticists. Surely there is much to be said for this idea, for many of the images and ideas used by the Jesus of the Gospels are similar to those found in apocalyptic works. In many respects, Jesus appears to be an "incarnation" of that Teacher of Righteousness so lauded by the Dead Sea sect.

Others, like S. G. F. Brandon, connect Jesus with the zealot movement. Here again, one can point to: 1) Jesus' disciple who was a zealot, 2) Jesus' remark about coming not with peace but with a sword, and 3) his crucifixion for supposed revolutionary activities. If one assumes, as Brandon does, that the Gospels were "doctored" in order to conceal from the Romans Jesus' overt connection with zealotry, a good case can be made for this position.

Still others, paying special heed to Jesus' teachings and interpretation of the Law see in his various statements reflections of both the wisdom tradition and the work of the Pharisees. Some scholars would take him to be a legal absolutist who interpreted the Law in its most rigorous sense. In this case, he would stand somewhat to the right of the famous Shammai who will be discussed shortly. Others find in his use of parables and epigrams a continuation of the flexible and urbane tradition of the wise man.

There are those who maintain that Jesus sought to reform Judaism and never intended to found a church for the Gentiles. Others see the work of the apostles — particularly Paul — as a logical outgrowth of Jesus' essential message. Both those who claim that Jesus was a profound supporter of the Torah and those who insist that his teachings point to the inadequacy of the "Old Covenant" seem to have legitimate grounds upon which to stand.

After reviewing the many interpretations of Jesus offered by Christians and non-Christians alike, one must conclude that the Jesus who appears in the Bible can never be fully separated from our apprehension of him. Every interpretation says as much about the interpreter as it does about Jesus. Orthodox Christians see in him an absolutely unique person, the Son of God incarnate. Humanists have often viewed him as a much misunderstood teacher of love and social justice. Occultists point to his magic and parapsychological powers as central. Jews may find him to be a badly interpreted or perhaps misguided Rabbi.

Part of the difficulty lies in the fact that our sources concerning Jesus and his era are both severely limited and invariably biased. Nor have modern discoveries of the Dead Sea Scrolls, the Zadokite Fragments, etc., really clarified the situation. Instead, they have only introduced perplexing new dimensions to the problem. At this juncture, and perhaps forever, Jesus confronts man as a question mark, eliciting from each person his own, individual response (see V.A).

From what we can gather from early sources, the "Way of the Nazarene" started as a sect within Judaism. Early Christians continued to attend synagogue and Temple; many observed the Jewish Law. Paul, however, who began his career as a Pharisee and student of Gamaliel I, opened the sect decisively to the Gentiles by maintaining that salvation is to be found through faith in Jesus the Christ alone, not through obedience to the Law. For him, Rabbinic Judaism had been heading in exactly the wrong direction. Paul reasoned that once one sees that the Law is absolute and cannot be obeyed literally, one is forced to admit that man must depend entirely upon the mercy of God. The revelation of that mercy came to Paul in the person of Jesus.

The idea that the Law is so demanding that it cannot be obeyed was not peculiar to Paul and the early Christians alone. The book of II Ezra (in the Roman Catholic canon: IV Esdras), a Jewish apocalyptic work which deals profoundly with the problem of theodicy, makes a similar point. Ezra carries on a dialogue with the angel Uriel who speaks of the Last Judgment when the righteous will triumph and the unrighteous will perish. Ezra, however, repeatedly returns to the central question: Are there any righteous? Has anyone really fulfilled the demands of the Torah? The angel out-talks Ezra, but doesn't really answer his question. Over the whole discussion there hangs a dark cloud: Even if God intervenes on behalf of the righteous, will anyone in the last analysis benefit? Are not all men corrupted with sin?

In fact, Paul answers "Ezra's" question by saying that although there are no righteous men, God will forgive those who believe in Jesus and will impute to them the righteousness which they lack. This message of Paul (Israel with Jesus but without the Law) held great attraction for both Gentiles who had long been intrigued by Israel's great tradition but could not stomach Jewish legalism and many Hellenistic Jews, who found the Law an impediment to a full life in a predominantly Gentile society. Significantly, Paul, throughout his life, continued to visit and preach in synagogues, finding there both eager listeners and vitriolic critics. While many Christians in Palestine remained also Jewish, Christians in other parts of the world became increasingly independent of the synagogue, eventually developing a unique institution of their own, the church.*

---

*For New Testament attitudes toward Judaism, *see* Document V.A

The Traditions of the Rabbis

While Christians were taking the traditions of Israel in a radically new direction, the Rabbis of Judaism continued to explore, methodically and painstakingly, The Law and the Prophets. For the faithful Jew, the Torah was God's Word which could not be abandoned simply because some self-proclaimed Messiah had died on a cross. The Law must be obeyed and to do that Jews had to know exactly what it meant and implied.

The traditions of the *sopherim* which began in the Persian period were carried on and developed with monumental acuteness by lay scholars who came to be called the *Tannaim*. In fact, while Jesus was still a boy, two of the greatest interpreters of the Law, Hillel (ca. 60 B.C.-20 A.D.) and Shammai (first century A.D.) disputed various points of the Law in Jerusalem, forming about them the two schools, Beth Hillel and Beth Shammai, which were to dominate Rabbinic thought for several centuries.

Hillel was a Babylonian Jew who had come to Judah as a young man and had soon risen to prominence as an interpreter of the Law. Generally his views were liberal and humane, though there are several examples of his strictness which can be cited. Shammai was a Palestinian Rabbi whose attitudes were those of a strict constructionist. For instance, Shammai (like Jesus) believed that adultery should be the only ground for divorce. Hillel, on the other hand, took a much less rigorous view, pointing out that the one place in the Law (Deut. 24:1ff) which treats divorce is, to say the least, ambiguous. As the Talmud indicates, Hillel's views were generally accepted while Shammai's were not. The opinions of both, however, are frequently included in the Talmudic text.

According to the Mishnah (Pirke Avot, chapter one), Hillel and Shammai were but one dual link in a chain of tradition stretching from Moses to the famous Johanan ben Zakkai of whom we shall have more to say later in this chapter. As shall be seen, it was this tradition of the *Tannaim,* so acute, so argumentative, so all-inclusive, which was eventually to win the day in Judaism itself. Despite all of the bloody warfare, sectarian squabbling, and doomsday predictions, the Rabbis kept at their work, methodically developing an understanding of God's will which was to undergird Judaism for centuries to come.

Philo Judaeus

While Palestine was wracked with political turmoil and the Rabbis argued hard points of the Law, quite another sort of spirit was blossoming in Alexandria, Egypt. Philo Judaeus (20 B.C.-40 A.D.) was born into an aristocratic Jewish family in one of the largest settlements of Jews outside the homeland itself. There Philo was educated not only in the traditions of his people but also in the thought and style of the Greek and Hellenistic philosophers. In fact, he undoubtedly knew more about the ideas of the ancient Hellenes and their successors than he did about his own Jewish tradition.

Philo lived in two worlds. In Alexandria, the Jewish minority, though considerable in number, was despised by the Greek-speaking Gentiles and hence was ostracized and became a world unto itself. This situation might well serve as a symbol for all of Philo's thought, for he was haunted by a sense of alienation and bondage. His self-appointed task was to heal this cultural schizophrenia by proving to Jew and Gentile alike that ultimately the wisdom of the Greeks and the righteousness of the Jews amount to the same thing.

Philo's thought is very difficult to summarize, for much of his writing consists of lengthy *midrashim* (expansive interpretations) upon Scripture. (For an example of Midrashic interpretation, *see* III.C). Thus, the form of his works is thoroughly Jewish. Stylistically, however, he writes in a florid Hellenistic manner, often saying little with a good many words. If one can forgive him the sin of verbosity, however, a unique and thoughtful spirit shines through (*see* III.B).

Philo, as an interpreter of Scripture, believed that the Bible not only has a literal, historical meaning but also a figurative and spiritual one. His treatment of the text's literal purport is usually clumsy and not too well-informed — he obviously wasn't much interested in historical details — but when he turns to what he considers the deeper truths of Scripture, the real Philo emerges.

In order to explicate the spiritual and philosophical truths which the canonical books reveal, he resorts to the now much abused allegorical method which he borrowed from the Stoics. In his hands historical narratives are turned into allegories with a meaning which transcends Israel's nationhood and particularity. Abraham, Isaac, and Jacob, for instance, become, through his allegorizing, stages of the soul as it rises to a knowledge of God.

What Philo discovers in Scripture is, predictably, his own particular synthesis of Platonic, Stoic, and Neo-Pythagorean thought. Essential to this synthesis is the dichotomy between spirit and matter and between the world and God. God, for Philo, is absolutely transcendent, beyond all earthly wisdom, virtue, perfection, or language. Occasionally the author employs the familiar Biblical anthropomorphisms when speaking of God, but he knows he speaks metaphorically. In the last analysis, God can only be spoken of metaphorically. God so transcends the world that he himself has no direct connection with matter at all.

The great abyss between God and the material world is bridged by various potencies *(dynameis)* which proceed from him and through which he created and governs the world. These potencies are equated with both Platonic ideas and the angels which had become so popular in Judaism. They are united in the *Logos* (Word) which is variously described as an idea in the mind of God and as a "second God" who expresses in this world the will of the hidden and transcendent One. In many respects, the *Logos* of Philo is reminiscent of Wisdom in Proverbs and Ecclesiasticus.

Scholars in the past have heatedly debated the question as to whether the writer of the Gospel of John utilized Philo's idea when he proclaimed Jesus to be the *Logos* (Word) made flesh (John 1:1ff). Whether "John" knew of Philo's ideas or not, however, is ultimately of little consequence. What is of consequence is that the notion of a somehow-divine intermediary who could lead man to God was common in both apocalyptic and wisdom literature. All of these writings strongly assert the oneness of God; yet that very transcendent oneness implies the need for a mediator. Philo carries forward this idea in a thoroughly metaphysical direction, maintaining that the principle of mediation can be known through the intellect. In contrast, what is unique about Christianity is that the mediation takes place, not through an abstract principle, but through an historical human being.

Matter, for Philo, is the culprit, the source of evil and sin in the world. Unfortunately, man's spirit is trapped in matter and can be very easily led astray by the love for material things.

This is where both Greek philosophy and the Jewish law come in. Both are effective and complementary means through which the spirit can free itself from the prison house of matter to rise to the contemplation of God. That is, in effect, what the great allegory of the Exodus is all about. Just as Israel escaped from slavery under the Pharaoh, so man, following the heavenly *Logos* revealed in both the philosophers and the Jewish Law, can attain an apathy in regard to sensuous desires and flee the bondage of the senses. The pilgrimage is difficult and demanding, but at the end there is that final moment when the individual experiences the ecstasy of the pure spirit and becomes one with the One. Reason may play an important role in the control of desires, but ultimately the end of man is supra-rational.

Philo himself was no recluse; he was a leader of the Alexandrian Jewish community who even traveled to Rome to plead the cause of his people before a threatening Caligula. Nevertheless, he was attracted to the simple, austere life of the mystic. In his writings he speaks with approval of Jewish ascetic communities, both in Judah [the Essenes] and in Egypt [the Therapeutae] (*see* IV.C). How long these communities continued we do not know. Neither do we know much about their nature and influence. It is usually assumed that Jewish monasticism was a momentary aberration, but this may be but one of those distortions of history perpetrated by those Jewish leaders who found ascetic mysticism antithetical to the way of Judaism.

It is also often asserted that Philo, himself, was "one of a kind" and had little influence upon subsequent generations of Jews. Perhaps. But we also learn from Philo that before him there had been other similar Jewish thinkers upon whom he often drew for insight and inspiration. The fact that we have no writings from followers of Philo does not mean that none existed. If truth be told, we would not have the voluminous writings of Philo himself were it not for the fact that early Christian theologians preserved them. How many other Jewish writings of this sort have been lost, we do not know.

It is at least the case that when Jewish theologians like Saadya Gaon began to develop a philosophical theology in the early Middle Ages, they showed no awareness of Philo's work. If Philo did develop a school of thinkers which carried on his work, it left little impression upon the course of Jewish life and thought as we now know it. Rather, it was upon the Christian theologians of Alexandria that Philo had the most influence. Men like Clement of Alexandria and Origen, though by no means mere copiers, were to transform his Jewish enterprise into a thoroughly Christian undertaking.

In any event, it can be asserted with confidence that Philo was the first Jewish theologian to attempt a synthesis of Israel's faith and Hellenistic wisdom, whose writings have been preserved. Although a frustrating stylist and a sometimes ill-informed exegete, he stands as a primary example of Hellenistic Judaism and as a harbinger of things to come (*see* III.A and IV.C).

The Revolution of 66-70 B.C.

Meanwhile, in Judah tensions grew ever more severe. Rapacious Roman procurators, vacillating Jewish puppet rulers, heavy taxes, and wide-spread poverty fanned the flames of zealotry, turning even moderates into revolutionaries. The growing little Christian sect was but a minor, though annoying, thorn in the side of those Jews who fought desperately for the cause of restraint and reason.

One bright spot in this chaotic time was the rule of Herod Agrippa (41-44) who was appointed King of Judaea by Caius Caligula, replacing the Roman procurator with home rule. His death, however, brought a new series of procurators who were even more venial and inefficient than those before them. Perhaps the worst was Gessius Florus (64-66) whose cupidity and violence pushed both extremists and moderates to a point of no return. When Florus massacred a deputation of moderate leaders for no good reason, the whole nation ignited into flames.

Some zealots, led by one Eleazar, attacked Jerusalem and were successful in seizing the Temple area. Others, under the direction of Menahem, the son of Judas of Galilee, captured Masada, a fortress retreat on a butte overlooking the Dead Sea which had been built by Herod the Great. Before long, Roman troops were being slaughtered and, though the revolutionaries quarreled viciously among themselves, much of Judah soon came under their control.

Cestius Gallus, the proconsul in Syria who had jurisdiction over the region, recognized the seriousness of the uprising and marched into Judaea with some 40,000 men. Because of delays, winter weather, and determined resistance, however, he was forced to retreat, leaving behind some 6,000 dead and huge quantities of war material useful to the defenders. With such a victory in hand, even the most moderate joined the zealot cause and there was much talk of a new era of freedom comparable to that under the Hasmoneans.

The Romans, however, were not so easily dismissed. Nero soon dispatched Vespasian, a trusted general, with 50,000 men and unlimited power to crush the revolt. Vespasian moved coolly and carefully, securing first all of the outlying provinces. In so doing, he captured Flavius Josephus, the Jewish commander of Galilee who was later to write a vivid and detailed account of the whole war. Much of our knowledge of this era comes from his *Wars of the Jews* which to this day makes exciting reading.

By the middle of 68 A.D. nearly all resistance was crushed outside of Jerusalem itself. Vespasian now began what portended to be a long and brutal seige, but was diverted — it appeared to some providentially — from his goal by the sudden death of Emperor Nero. Vespasian returned to Rome to vie for, and eventually receive, the Roman emperorship.

The war, however, was not over. Vespasian dispatched his son Titus with troops and before long the siege of Jerusalem was again initiated. Titus called for surrender, but the zealots would hear none of it. For months, despite internal struggles and dwindling supplies, the defenders held on valiantly. Eventually, however, the Roman war machine did its work and the triple walls of Jerusalem were breached. The defenders retreated to the Temple area itself where, after another siege, they were finally massacred. In the process, the Temple was burned and gutted and, in a stroke, Judaism's cultus came to an end. After 70 A.D. the holy center was never again to be rebuilt. All that remains of it today is the famous Wailing Wall of Jerusalem where, for centuries, Jews have come to lament the loss of this symbol of Jewish strength and unity.

Resistance at Masada was to continue for some time, but eventually Roman siege techniques subdued even this impregnable fortress. When the Romans finally succeeded in reaching the top of the butte, they found only a few women and children alive. All the defenders had committed suicide rather than endure enslavement by the Romans. Modern archaeologists — in particular Yigael Yadin — have explored Masada and have found not only the remains of Herod's pleasure palace but the actual bones of those plucky defenders. The huge earthen ramp built by the Romans to attack the fortress remains to this day as mute testimony to the determination of both Jews and Romans.

Titus returned home in triumph, building in Rome a triumphal arch to commemorate his victory. On it can still be seen a procession of Jewish slaves being led captive into the Empire's capital. Also in evidence are Roman soldiers carrying the sacred menorah and other paraphernalia from the Temple. The Age of the Second Temple was at an end.

The Rabbis Carry On

During the initial siege of Jerusalem under Vespasian, Johanan ben Zakkai, a Rabbinic leader who was not basically anti-Roman in attitude, escaped from the city of Jerusalem. According to tradition, he was carried out in a coffin, as though dead. Once safely outside the walls, he met with Vespasian, predicted that the general would become the next Roman Emperor, and asked that he be allowed the town of Jabneh (Jamnia) and its academy. Vespasian, perhaps out of simple surprise, granted his unusual request.

Thus was founded the most important Jewish institution to exist immediately after the destruction. Johanan ben Zakkai had been for sometime one of the most vocal spokesmen for the Rabbis against the Sadducees. Probably a student of Hillel, he strongly supported the Oral Law and, both before and after 70 A.D., helped to develop it in a variety of ways. At Jabheh he gathered around him a group of lay scholars who formed the *Beth Din Ha-Gadol*, the successor to the now defunct Sanhedrin.

The new organization, of course, had none of the official power and responsibility wielded by the old juridical assembly. It was not recognized by Rome and had no civil power to enforce its regulations. Jews who disagreed with its rulings were, in a sense, free to do so and we can imagine that remnants of the Sadducean party went entirely their own way. Nevertheless, Johanan ben Zakkai as *Nasi* laid down numerous *taqqanoth* (ordinances) and was able, through the force of moral and religious suasion, to gain general acceptance of his pronouncements, at least in Palestine.

Many of these *taqqanoth* reveal the way in which Johanan sought to reconstitute a Judaism bereft of its central cultus. As an anti-Sadducee, the new Nasi does not seem to have lamented unduly either the demise of the High Priesthood or the loss of the Temple. Unlike many of his contemporaries he did not yearn for the rebuilding of the Holy Place. Instead he worked to limit any priestly prerogatives which still obtained and to appropriate for general use many of those customs which once were exclusively used in the Temple. In so doing, he turned Judaism ever more into a world religion which could survive and thrive without homeland or Temple. In a sense, the Temple was replaced in the "center" by the Rabbinic academy which united Judaism through a common law.

It is usually assumed that Johanan ben Zakkai and his many colleagues and disciples were primarily Pharisees and there may be some truth in this. Surely the new assembly was profoundly anti-Sadducean in nature and often took a rather Pharisaic stance. At the same time, it should be noted that the Talmud sometimes includes rather derogatory remarks about the Pharisees and indicates that at least some Pharisees, after the fall of Jerusalem, refused to submit to the authority of the *Beth Din Ha-Gadol* and its Nasi. It is an open question whether before 70 A.D. the Pharisees and the moderate Rabbis can be lumped together, or whether the Pharisees, even at that time, constituted a sect group which was separatist in outlook and radically rigorous in its legal approach.

Before the fall of Jerusalem, the position of Nasi in the Sanhedrin seems to have been an inherited one, held successively by the descendants of Hillel: Simon I, Gamaliel I, and Simon II. There is some question, therefore, as to why Simon II's son, Gamaliel II, did not immediately become Nasi at Jabneh. Probably this was due to the fact that Gamaliel had been anti-Roman during the revolution of 66-70 and hence was, for a time, under suspicion by the Romans. His leadership, therefore, might have wrecked the venture before it was even started.

In any event, sometime between 80 and 90 A.D. Johanan retired from (or was relieved of) his office and was replaced by Gamaliel II. Thus the academy was again headed by a man who could trace his lineage back not only to the famous Hillel but ultimately to King David himself. The house of David, which God had promised would last forever (II Samuel 7:12-16), therefore continued in authority.

A number of Gamaliel's accomplishments bear mentioning. Beside solving several tricky problems connected with the organization of the Jewish calendar — problems which were very important for the establishment of the times for festivals — he also labored to develop a standard prayer service for public use in synagogues. In this connection, the content and order of the *Amidah*, "the Eighteen Benedictions," were standardized. This was of no little consequence, for the *Amidah* became in Judaism the prayer *(tefillah) par excellence.* Gamaliel decreed that the *Amidah* should be recited three times daily by all Jews. In its revised form, it became one of the main pillars of Jewish public worship, comparable to the Christian Lord's Prayer (*see* I.A).

Gamaliel and his fellow Rabbis were also responsible for another major decision, this time concerning Scripture itself. We have already seen that the Law and the Prophets gained final, authoritative status during the fifth and third centuries B.C., respectively. During the Inter-testamental period, other works had also commended themselves to Jews as useful and many collections of Scripture already included them. By the time of Jesus, the book of Psalms, in particular, was already regarded as having canonical status. This "Hymn book of the Second Temple" was so widely used for both liturgical worship and personal devotion that the Rabbis had no need to formally canonize it. In fact, by 90 A.D. the task of the Rabbis was not so much to choose new works as to exclude those which they found objectionable.

Obviously, all Christian writings plus those which seemed to favor a Christian interpretation were anathema and were excluded automatically. The twelfth Benediction of the *Amidah* expresses well the Rabbinic attitude toward that sect:

> Benediction 12. For the renegades let there be no hope, and
> may the arrogant kingdom soon be rooted out in our days,
> and the Nazarenes and the *minim* perish as in a moment and

be blotted out from the book of life and with the righteous may they not be inscribed. Blessed art thou, O Lord, who humblest the arrogant.[1]

Even though they included the book of Daniel in the canon, the Rabbis were also suspicious of those apocalyptic works which either promoted obscurantist interpretations of Scripture or which encouraged zealotic dreams for a Messianic victory over the Romans. They had had enough of such bloodshed, at least for the time being, and were quite willing to put the restoration of Jerusalem in God's hands.

Benediction 14. And to Jerusalem, thy city, return in mercy, and dwell therein as thou has spoken; rebuild it soon in our days as an everlasting building, and speedily set up therein the throne of David. Blessed art thou, O Lord, who rebuildest Jerusalem.[2]

Although many of the works selected came from the post-exilic period, only those books which were purported to have been written before or during the time of Ezra were selected. Thus works like "the Wisdom of Jesus ben Sirach" and the books of the Maccabees found no place in the Rabbinic list of those books which "pollute the hands" (i.e., are holy). After some controversy and debate, therefore, the canon of the *Kethubiim* (Writings) came to include the following:
1. Job. A book of wisdom dealing in depth with the problem: why do the righteous suffer?
2. Psalms. A collection of 150 psalms which express in their verses many varieties of Jewish piety. Perhaps no single book has been more influential in the shaping of Jewish and Christian attitudes toward God and man.
3. Proverbs.
4. The Megilloth. These are five short scrolls traditionally read on five festival days. They include:

   a. Ruth. A story of the Moabitess who became the ancestress of King David. Read on *Shevuoth* (Pentecost).

---

[1] C. K. Barrett, ed., *The New Testament Background: Selected Documents* (New York: Harpet and Brothers, 1961), p. 167.

[2] *Ibid.,* p. 163.

b. The Song of Songs. A love song which was interpreted allegorically to refer to the love of Israel for God. Read on *Pesach* (Passover).

c. Lamentations. A series of five poems lamenting the fall of Jerusalem. Read on the 9th of Av.

d. Ecclesiastes. Read on *Succoth* (Tabernacles).

e. Esther. A highly nationalistic account of the victory of Esther and Mordecai over Persian anti-Semites. Read on Purim.

5. Daniel.

6. I and II Chronicles.

7. Ezra and Nehemiah.

By the time these decisions were made, the Christian Church had already become accustomed to using Greek translations of the Old Testament which included, besides these books, at least fifteen other works and additions to works which were not accepted by the Rabbis at Jabneh. Therefore, until the Reformation of the sixteenth century all Christian Bibles contained such works as III and IV Esdras, Tobit, Judith, the Wisdom of Jesus ben Sirach, I and II Maccabees, etc. Eventually some of the Protestant Reformers (particularly the Calvinists) counselled a return to the Jewish canon and excluded what came to be called "The Apocrypha" from their Bibles. Roman Catholics, however, have retained these books, while Anglicans and Lutherans regarded them as of edifactory value. Even the Calvinists retained the order of the Greek Bible and hence did not preserve the clear-cut distinction between the Prophets and the Writings manifest in the Hebrew Scriptures.

Beside the decisions made concerning calendration, prayer, and canon, the assembly of Gamaliel is also known for its halakic (legal) interpretations. In the Talmud several laws concerning the rights of women, agriculture, and ritualistic matters are attributed to Gamaliel. In the main, these new rulings can be characterized as neither lenient nor stringent, though the assembly clearly wished to provide better justice for the "weaker sex."

The question of who succeeded Gamaliel in office is hotly disputed, but there is at least a reasonable basis for believing that Eleazar ben Azariah and then the famous Rabbi Akiba were primary leaders for relatively short periods of time. Akiba may have only been acting Nasi, but even so he demands more than a minor place in the history of the period, for it was he who began the process of organizing and pruning the vast halakic material which had developed during and after the Second Temple period. Thus he initiated a movement which was to culminate the Mishnah of Judah Ha-Nasi at the beginning of the third century. Akiba organized the Oral Law in various categories, selected the most important *halakoth* for special preservation, and thus revolutionized the whole process of Jewish education.

Akiba is also to be remembered for his method of interpreting Scripture. Unlike many of his contemporaries, who argued that Scripture speaks the language of common man and thus should be understood according to its most obvious sense, Akiba maintained that every word, every letter of Scripture has special significance which the exegete must discover. For him, the Torah was God's law and hence each minute detail was of special importance. If a word was obscure or an idea repeated this implied to him that something special was being communicated.

Although Rabbi Akiba's attitude frequently led to the most contorted results, it was found particularly attractive by many followers who were able, through it, to discover numerous, hidden truths in the Law. Parenthetically, the same techniques were also employed by Jewish mystics and occultists to find in Scripture all sorts of apparently non-Biblical ideas. It is no wonder that Rabbi Akiba's name came to be associated with the esoteric tradition of Judaism.

The Revolt of Bar Kokhba

Akiba is also known for his political activity which ended in his martyrdom. After the destruction of the Temple, many Rabbis turned with horror from any form of zealotry, seeking to live in peace with the Romans. The rather pacific tone of the Rabbinic writings, however, should not blind us to the fact that in Palestine and throughout many parts of the Diaspora there were militant Jews, hungry for new conflict with Rome. These people were frequently stirred up by the Parthians who found it useful to foment rebellion in the Roman Empire and hence keep her western enemies at bay. There is evidence, in fact, that although Parthia officially stayed out of the civil war which erupted in 66 A.D., she allowed Jewish troops from

Adiabene to fight with Palestinian forces against the Romans. It may be that the zealots held out for so long in 70 A.D. because they hoped for Parthian intervention.

Parthia had a large and influential Jewish minority within her boundaries. Indeed, several areas were, at times, governed by Jewish officials. Generally, the Jews in Parthia were loyal to their government and often occupied positions of influence. By the first third of the second century, the Jewish community in the Parthian Empire had its own Exilarch, a son of David, who ruled over the Jewish communities there and who, as a consequence, rivaled the Palestinian Nasi in importance. As we have already said, the latter made claims to Davidic descent too, but he also had to admit that the Exilarch's line of descent was more prestigious.

In any event, when Trajan invaded Parthia in the second decade of the second century, Jews in Cyprus, Egypt, and Cyrenaica revolted, slaughtering Gentiles in great numbers, and hence drawing Roman attention away from the Parthian campaign. The revolts were so bloody and so out-of-hand that Jews ever after were forbidden to set foot on Cyprus or Cyrenaica under penalty of death. In Egypt too the revolt left permanent scars which were never quite erased. It was at this time that the Gentiles, in response, destroyed the heterodox temple in Leontides.

Sensing a "fifth column" in their midst, the Romans looked with suspicion on the whole Jewish population and, it would appear, decided to solve the problem once and for all. The Emperor Hadrian (117-138 A.D.) began his reign by showing apparent friendship for the Jews but before long things took a turn for the worse. Hadrian gave orders for the erection, on the site of the Jewish Temple, of an edifice dedicated to the worship of Capitoline Jupiter. He also issued general laws forbidding the mutilation of the body and hence, either consciously or inadvertently, banned circumcision.

The Jewish community in Palestine, under the leadership of one Simon bar Kokhba (whose name we now know was Bar Kosiba), revolted once more. Rabbi Akiba greatly encouraged the rebellion by proclaiming this leader to be none other than the Messiah himself. For three and one-half years Bar Kokhba and his followers fought on, defeating the best Roman troops sent against them. Eventually, however, the unavoidable occurred. In 135 A.D., Roman troops under Severus attacked Bar

Kokhba at Bethar, a few miles southwest of Jerusalem. The revolutionary met his death and thus his attempt to create a new independent state was quelled.

Persecutions now began in earnest. Hadrian suppressed the *Beth Din Ha-Gadol*, issuing an order banning both the teaching of the Torah and the practice of its observances. So many disobeyed the Roman edict and hence were martyred that a council of sages, meeting at Lydda, announced that in order to save his life a Jew might violate all commandments except those forbidding idolatry, murder, and incest. This decision was to have profound effects upon Judaism, for it became a standard for conduct under growing Gentile persecution. Akiba, however, continued to teach publicly and hence met a martyr's death. It is said that Roman soldiers used pinchers to pull his living flesh from his bones.

The Creation of the Mishnah

After Hadrian's death in 138 A.D. the anti-Jewish laws were annulled by Antonius Pius and the Rabbis were able to reconvene, this time at Usha in Palestine. Eventually the line of Hillel was restored to leadership in the person of Simon ben Gamaliel II, but he was basically a weak Nasi who very nearly was expelled from office by Rabbi Nathan and Rabbi Meir.

Happily for Judaism he retained his position, for although he was hardly a great scholar, his son Judah I (circa 170-217 A.D.) was one of the best. Through his efforts, the Oral Law was arranged and codified and a whole new era of scholarship began. Judah I's position, however, was far from secure when he took office. Even though the Nasi is said to have been on friendly terms with the emperor, Roman persecution occurred intermittently. Even more disconcerting, perhaps, was the apparent threat to the preeminence of the Palestinian Nasi's position from the Exilarch of Babylonia. In a number of Talmudic passages rivalry is clearly in evidence between Judah Ha-Nasi and Hiyya, a Babylonian Rabbi who was a member of the *Beth Din Ha-Gadol* and who frequently reminded Judah of the status of the Exilarch.

Nevertheless, Judah was not only to survive in these circumstances but to preside over the formulation of the Mishnah, one of the most important documents in Jewish history. Following the lead of Rabbi Akiba, Judah and his academy selected, organized, and edited the numerous *halakoth* developed over the centuries, thus producing a collection of traditional legal judgments which was to serve Judaism well from that day to this.

Other traditions not chosen by him for the Mishnah are fortunately preserved for us in both the *Tosephta* and *Berkaioth.* Both these collections are of importance, for they help to show how Judah did his work by revealing what he left out of his collection. Clearly, Judah sought to produce a synthesis of various schools of thought. Frequently, he omitted the arguments for a particular point of view in order to keep his collection from becoming too unwieldly. The legal judgments themselves are also often abbreviated in the Mishnah, one may suppose for the sake of conciseness.

The term "legal judgments" is more appropriate than "laws," because frequently the Mishnah includes contradictory opinions and sometimes leaves issues unresolved. It offers, therefore, guidelines for judgment rather than final, definitive answers and calls upon succeeding generations to study further in order to decide which opinion is best. This characteristic of the Mishnah is important for it reveals that the Jewish attitude toward law could be exceedingly flexible and open to new arguments. This quality has allowed Judaism to continue for centuries the development and alteration of its interpretation of the Torah.

Unlike Midrashic writings which are essentially a running commentary on Scripture, the Mishnah, while alluding to appropriate texts from the Torah, is bound by neither the order nor even the exact requirements of Mosaic Law. The *Mishnaoth* (individual paragraphs) are arranged topically, though some topics obviously overlap. When an ordinance of the Torah itself is found to be at variance with a more general commandment or ordinance, the former is annulled. For instance, though Sabbath Laws are strictly interpreted and enforced, they are abandoned in cases of sickness, danger, etc. Throughout the Mishnah we find expressed an overarching concern for the poor and down-trodden, a concern which operates to ameliorate the Law at a number of points.

The Mishnah of Judah Ha-Nasi is divided into six *Sedarim* or orders. These are each divided into *Massechtiyot* or tractates. There are, in all, sixty-three such tractates. The tractates are divided into *Perakim* (chapters) which, in turn, are subdivided into sections called *Mishnaoth* or *Halakoth*. A brief summary of the Sedarim and their contents will at least give an overview of the vast amount of material involved.

I. Zeraim (Seeds). The eleven tractates in this Seder deal with benedictions and prayers (man's response to God's gift of food), agriculture and fruits, the Sabbatical year, tithes and offerings to the priests.

II. Mo'ed (Festivals). These twelve tractates concern the Sabbath, High Holy Days, Passover, the Temple tax, the festival of Succoth, fast days, Purim, etc. The tractate "Shabbat" is the longest in the Mishna.

III. Nashim (Women). Seven tractates deal with marriage, betrothal, divorce, levirate marriages, vows, etc.

IV. Nezikim (Damages). In ten tractates what we might call civil and criminal law is discussed. Included in this Seder is the tractate Abot, the "Ethics of the Fathers," a rich source for ethical teachings in the Mishnah.

V. Kodashim (Sacred Things). Laws related to the Temple and its sacrificial cultus are elaborated in eleven tractates. Even at the time of Judah Ha-Nasi much of this material was no longer immediately relevant, for the Temple had long since been destroyed.

VI. Tohorot (Purifications). The twelve tractates in this Seder deal with various impurities of body and things.

There is no possibility in this brief summary of Jewish history to include further analysis of this massive work, but a few selected quotations may provide at least a clue as to the style and technique of the Mishnah.

Yevamot 6:6

> No man may refrain from fulfilling the mitzvah of: "Be fruitful and multiply", (Genesis 1:28) unless he already has children. According to the school of Shammai, he must have two sons. According to the school of Hillel, a son and a daughter, for it is written, "male and female created He them" (Genesis 1:27). If he marries a woman and lives with her ten years, and she bears no child, he is still not permitted to refrain from fulfilling the mitzvah. If he divorces her, she may be married to another man, and the second husband may live with her for ten years. If she has a miscarriage, the time is reckoned from the date of the miscarriage. The duty "to be fruitful and multiply" is incumbent upon the man, but

not on the woman. R. Johanan b. Baroha says: of both it is
written: "And God blessed them and God said unto them,"
be fruitful and multiply' "*

Hullin 8:3

If a drop of milk falls on a piece of meat cooking in a pot and
there is enough milk to flavor the piece of meat, it is forbidden. If the pot is stirred, it is forbidden if there is enough
milk to flavor all the contents of the pot. (*Ibid.*, p. 252).

Eduyot 1:4

Why do they record the opinions of Shammai and Hillel
which did not prevail? In order to teach future generations
that a man should not persist in his opinion, for even "the
fathers of the world" did not have all their opinions prevail.
(*Ibid.*, p. 232).

Horayot 1:1

If a Bet Din ruled that any mitzvah of the Torah could be
transgressed, and an individual proceeded and acted in error
following their ruling, whether they acted and he acted with
them, or whether he acted after them, or even if they did not
act and he did, he is exempt, because he relied on a ruling of
the court. If a Bet Din ruled erroneously and a member of the
court knew that they had erred, or a disciple who was capable
of deciding matters of Torah knew they had erred and still
went and acted on their ruling, whether they acted and he
acted with them, or they acted thereafter, or whether they
did not act at all but he did so, he is liable since he did not
have to depend on the ruling of the court. This is the general
rule: Anyone who can rely on himself is liable, but anyone
who must depend on the court is exempt. (*Ibid.*, p. 37).

The Age of the Amoraim

With the work of Judah Ha-Nasi the so-called Tannaic
period of Judaism came to an end. After this time, although
many Jews continued to live in Palestine, the center of gravity
shifted to Babylonia. Many of the foremost Rabbis, harried by
Roman persecution, traveled eastward to continue their
labors; the *Beth Din Ha-Gadol* in Palestine became but a

---

*Eugene J. Lipman, tr. *The Mishnah, Oral Teachings of Judaism* (New York:
Norton, 1970), p. 161.

shadow of its former self. Abba Arika (175-247), a disciple of Judah Ha-Nasi, went to Babylonia in 219, founding there the famous school at Sura. Another disciple of Judah I, Rabbi Samuel (180-250), established a rival school at Nehardea. Still a third academy was eventually began in Pumbeditha in 258.

In both Palestine and Babylonia, teachers called *Amoraim* (speakers) worked through the Mishnah line-by-line, discussing in detail the meaning and implication of each word and sentence. Thus, in a relatively short space of time the Mishnah became the focal point for Jewish learning and discussion. Gradually, around the now-written "Oral" Law there developed a new oral tradition of considerable extent which came to be called Gemara (completion).

Unlike the Mishnah, the Gemara is in Aramaic and not in Hebrew, the classical language of Israel which Judah Ha-Nasi sought to perpetuate. Gone also are the terseness and conciseness of Mishnah. The Gemara, to be sure, seeks to summarize arguments and sometimes can be painfully abbreviated. Nevertheless, there is an expansiveness about the Gemara which cannot be denied. The Amoraic traditions of both Palestine and Babylonia are laced freely with all sorts of stories, legends, and traditions which are woven into the fabric of discussion. Much of our knowledge of this whole long period, in fact, comes from this *aggadah* which provides us with many glimpses of both the Tannaic and Amoraic periods.

Needless to say, the historian must examine these traditions with great care, for many of them reveal more about the imagination of the Amoraim than they do about historical fact. Still, imbedded in the text are many stories of historical worth which, if used carefully, can help to illumine the whole period. A few examples will show the variety of aggadic material available:

Shabbath, 56b

> Rab Judah said in Samuel's name: When Solomon married Pharaoh's daughter, Gabriel descended and planted a reed in the sea, and it gathered a bank around it, on which the great city of Rome was built. In Baraitha it was taught: On the day that Jeroboam brought the two golden calves, one into Bethel and the other into Dan, a hut was built and this developed into Greek Italy.*

---

*Rabbi I. Epstein, ed., The Babylonian Talmud, Vol. I (London: Soncino Press, 1938), p. 264.

Shabbath 156b

From R. Akiba too (we learn that) Israel is free from planetary influence. For R. Akiba had a daughter. Now, astrologers told him, on the day she enters the bridal chamber a snake will bite her and she will die. He was very worried about this. On that day (of her marriage) she took a broach (and) stuck it into the wall and by chance it penetrated (sank) into the eye of a serpent. The following morning, when she took it out, the snake came trailing after it. 'What did you do?' her father asked her. 'A poor man came to our door in the evening,' she replied, 'and everybody was busy at the banquet, and there was none to attend to him. So I took the portion which was given to me and gave it to him.' 'You have done a good deed,' said he to her. Thereupon R. Akiba went out and lectured: 'But charity delivereth from death': and not (merely) from an unnatural death, but from death itself. (*Ibid.*, Pt. II, Vol. I, p. 801).

Baba Mezi'a 85b

Elijah used to frequent Rabbi's academy. One day — it was New Moon — he was waiting for him, but he failed to come. Said he to him (the next day): 'Why didst thou delay?' — He replied: '(I had to wait) until I awoke Abraham, washed his hands, and he prayed and I put him to rest again: likewise Isaac and Jacob.' 'But why not awake them together?' — 'I feared that they would wax strong in prayer and bring the Messiah before his time.' 'And is their like to be found in this world?' he asked. — 'There is R. Hiyya and his sons,' he replied. Thereupon Rabbi proclaimed a fast, and R. Hiyya and his sons were bidden to descend (to the reading desk). As he (R. Hiyya) exclaimed, 'He causeth the wind to blow,' a wind blew; he proceeded, 'he causeth the rain to descend,' whereat the rain descended. When he was about to say, 'He quickeneth the dead,' the universe trembled, (and) in Heaven it was asked, 'Who hath revealed our secret to the world?' 'Elijah,' they replied. Elijah was therefore brought and smitten with sixty flaming lashes so he went, disguised himself as a fiery bear, entered amongst and scattered them. (*Ibid.*, Pt. IV, Vol. I, p. 492).

Baba Bathra 12b

R. Johanan said: Since the Temple was destroyed, prophecy
has been taken from prophets and given to fools and
children. How given to fools? — The case of Mar son of R.
Ashi will illustrate. He was one day standing in the manor of
Mahuza when he heard a certain lunatic exclaim: The man
who is to be elected head of the Academy in Matha Mehasia
signs his name Tabiumi. He said to himself: Who among the
Rabbis signs his name Tabiumi? I do. This seems to show
that my lucky time has come. So he quickly went to Matha
Mehasia. When he arrived, he found that the Rabbis had
voted to appoint R. Aha of Difti as their head. When they
heard of his arrival, they sent a couple of Rabbis to him to
consult him. He detained them with him, and they sent
another couple of Rabbis. He detained these also (and so it
went on) until the number reached ten. When ten were
assembled, he began to discourse and expound the Oral Law
and the Scriptures, (having waited so long) because a public
discourse (on them) should not be commenced if the audience
is less than ten. R. Aha applied to himself the saying: If a
man is in disfavour (with Heaven) he does not readily come
into favour, and if a man is in favour he does not readily fall
into disfavour (*Ibid.,* Pt IV., Vol. II, p. 60).

The extent to which any of these stories can be described as
historical is, in a way, immaterial. Even though legend may
triumph over fact in all of them, each, in its own way, reveals
post-Mishnaic attitudes toward Rome, astrology, prophecy,
etc. The third quotation, though obviously mythical in content, expresses very well the tension which existed between
Rabbi Judah Ha-Nasi and Rabbi Hiyya. The patient scholar
who is willing to listen carefully to the Talmudic dialogue can
derive abundant information about the life and thought of
Jewish people between the third and the sixth centuries.

The picture that emerges is one of a people deeply devoted to
the Law and its implications and yet also very much influenced
by their contemporary surroundings. Magic, astrology,
mythology, and all sorts of occult practices are mentioned and
not all assessments given are negative. At the same time, the
modern reader must be impressed by the acuteness of the legal
reasoning, the questioning frame of mind, and the compassion
shown for those in need. Although the Gemara, like the

Mishnah, contains many judgments and rules, the Gemara is not a legal code. Rather it is a portrait of great numbers of intelligent men who asked repeatedly: How does God want us to live now?

Although the major centers for intellectual activity were in Babylonia after the time of Judah Ha-Nasi, Rabbinic activity in Palestine did not end. There the Rabbis developed their own Gemara. Perhaps because the threats to the continued existence of Judaism in that area were so much greater, the Palestinian Talmud was written down and codified first. By the middle of the fourth century, the Palestinian Talmud, i.e., the Mishnah plus the Palestinian Gemara, was complete. This work was finished none too soon. In A.D. 425 the Christian Emperor Theodosius II abolished the patriarchal office which had been held by the head of the academy and that venerable tradition of scholarship came to a momentary end.

The much more extensive and authoritative Babylonian Talmud took considerably longer than its Palestinian counterpart to complete. Layer upon layer of halakic and aggadic material was added until the work of editing and redacting was undertaken by Rab Ashi of the Sura Academy in the fifth century. His successors carried on his labors until, in about 500 A.D. the work was completed by Rabina II, the last of the Amoraim. Again, the codification of the Gemara took place under threat, this time by the fire-worshipping Mazdeans of Iran and Babylonia who had become increasingly suppressive since their take-over politically in the third century. Ironically, then, it was anti-Jewish persecution which led to the formulation of Judaism's greatest post-Biblical masterpiece.

Among the documents which men around the world have produced, the Talmud is unique. It is a collection of laws and judgments; yet it is much more than that, for it incorporates the insights, piety, and wit of generations of scholars who, wrestling with crucial contemporary problems, sought for answers both hidden and explicit in God's word. No one can just read the Talmud. To try to do so would be like trying to read through the Congressional Record of the United States. Instead, the Talmud is a work which is to be studied and meditated upon over the years. To this day, shopkeepers and farmers, servants and financiers meet together in synagogues to pour over the text, to learn what Judaism is all about, and to debate what, for the present, the implications of the Law are.

After the Bible, the Talmud has served as the most authoritative work to which Jews could appeal for guidance. Indeed, in certain respects, the Talmud has had preeminence over even Scripture, for the Torah has most frequently been read with Talmudic eyes. At the same time, the Talmud is no seamless robe but contains within it a great variety of differing, even contradictory opinions. This very inconsistency has meant that Judaism has been able to maintain its flexibility through the centuries and hence has been able to retain within i s ranks men of decidedly different points of view.

The Mystical Tradition

Since the development of Mishnah and Gemara was so crucial for the further development of Judaism, most historians of the Jews have concentrated much of their attention upon this Rabbinic movement. Because these efforts were confined to a few academies in Palestine and Babylonia, however, we must ask: What else was going on?

Clearly, by this time there were Jewish communities all over the world — from northern Europe to China. Recent discoveries of what looks to be Hebraic writing in Tennessee reveal that there may have even been a community of Jews in America during the period of the Roman Empire! What immediate effects did the work of the Rabbis have upon the far-flung settlements of the Diaspora? Was their labor the only major intellectual movement or were there others? Did all of the other sects of Judaism suddenly disappear with the fall of Jerusalem to Titus or did many of them survive?

Unfortunately, information is severely limited and we can, for the most part, only guess. There are at least hints in the Talmud and early Christian writings that certain groups of Pharisees, like the Baptist Pharisees, did survive outside the Rabbinic mainstream. It is also quite likely that Sadduceanism did not die immediately but continued on in attenuated form, perhaps providing the nucleus for the Karaite movement which we shall discuss in the next chapter. As already indicated, it is quite possible that Hellenistic Judaism a la Philo may have continued in Alexandria and elsewhere.

More direct evidence is available concerning the continuation of certain ideas found in the apocalyptic literature by esoteric thinkers within Judaism. Gershom Scholem, in his epoch-making works concerning Jewish mysticism, reminds us that while the Rabbis were pouring over the legal corpus of ancient Israel, there were those who found more interest and inspiration in the bizarre imagery of Ezekiel and in the secret wisdom *(kabbalah)* which, some claimed, had been passed down from the time of Abraham. This is not to say that the Tannaim and Amoraim themselves were not interested in the mystical side of their faith. There are many passages in the Talmud which show close acquaintance with all sorts of mystical symbols and ideas. During this period, however, there were authors who developed these ideas in a much more direct and systematic way. It is to these thinkers which we now must turn.

Among those works which express what Scholem has termed *merkabah* (throne) mysticism are "The Visions of Ezekiel," "The Lesser Hekhaloth," "The Greater Hekhaloth," and the *Shiur Komah*. In all of these there is great emphasis placed upon ecstatic flight up through the seven heavens (which are populated by hostile and friendly angels) to the final transcendent level where God sits upon his throne *(merkabah)*. Apparently, certain postures (sitting with one's head between one's knees) and various incantations were used to achieve this flight. The literature is full of detailed information about what the ecstatic will encounter and the dangers he must avoid. Considerable emphasis is also placed upon the various palaces *(hekaloth)* through which the traveler must pass as well as upon the guiding angelic forces. The books reveal those words which must not be said, lest disaster befall the "traveler," and those powerful incantations and phrases which will get one through the innumerable dangers to be confronted (*see* II.A).

The final vision of God upon his throne is by no means easy to achieve and demands both great knowledge and great psychic stamina. Unlike most mystics, however, the *merkabah* ecstatics do not see the end of their quest as absorption into God or as the loss of self. Rather the culmination of the journey is a vision of God who throughout remains transcendent and aloof from creation. God may be seen in his radiant splendor and certain thaumaturgic secrets may be learned, but man remains man and God, God.

One rather striking work, *Shiur Komah*, offers to the reader an extraordinarily anthropomorphic description of God upon his throne. Although the units of measure are not wholly comprehensible and it is implied that the immensity of God's dimensions are not really understandable to mortal man, the work does indicate that God has an anthropomorphic form and that man, though minute in comparison, is made, quite literally, in God's image.

Another influential work, *Sepher Yetzirah*, offers in a few, brief pages clues to an occult understanding of creation based upon the ten *sephiroth* and the twenty-two letters of the Hebrew alphabet. The *sephiroth*, though not clearly defined in the work, appear to be both the attributes of God and yet emanations from him.

> 4. Ten ineffable Sephiroth, ten and not nine, ten and not eleven: understand with wisdom and apprehend with care; examine by means of them and search them out; know, count, and write. Put forth the subject in its light and place the Formator on His throne. He is the only Creator and the only Formator, and no one exists but He: His attributes are ten and have no limits.

> 6. Ten ineffable Sephiroth: their appearance is like that of a flash of lightning, their goal is infinite. His word is in them when they emanate and when they return; at His bidding do they haste like a whirlwind; and before His throne do they prostrate (themselves).*

These are paths of wisdom through which man can rise to God, the intermediaries between God and creation.

The twenty-two letters, by their very sounds, reflect the mysteries of the cosmos. From the three "mother letters," *aleph, mem,* and *shin,* flow air, water, and fire respectively. Seven double letters (i.e., those which can be pronounced hard or soft) relate to the seven heavens and planets. The twelve remaining letters represent the signs of the zodiac and the months of the Hebrew year.

Just how the *Sepher Yetzirah* was used is unclear, for its language is obscure and perplexing. Perhaps it was employed for magical purposes. In any event, it sets forth, albeit in a veiled fashion, categories of thought which were to influence the course of Jewish mystical and occult thought throughout

---

*Rabbi Akiba ben Joseph, *The Book of Formation (Sephir Yetzirah)*, trans Knut Stenring (New York: Ktav Publishing House, 1970), p. 17.

the Middle Ages. Parenthetically, the Tarot deck which has become popular once more in recent years reflects many of the secrets contained in the *Sepher Yetzirah*.

Until quite recently most modern, critical scholars dated these mystical works in the early Middle Ages and therefore considered their attribution to men like Rabbi Akiba and Rabbi Ishmael as entirely spurious. More recent investigation by Scholem, however, has demonstrated the probability of a much earlier date, thus placing them within the context of the Gnostic movement which pervaded Jewish, Christian, and pagan thought from the second century onward.

Unlike the Christian gnostics, who moved in a highly heretical direction by maintaining that beside the God of this world (the God of the Old Testament) there is a higher, hidden God whom Jesus made known, the Jewish mystics seem fastidiously orthodox. They assert strongly the oneness of God and occasionally express their full acceptance of the Mishnaic ordinances. Therefore, there seems to be no reason to think that they were anti-Rabbinic heretics. The attribution of the writing down of the *Sepher Yetzirah* to Rabbi Akiba may still be difficult to accept, but it is no longer unreasonable to think that the merkabah mystics represent the inner, ecstatic face of the Amoraic movement.

Sober, rational Rabbis of later ages, embarrassed by what they have regarded as superstition, have often tried to minimize such mysticism and have laid full stress upon the legal side of the Talmud alone. Nevertheless, throughout the years mysticism and the occult have not been entirely forgotten within the Jewish tradition. In the next chapter we will have occasion to examine more fully the development of such tendencies in the medieval period.

Judaism in the Roman and Persian Empires

Before turning to the new age which dawned after the close of the Talmud, it may be appropriate to look briefly at the situation of Judaism in the Roman and Persian Empires following the Bar Kokhba cataclysm. Needless to say, it is quite understandable that the Roman leaders, after experiencing the several Jewish riots and revolts which marred the first and second centuries A.D., looked with suspicion upon their

Jewish subjects. To the Romans, the Jews appeared as a fifth column movement operating in behalf of their Eastern enemies or, if not that, as at least a non-conforming minority which just would not blend into the Empire.

It is also understandable that the Jews, having experienced harsh Roman taxation, rapacious governors, and military brutality, looked upon Rome as a modern "Edom." Despite an occasional pro-Roman Nasi and a few olive branches proffered by various emperors, relations between Romans and Jews were seldom very cordial. After the era of Judah Ha-Nasi many Jews simply moved eastward, settling with their fellow Jews in Mesopotamia.

There, conditions were considerably better. The Neo-Persian, Sassanian Empire, which was founded in 226 A.D. continued the tradition of the Exilarch and generally treated the Jews justly. Taxation was, on the whole, less burdensome than under the Romans and Jews were allowed to hold high places in government. As we have seen, with the *Amoraim* Jewish intellectual life flourished in comparative freedom. Those Jews who remained in the Roman Empire tended to look more and more to Persia as a source for inspiration and encouragement.

The rise of Christianity only made the situation of Roman Empire Jews that much worse. From the very beginning, Christianity had found many converts among Jews of the Diaspora, particularly among those former Gentiles who had previously either converted to Judaism or had remained "God fearers," i.e., those who had sympathy for Judaism but were uncircumcized. During the Hellenistic age Judaism had become a missionary religion and had made many converts all over the Empire. Christianity's initial success among the "new Jews" forced Judaism to reconsider its whole missionary program. Long before the government officially banned the conversion of Christians to Judaism, the Jews had already ceased their missionary activity and had opted for a program of survival based upon ethnicity rather than rapid growth through conversions.

Not only did Christianity convert many Jews, particularly in Asia Minor and North Africa; Christian antagonism to Judaism put the mother faith continually on the defensive. In many respects, Christianity and Judaism were (and are) much alike. Both accepted the Law and the Prophets as canonical; both traced their religious lineage back to pre-exilic Israel.

Precisely because they held many beliefs in common, however, conflict was bound to result. Christianity claimed to be the rightful heir of the Old Testament tradition, the New Israel born out of the ashes of the old. The destruction of the Temple in 70 A.D. was taken by Christians as a sign that a new age, the age of Jesus, the Messiah, had begun. For Christians, the Jews were a deviant group which would not accept God's will for the new age. In Jesus, God had offered his new covenant, but the Jews had not accepted it. Instead, most maliciously, they had condemned the Messiah to death. Using the allegorical and other hermeneutical methods developed by the Rabbis, Christians searched the Scriptures to demonstrate their case.

The Jews, in turn, regarded the Christians as deviates who had introduced notions not at all in accord with the Hebrew Scriptures. The doctrine of the Trinity looked to them like tritheism; the doctrine of the incarnation, like blasphemy. Christian repudiation of the relevance of Mosaic Law in the new age appeared to Jews as a radical and unwarranted denial of God's eternal will for man. To the Jew, Christianity seemed a most distasteful synthesis of some ancient Jewish ideas and pure paganism.

The long debate which ensued brought out the worst in each party. Love and mercy, qualities extolled by both Jews and Christians, were seldom in evidence on either side. The Jews tended to shut themselves off, disdaining debate and distrusting any sign of reconciliation. The Christians, in their turn, offered bitter diatribe after bitter diatribe, at times attacking Judaism even more severely than paganism.

What a blow it was, therefore, when, in the fourth century, Constantine began the process whereby Christianity was to become the official religion of the Empire! Until the fourth century Judaism and Christianity had each known its hours of persecution and martyrdom. It is quite amazing, however, how quickly the Church of the saints and martyrs forgot what it was like to be suppressed and harried. While candles burned in memory of those saints who died under Roman persecution, the Christian emperors acted to suppress their Jewish brethren with little sympathy at all for those who, committed as they were to the transcendent Reality, refused to relinquish their faith.

All of this was, in a way, understandable. Christianity was proclaimed the religion of the state in order to provide a common religious unity parallel to the political one. Most of the pagans, at least overtly, submitted to this new vision of "one nation under God," but the Jews would not. They alone were the one major group which would not unite in common allegiance to the God revealed in Christ. Hence they were regarded not only as religiously deviate but as politically insubordinate (*see* V.B). Although Judaism was never quite outlawed, Jews in many areas were forbidden to build new synagogues and considerable pressure was put on them to conform. Since the Empire fought one war after another with Persia, the Jews were also frequently suspected of aiding and abetting the enemy.

Unfortunately for the Jews of the East, the Persians also began to think along similar lines. That is to say, while the Roman and then Byzantine Empire became increasingly "Christian" in its attitudes, the Sassanid dynasty increasingly emphasized Zoroastrianism as its official religion. By the fifth century, the governmental pressures for religious conformity became severe. To be sure, the Jewish community in Babylonia was much larger proportionally than it was in the Roman Empire and had a long tradition of prestige and political power which could not easily be set aside. Still, governmental insistence was intense and despite long-standing Jewish loyalty to the Persian government, there were examples of vicious persecution and harassment.

In both East and West this emphasis upon religious unity as a basis for the state was a sign of weakness, not strength. Somehow the vigorous, forward look of both Empires had given way to economic stagnation and political decay. The quest for absolute religious unity was but a grasping after straws, a sign that neither state could stand the healthy give-and-take of contrary opinions. Before long, a new and quite unexpected force was to take advantage of this stagnation, transforming the whole Mediterranean world into something decidedly new. In 570 A.D., just seventy years after the closing of the Talmud, Mohammed was born.

Judaism's year begins in the fall, on the first day of Tishri, the seventh lunar month, with Rosh hashana. On the tenth day of that same month falls Yom Kippur, the Day of Atonement when all pious Jews seek to cleanse themselves of their sin through prayer and fasting. Although not mentioned in the Torah itself, this day above all others is considered the holiest of days by Jews. It is the day when all sins of the past are laid bare before God so that He may "cover them over." Pictured here is a Torah scroll containing both the Law according to which Israel is judged and the promises of hope by which the people of God live.

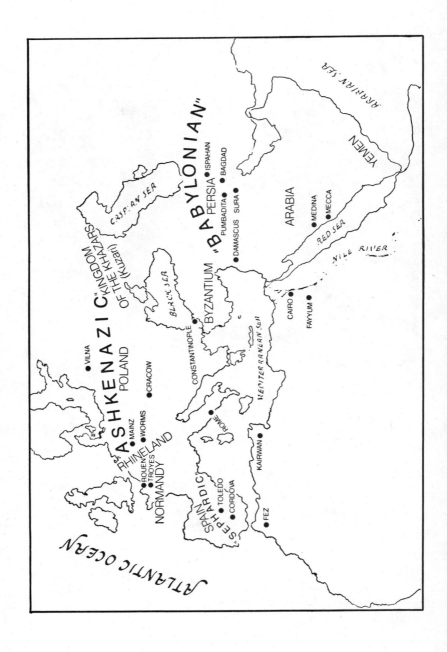

3

FROM MOHAMMED TO THE EXPULSION FROM SPAIN (570-1492 A.D.)

Long before the sixth century, when the Arabian peninsula gave birth to one of the world's great religions, Jews had settled along the Red Sea, in Arabia, Yemen, Ethiopia, and perhaps even further south. In a culture of rather backward polytheism, they had maintained themselves as merchants, caravaneers, and farmers, in outward appearance little different than their neighbors. The state of the Jews in this whole area was certainly not "advanced," according to the standards set in Babylonia, but they clung to their traditions and that, in itself, promoted higher standards of literacy and intellectual life than those known to their neighbors.

This is not to say, however, that Arabia was merely a back water area, isolated from the surrounding world. On the contrary, the Arabian peninsula had been engaged in trade with both east and west for centuries and was characterized by a rather cosmopolitan atmosphere. Still, the religion of the region was that of the desert Bedouin and featured sacred stones, a host of male and female deities, and an accent upon tribalism.

Many reasons have been given for Mohammed's religious revolution, not least among which is that he came into contact with Jews and Christians and felt that his own backward culture needed to be modernized along monotheistic lines. This sense of cultural and religious inferiority may, indeed, have stimulated Mohammed to start thinking and undoubtedly caused him to adopt various Judaeo-Christian beliefs and practices. At the same time, it must be recognized that Mohammed was much more than a mere copier; he was an ecstatic who received revelations from the angel Gabriel. Had it not been for his visionary and auditory experiences, he probably would have remained an illiterate camel driver who had the good fortune to marry rich.

Mohammed regarded himself, not just as a reformer, but as the seal of the prophets, the last of a long line of God-inspired men stretching back to Abraham himself. Therefore, he was willing to endure persecution, hardship, and peril because he knew he was right. The angel of Allah had spoken.

Because the Jews also believed in one God and in his prophets, Mohammed regarded them as natural allies against his heathen foes. The Jews were his brothers; while they were descended from Abraham through Isaac, the Arabs were descended from Abraham's older son, Ishmael. Both Arabs and Jews, therefore, are, according to Islam, recipients of God's blessing to Abraham. During the course of his revelations, Mohammed [or was it Gabriel?] introduced a number of practices of Jewish origin. Mohammed taught his followers initially to face Jerusalem when they prayed, to refrain from eating pork, and to celebrate the Day of Atonement. Apparently, the prophet believed that by so doing he could win the Jews over to his cause. When they refused to be convinced, however, and even criticized his interpretation of the Scriptures, he turned against them, and, quite bitterly, attacked them with force of arms. Jerusalem remained important for Islam, but now believers were instructed to face Mecca when praying. The Day of Atonement was replaced by the sacred month of Ramadan. Jewish tribes, his hoped-for allies, were driven out of Medina. It appeared, therefore, that Islam and Judaism, though similar in many ways, would coexist even less amiably than Christianity and Judaism (see V. C).

The truth of the matter, however, was rather the reverse. As the Arabic forces united under the banner of Islam pushed out of the peninsula, they conquered an immense territory which no army of Bedouin tribesmen could hope to retain by military power alone. In a few short years, Syria-Palestine, Mesopotamia, Persia, Egypt, and North Africa had submitted to their violent advances. Both Byzantium and Persia, exhausted by long wars with each other, simply collapsed. Within a century, Spain had also fallen before the Islamic forces and the Muslims threatened even the bastions of France.

To conquer by force is one thing, but to govern by force is another. Therefore, the Arabs had to adopt a much more conciliatory view toward both Christians and Jews within their vast domains in order to keep the peace. It is true that the "Pact of Omar," which set forth the position of non-Muslims in a Muslim society, placed some onerous burdens upon the "unbelievers." Both Christians and Jews were required to pay a special tax and were forbidden to ride horses or carry swords. They were also officially required to wear a special badge identifying themselves as infidels.

In actual practice, however, both Christians and Jews were usually treated quite well and were allowed to hold positions of respect and honor in society. While Christian clergy and laity in the remaining Byzantine territory often urged and implemented vicious suppression of Jews in the name of religious uniformity, Islam, in general, learned the art of coexistence and often closed its eyes to its own repressive dicta. It is not surprising, then, that under Muslim rule Judaism blossomed once again.

The Age of the Geonim

After the victory of Islam, Babylonian Jewry, repressed for a time by the Zoroastrians, was resurrected to new life. The position of Exilarch was preserved by the Muslim rulers and Judaism retained its status as a more-or-less self-governing minority. Perhaps ever more important than the Davidic Exilarch were the heads *(Geonim)* of the Jewish academies at Sura and Pumbeditha. These men, who ruled over the vital intellectual life of Babylonian Jewry, were to become, in effect, the teachers of worldwide Judaism.

From all over the world, Jewish communities sent legal, moral, and liturgical questions to which the *Gaon* of Sura, in particular, offered authoritative *responsa.* In this way, despite the far-flung nature of Judaism, a modicum of uniformity of thought and action was maintained. The fact that Islam had united so much of the world in one great empire greatly facilitated communication. Messengers from the Gaon traveled throughout the Islamic world and beyond, carrying not only the *responsa* from the head of an academy, but also instructions in Talmud. It was doubtless through their influence that the Babylonian Talmud, in particular, became almost universally recognized as the authoritative source for Jewish law, wisdom, and practice.

Among the *responsa* which have been preserved are at least two which bear special mention. In 860 a certain community sought advice concerning the ordering of synagogue worship. The Gaon, Rav Amram, replied with his famous *Seder* or *Siddur* (arrangement) through which he indicated how he believed the traditional prayers should be ordered. This *responsa* was copied many times and became a major source for unifying Jewish liturgical practice. Sixty years later, Saadya Gaon offered a similar *responsa* for an Egyptian synagogue, reiterating much of what Rav Amram had said.

Another famous *responsa* was offered in the tenth century by Sherira, one of the last of the great Geonim. A community at Kairwan in North Africa had written to him, asking for information about how the Talmud came into being. In response, Sherira offered a lengthy description of both the various individuals mentioned in the Talmud and the academies which brought the Talmud to birth. His explanation remains as one of our chief sources for understanding the Talmud and its many personalities.

While the academies of Babylonia continued to legislate for much of the Jewish world, the academies in Palestine, now free of Christian meddling, also began to flourish once more. Perhaps because of Muslim influence, the Palestinians developed a poetic tradition *(piyyut)* through which the deep feelings of Jewish piety were expressed. Jose ben Jose and Eleazar Kalir, in particular, composed poetry for almost every important Jewish festival day *(see* II. B). Millions of Jews in the twentieth century still chant Kalir's poetry in worship.

Scholarly work was also important in the Palestinian academies. Not only did these schools produce abundant aggadic material; they also labored diligently to produce a standardized text for the Hebrew Scriptures. Hebrew, for centuries, had been written with only consonants. That is to say, the reader was expected to be able to supply the missing vowel sounds when reading. Due to the nature of the language, this is not as difficult as it sounds, for vowels are more fluid in Hebrew than they are in Indo-Aryan languages. Nevertheless, this mode of writing did mean that disputes could arise concerning exactly how a word should be pronounced and hence concerning what a particular phrase meant. In both Babylonia and Palestine, scholars came to the conclusion that to guard against error, vowel sound ought to be indicated so that all Jews could agree upon the exact meaning of the text. Eventually, the system adopted in Palestine proved to be the more usable and was universally adopted. Over the years, textual scholars (known as the Massoretes) labored to produce a standardized text. The fruit of their labors was the Massoretic Hebrew text which is used by both Cfristians and Jews to this day.

The work of the Massoretes did have one negative effect. The universal acceptance of their work meant the destruction of texts with variant readings which may have had a long tradition of their own. Until quite recently it was difficult to know anything about the variations of text extant in the pre-Massoretic times. The discovery of the Dead Sea Scrolls, however, has given to scholars some Biblical texts which antedate the Massoretic text by centuries. Although these finds have demonstrated that the Massoretes did their work well, they also have revealed some surprising variations quite unknown until the twentieth century.

Messianists and Karaites

Although life under Islam was generally tolerable, it would be amiss to imply that there were no significant problems. Muslim rulers did at times act despotically and sometimes worked militantly to convert the Jews to Islam. The Jews, in their turn, also occasionally chafed against Gentile rule and sought for more freedom. For instance, not long after the Islamic conquest of the Middle Eastern heartland, Messianic ideas began to bubble up, particularly in Babylonia. About the year 700, a self-proclaimed Messiah, Abu-Issa of Ispahan, gathered an army of Jews with the intent of throwing off the Muslim yoke and leading his people back to Palestine. When his miraculous power failed him, however, the revolt was crushed and the would-be Messiah committed suicide. Judghan al-Rai attempted a similar venture somewhat later with similar results.

Such Messianic movements, which expressed discontent with both Islam and the leadership of the *Geonim,* died quickly but revolution lurked beneath the surface. In about 760 another sort of revolt took place, this time within Judaism, which was to have lasting disruptive effects.

Anan ben David was, according to his own opinion, the rightful heir to the Exilarchate but he was passed over and the position given to a younger brother. Anan, however, was not so easily dismissed. He attacked, in the name of Scripture, not only the contemporary Gaon but the whole Talmudic tradition. Although Anan was thrown into prison as a traitor by the Muslim rulers, his words caught fire and his message spread rapidly. Many Jews, both intellectuals and common men, flocked to his side in protest against the authority of the now-written oral law. Thus arose the Karaite movement which was to divide Judaism for centuries and which still exists, in diminished numbers, today (*see* IV. D).

The Karaites, like the Sadducees before them, rejected the vast proliferation of law and binding custom which the Talmud represented and called upon Jews to return to the Mosaic Law alone. Repelled by the results of the monumental labors of the Tannaim, Amoraim, and Geonim, they held up the Hebrew Scriptures as a sufficient guide for faith and practice. Before long, the movement had spread to many other parts of the Jewish world, threatening to split in two Jewish communities everywhere.

In many respects, Karaitism was an attractive movement, particularly for the intellectual, for it was easy enough to demonstrate that many of the rules of Jewish life which had developed were not "Biblical" in the strict sense at all. At the same time, because the movement rejected the ameliorating influences of tradition, it often turned out to be much more harshly legalistic than Talmudic Judaism had ever been. The Torah, for instance, prohibits the kindling of a fire on the Sabbath (Exodus 35:3). This implied to the Karaites that even on a snowy Sabbath in January a Jewish family must survive without light or heat—not a very happy thought for Jews living in Germany or Russia! Their interpretations of what constitutes incest and how far one should travel on the Sabbath were equally rigorous.

Nevertheless, the Karaite schism continued in full-strength for centuries. Only gradually did enthusiasm wane and the movement become a minor Jewish sect. One effect which this disruption had was to make non-Karaite Jews even more fervent in their affirmation of Talmudic principles. Ironically, then, it may have been the Karaites who fixed for the Talmud its place of preeminence in Jewish life. Their very excesses made the opposition fear the label Karaite. Thus, in a sense, Anan ben David accomplished exactly the opposite of what he set out to do.

Saadya Gaon (882-942)

The strength of Karaitism during the centuries to follow is well illustrated by the life of Saadya ben Josef al-Fayyumi, one of the greatest thinkers Judaism has ever produced. Saadya was born in Fayyum in Egypt in 882. There he received his education and first came into contact and conflict with the Karaites. Significantly, the Karaites were so strong in the Egyptian Jewish community that Saadya was forced to leave his homeland at the age of thirty to take up residence first in Palestine and then in Babylonia. Fortunately for traditional Judaism, he was not easily silenced and devoted much of his energy as a scholar to a cogent attack upon Karaitism and all it stood for. More than anyone else Saadya delivered to Karaitism an intellectual *coup de grâce* from which it never quite recovered.

Saadya, however, was much more than an anti-Karaite pamphleteer. By any standards, he was a genius of his age who "turned to gold" almost everything he touched. After arriving in Babylonia he joined the academy at Sura. When the Gaon died in 928, Saadya, already recognized for his superior intellectual abilities, was elected to that highly prestigious post. Few have served Judaism with more distinction.

Among his many accomplishments as a scholar was his translation of the Hebrew Scriptures into Arabic. In this, he not only gave to the Arabic world a version of Scripture which has been used until today; he also greatly furthered the study of Hebrew grammar and lexicography. Had he done nothing else, he would deserve mention in any history of the Near East.

Saadya, however, is best known for his philosophical and theological writings, for through them he became the father of Jewish theological thought in the Middle Ages. Maimonides may be better known to the world, but his vision of a synthesis of Greek learning and Hebrew tradition leans heavily upon Saadya's work.

When Saadya came to Baghdad in the tenth century, he entered the heartland of "Western" intellectual culture. After a moment of intellectual glory under the auspices of Charlemagne in the ninth century, Western Europe was again in the clutches of a Dark Age. In Babylonia, however, the torch of learning burned brightly and scholars debated questions which had not even been conceived by Western Europeans.

Much of the intellectual ferment in evidence in Babylonia at the time was due to the healthy give-and-take between Muslims, Zoroastrians, Jews, and Christians and to the revival of Hellenic learning in the Baghdad academies. When Justinian closed the Greek academies in Athens in an attempt to suppress heresy, the academies moved, bag and baggage to the "enemy camp" and set up shop in Babylonia. After the sixth century, then, the task of preserving and interpreting the ancient Greek texts was carried on under the auspices of the Persians.

When the Muslims conquered the Persian Empire, it was only a matter of time before they too became interested in philosophy, if only because both Plato and Aristotle seemed to provide a rational basis for many of the doctrines which Muslims held most precious. Had not both Plato and Aristotle demonstrated the existence of one God? Had they not shown that through reason one can arrive at some of the truths of revelation? Would it not be appropriate to utilize their arguments in the service of the faith?

By the eighth century, a group of Muslim intellectuals called the Mu'tazilites were already working on the problems of reconciling the claims of reason and those of revelation. In so doing, they incurred the wrath of the orthodox by questioning the anthropomorphic attributes of God, by emphasizing man's free will vis a vis predestination *(kismet)*, and by implying that God's justice limits the infinitude of his power. Eventually, the orthodox triumphed over these synthesizers, but from the debates grew a flourishing scholastic tradition in Islam (the *kalam)* distinguished by such luminaries as Al-Farabi (d. 950), Ibn Sina (d. 1037), and Ibn Rushd (d. 1198).

When Saadya produced in 933 his famous work, *Sefer Ha-Emuot we Ha-Deoth (The Book of Beliefs and Opinions)*, he was not writing in a theological vacuum, for questions concerning the relation between Greek philosophy and religious faith were very much in the air. His accomplishment was to produce a work which was both well-informed by Greek, particularly Aristotelian philosophy, and yet supportive of the central ideas of traditional Judaism.

Saadya, in this work, begins by identifying four sources for human knowledge: 1) sense perception, 2) reason, 3) rational deductions from the data provided by perception and reason, and 4) tradition. According to Saadya, man, through a careful use of reason, can arrive at firm theological and ethical conclusions—conclusions which are quite consistent with the content of revelation. This he demonstrates by "proving" the existence and oneness of God, the doctrine of *creatio ex nihilo,* etc. Indeed, his aim is to show that the central truths of the Jewish tradition can be arrived at through sense perception and reason alone.

Why then does man need a revealed tradition at all? The problem is that men are often either too busy or too lazy to use reason or they use it incorrectly and hence arrive at faulty conclusions. God has given man the tradition in order so provide for those whose reason has not been exercised fully enough. In a sense, a modern scientist could use the same argument. That is, all the contents of a scientific tradition are derivable through careful investigation, but no student has the time to start *de novo*. Science would not get very far if each generation had to begin anew. The difference, of course, is that while the scientific tradition arose initially through the use of reason, Saadya's tradition was given by God through revelation. This difference is somewhat minimized, however, by Saadya's contention that if a tradition is not reasonable, it is false revelation. Happily, he found no such false traditions within Judaism, though he was quick to point out the inconsistencies of Zoroastrian dualism and Christian Trinitarianism.

Despite Saadya's early date, his work still makes highly profitable reading today. Some of his arguments may appear peculiar, for he utilized the natural science of his day when making his case. Nevertheless, it is astonishing to discover that the arguments of such a late-comer as John Locke are already well-developed by him. In his formulation of the relation between reason and revelation, he set the stage for the whole of Jewish and Christian scholasticism.

Besides his *magnum opus*, Saadya produced as well numerous *responsa* and Midrashic commentaries on Scripture. Also preserved is his commentary on the *Sepher Yetzirah*, that esoteric Kabbalistic work already mentioned in chapter 2. For all of these Judaism is deeply indebted. Of a somewhat less positive nature, however, was his bitter quarrel with the reigning Exilarch which sent Saadya into exile for a time and produced within the Jewish community considerable suspicion of their titular head. Saadya was probably both morally and intellectually correct in his struggle to remove the abuses of the Exilarch, but the whole controversy led Jews all over the world to lose faith in that central Davidic institution which had unified them for so long. After Saadya, the preeminence of the Exilarch as well as that of Babylonian Jewry began to wane. The Geonim continued to offer authoritative *responsa*, but somehow the Jewish vision of the glories of Babylonian Judaism faded. Within a few years, the center of intellectual life had shifted to Spain.

The Golden Age in Spain

Jews had lived in Spain for centuries — perhaps since the days when the Phoenicians established colonies there — and had experienced both modest prosperity and vicious persecution on the Iberian peninsula. The Christian Visigoths, once converted to Roman Catholicism, had been particularly oppressive, demanding after 600 A.D. that all Jews be baptized forthwith. Therefore, when the forces of Islam conquered much of the land in 711, the decimated Jewish community welcomed them gladly.

A few decades later, in 750, the Abbasids overthrew the Umayyad caliphate which had ruled the Arab world from Damascus and moved the capital of the Muslim world eastward, to Baghdad. Abd Ar Rahman, a member of the house of Umayyad, escaped the massacre which destroyed most of his family and fled to Spain. There, in 755, he established a separate caliphate which was to vie with the Abbasids (and later also with the Fatamids of Egypt) for preeminence in the Arab world. The Umayyad rulers welcomed Jews to their territory and encouraged them to enhance the economic, social, and intellectual life in Spain according to their own genius. Many Jews from North Africa and elsewhere migrated to the growingly prosperous region and were treated with considerable tolerance by their Islamic rulers.

It took some time for the impoverished Jewish community in Spain to "find its feet" but by the tenth century, leaders of real ability began to emerge. One of the most distinguished was Hasdai ibn Shaprut (915-970), a physician who eventually became vizier to the Caliph Abd Ar Rahman III. In that position he was able to found an academy for Talmudic study in Cordoba and to attract to it leading Jewish scholars. Thus began in earnest the illustrious tradition of intellectual supremacy among the Spanish Jews.

Solomon Ibn Gabirol (A.D. 1021-1058)

In the eleventh century, the Umayyad dynasty was overthrown and Spain split into a number of warring states. Still, the position of the Jews remained reasonably secure and, often holding political posts of importance, they continued to develop their own intellectual tradition. One of the first major Jewish thinkers of note — undoubtedly the first philosopher which Spain was to produce — was Solomon ibn Gabirol (1021-1058). Curiously, however, within Judaism itself he has been remembered primarily as a poet who contributed a number of religious lyrics, notably "The Royal Crown," to the traditions of Eastern Jewry (*see* II.C).

During the latter part of his life Gabirol wrote a work entitled *The Fountain of Life* which expresses a unique version of Neo-Platonic theology. In a sense, he sought in it to reconcile his Jewish faith and Greek philosophy, but, unlike Saadya, he developed his philosophical position with little reference to either the Bible or the Talmud. Hence, when his work was translated into Latin under the title *Fons Vitae* and his name was corrupted to Avicebron, Christian scholastics had no idea that they were reading a Jewish author. It was not until the nineteenth century that Solomon Munk identified correctly the true author.

Perhaps it was because Gabirol failed to emphasize the relation between his metaphysics and his Jewish faith that his major work was never fully translated from Arabic into Hebrew and never exerted great influence upon subsequent generations of Jewish thinkers. The fact that the influence of Aristotle increased considerably while the thought of the Neo-Platonists fell into increasing disfavor also may have contributed to the oblivion to which Gabirol was consigned among Jews. Among Christian scholastics, however, his formulation of the relation between form and matter and his emphasis upon the Divine Will were hotly debated throughout the Middle Ages. John Duns Scotus was particularly influenced by him and refers to his position on a number of occasions.

Although the writing of Gabirol is marred by verbosity — some would say philosophic puerility as well — his philosophy contains a number of unique ideas which bear mentioning. Like most Neo-Platonists, Gabirol saw the universe as flowing from God (the First Essence) like water from a fountain — hence, the title of his work. The doctrine of creation is reinterpreted as emanation, as a timeless flow of Being. Also like Plotinus and the other Neo-Platonists, he accepts a hierarchy of Being which descends from intellect to soul to nature to corporeality. Man, as the microcosm, reflects this whole hierarchy in his own nature. To know man is to know the universe.

Unlike Plotinus, however, Gabirol regards matter, not as non-being, but as the spiritual substance which undergirds all. It is the primary emanation from God. Intellect, as well as corporeal being, is essentially matter. Matter for him is like a mirror in which the form of God is reflected. Hence in the hierarchy of Being manifest in both the universe and man, we see the reflection of God.

Gabirol also, somewhat inconsistently but nevertheless profoundly, introduces the very non-Platonic idea of God's will. God is, for him, not just a passive and inert principle from which all flows. God has Will and that Will is reflected in the dynamic nature of the universe. Man, as the microcosm, reflects God himself, through the exertion of his own will. Thus, in a sense, Gabirol provides a metaphysical basis for a unique type of "will-mysticism." Through a contemplation of the mystery of his own will, man can rise to a knowledge of God, himself.

Bahya ibn Pakuda (11th Century)

One Jewish thinker who does reflect some acquaintance with Gabirol is Bahya ibn Pakuda who wrote a book called, *Duties of the Heart*, some time during the first half of the twelfth century. Unlike Gabirol, Pakuda was more interested in personal religion than in abstract metaphysics. His object was to examine the attitudes which the soul, as opposed to the outer man, should express. For Pakuda, religion is much more than obeying rules and regulations. The essence of religion is, for him, those qualities of faith, humility, trust, and repentance not visible to the naked eye.

Reason, of course, is one of the capacities of the inner man and as such serves to bring man to a knowledge of God. In this connection, Pakuda draws freely upon both the arguments of Saadya (and the *Kalam*) and the philosophy of Neo-Platonists like Gabirol to demonstrate the Oneness, Existence, and Eternality of God. Essentially, however, Pakuda's major emphasis is not upon the development of a philosophical system but upon those feelings of trust and dependence which arise when reason has done its work and which characterize the religious life. For him, faulty reasoning is not as dangerous as the love of pleasure and power. Speculation about the universe and its nature may be interesting, but far more essential for the good life are the control of the appetite and a deep inner conviction of the goodness and mercy of God.

Because of his interest in "practical Judaism," it is not surprising that while Gabirol's book was forgotten by all but the erudite, Pakuda's *Duties of the Heart* became one of the most popular ethical treatises in medieval Judaism. Christians and secularists, who have often maintained that Judaism is narrowly legalistic and concerned only with outward form, would do well to read this volume with care.

Other Jewish intellectuals of the twelfth century who deserve at least passing mention are Abraham bar Hiyya, a

Neo-Platonic ethicist, Joseph ibn Zaddik (d. 1149), a syn-
thesizer of Neo-Platonic and Aristotelian ideas, and Moses ibn
Ezra (1070-1138), a famous poet. Perhaps more important and
therefore deserving more attention are the Biblical interpreter,
Abraham ibn Ezra and the poet-philosopher Judah Halevi.

Abraham ibn Ezra (1092-1167)

Ibn Ezra, who lived from 1092-1167, traveled widely in
Europe and the Near East, carrying on his literary activity as
he sojourned first in one place and then in another. His major
claim to fame was his extensive interpretation of Scripture,
based upon a scientific and philological foundation. Some
acknowledge him to be the first modern Biblical critic for he,
long before modern criticism arose, questioned the Mosaic
authorship of the Torah and offered innumerable insights into
Hebrew philology. Sometimes his acute mind led him to the
brink of heresy. For instance, his analysis of the Hebrew word
bara, usually translated "he created," caused him to question
the whole doctrine of *creatio ex nihilo*, so central in both
Jewish and Christian theology.

Nevertheless, ibn Ezra was also very much a child of his
time. He accepted astrology as a respectable science and tried
manfully to reconcile the fatalism which it implies with the
free will of man. He also indulged in numerology and, despite
his own better judgment, sometimes succumbed to the temptation to allegorize the Scriptures and find in them hidden mean-
ings. Frequently, those secrets he uncovered look very much
like echoes from the metaphysics of Solomon ibn Gabirol.

Like many other men of his age, he was convinced that
reason is capable of achieving the knowledge of God through
the study of nature. Although he recognized in Scripture many
laws not easily derived through reason, he also believed that
nothing in the Law is against reason. Reason and revelation
are both consistent and interdependent, for through reason
man can learn to control his appetites, free his soul from the
tyranny of the body, and hence achieve what the Law commands.

Judah Halevi (1085-1140)

As we have intimated, Jewish intellectual life from Saadya onward was characterized by various attempts to come to grips with the claims of Greek philosophy and to synthesize the truths of reason and revelation. Thus, like Islam and Christianity, Judaism, at least in Spain, experienced an era of scholasticism. More traditional forms of study were not neglected — as we shall see, Maimonides, the greatest scholastic of them all, was also an eminent Talmudist — but certainly the major intellectuals were caught up in the scholastic movement.

The one major thinker who questioned this whole trend of thought was the physician-poet-philosopher, Judah Halevi. Halevi was born during the last quarter of the eleventh century in Toledo at about the time that this city fell into Christian hands. Happily, the new Christian kings initially adopted a tolerant attitude toward their non-Christian subjects and Halevi did not experience the horrors that Jews in Spain were later to know.

At an early age he exhibited genuine poetic gifts and, though he supported himself through the practice of medicine, soon became famous for his religious verse. As his poetry repeatedly reveals, Halevi was a man who felt his religion deeply *(see* II.D.). Hence, although well-trained in philosophy, he came to see that the abstract notions of the Greeks do not really express the depth of Israel's faith. Like the Christian theologian Tertullian, he asked of his fellow intellectuals the leading question: "What has Athens to do with Jerusalem?" His answer, which he developed at length in his famous *Kuzari*, is "not much."

About three or four centuries before the time of Halevi, the king, court, and many common folk of the Kazars, a Tartar kingdom of South Russia, were converted to Judaism. According to tradition, the king, wishing to modernize his kingdom by adopting some form of monotheism, listened carefully to representatives of Christianity, Islam, and Judaism before deciding which he would choose for himself. Halevi uses this historical event as a basis for a dialogue through which the Jewish spokesman expresses Halevi's opinions before the king of the Kazars and thus converts him.

Unlike the Christian and Muslim, the Jewish "Haber" appeals not to the arguments of reason but to the historical experience of the Jewish people. "We Jews," he says, "believe in the God of Abraham, Isaac, and Jacob, who took the children of Israel out of Egypt, supported them in the wilderness, gave them the land of Canaan and so on."* When the king asks why the *Haber* did not begin with a more philosophical definition of the faith the way the others had, he explains his position at length.

Halevi, in one sense, shows great respect for philosophy, maintaining that reason can discover many truths about the world. Man can, through reason, even come to a very general and abstract knowledge about God. But Israel's truth transcends such empty ideas, pointing instead to YHWH, the very concrete and special God who has dealt particularly with Israel. Like the philosophers, Halevi believes the anthropomorphisms of the Bible to be metaphorical, but he also maintains that Israel's knowledge of YHWH is far deeper and more religiously significant than that of the speculators. Even the Pharaoh could have known the God of the philosophers, but Moses heard YHWH speak "face to face."

But why Moses and not the Pharaoh? Why is it that both Christianity and Islam base their beliefs in such large measure upon the oracles of the Hebrew prophets? The fact is, says Halevi, that all peoples are not equal. The seed of Abraham is especially blessed with an unusual ability to know God. Just as some materials, like stone or wood are impervious to the sun's light while others, like ruby or crystal, are not, so some people are naturally "open" to God's revelations while others are not. Hence, the great prophets, who knew God far more directly and fully than the philosophers, were Jewish. Even what the Greek philosophers did know was based upon a tradition initiated by Israel and then passed on from the Israelites to the Babylonians to the Persians to the Greeks.

Moreover, Halevi maintains that the center of the earth, Palestine, provides more favorable conditions for the knowledge of God than any other place. For this reason, Jews

---

*Quoted in Isaac Husik, *A History of Medieval Jewish Philosphy* (New York: Meridian Books, 1959), p. 156.

all over the world yearn to return to the promised land where the center for "God-consciousness" is. If tradition is correct, this is actually what our poet-philosopher did in his later years, only to be run through by an Arab swordsman as he recited religious verse before the gates of Jerusalem.

Halevi, of course, was quite willing to admit that Israel's special powers have not made her more prosperous or successful according to the standards of this world. On the contrary, the Jews have suffered in this world for centuries and appear to be the most despised of men. Nevertheless, they are a special people upon whom all the rest depend for their knowledge of God.

The idea that the Jews are a "master race" and hence different from other peoples was, of course, a notion which philosophers found difficult to accommodate and which proved to be highly dangerous, particularly when appropriated by Gentiles in the twentieth century who turned the idea against Judaism. The idea that the land of Israel is somehow a sacred place, quite different from other areas, has also led to more than one bloody conflict. Still, one must admit that Halevi, in his emphasis upon the uniqueness of Israel and her message, was far more honest and true to the tradition than the philosophers who tried to show that Aristotle and Moses really say the same thing. Quite clearly they do not and it is to Halevi's credit that he was clear-sighted enough to see this. Furthermore, those who wish to attack his notion of the uniqueness of Israel must ultimately wrestle with the Bible itself. Surely the Bible is not merely a popularization of philosophy for the masses but presents its own very unique vision of God and man, a vision which emphasizes throughout the special place in human history accorded to Israel by God.

The Preeminence of Aristotle:
Moses Maimonides (1135-1204)

Despite Halevi's stringent and well-articulated critique of the religious knowledge which philosophy purports to provide, his voice remained unheeded as others, virtually inebriated by the supposed cogency of Greek (particularly Aristotelian) philosophy, worked to reconcile the reasoning of that philosopher and their own Jewish tradition. Aristotle had been known by, and influenced to some extent, virtually all of the philosophers we have discussed, but in general his thought had been mediated by Arabic thinkers whose formulation of Aristotle's position had a distinctly Neo-Platonic cast. With Abraham ibn Daud (b. 1110), however, Aristotelian influence becomes much more patent. The influence of such Arabic writers as Alfarabi and ibn Sina is still very much in evidence, but with ibn Daud Aristotle begins to emerge victorious over his Neo-Platonic interpreters. In his *Emunah Ramah (Exalted Faith)*, ibn Daud attacks Gabirol as introducing ideas dangerous to Judaism, proposing instead the reasoning and proofs of the Aristotelians. In so doing, he foreshadows in innumerable ways the work of the greatest of all the medieval Jewish thinkers, the incomparable Moses Maimonides.

Because much of Maimonides' philosophy is little more than an elaboration of ibn Daud's pioneering work, it may appear unjust to pass over the latter so abruptly in this brief survey. The truth of the matter is, however, that it was Maimonides and not his predecessor who both shook the Jewish world and profoundly influenced Christian thought during the thirteenth and fourteenth centuries. Ibn Daud may have been in some ways more innovative, but it is the name of Maimonides which has been upon men's lips.

Moses ben Maimon was born in Cordoba, Spain, in 1135, the son of a scholarly judge. The first years of his life were peaceful enough, but in 1148 the storm broke. Cordoba, the citadel of Jewish learning since the time of Hasdai ibn Shaprut, was captured, this time by fanatical Muslims from North Africa who demanded the immediate conversion of all Jews. To escape the unbearable choice of "conversion or the sword," the whole family departed, beginning a period of extensive wandering through southern Spain and then, curiously enough, to the homeland of the fanatics in Morocco. Even at this early time Maimonides demonstrated his precociousness by producing treatises on logic and the calendar.

Eventually, the family decided to go to Palestine, but when they arrived they found it to be occupied by Latin Crusaders who were no less zealous for converts than were their Muslim counterparts. Finally, the family found some rest and security within the Jewish community at Cairo. Misfortune, however, had not been wholly shaken off. Within a few months after their arrival in Cairo, Moses' father was dead. His brother David, who traded in precious stones, was drowned at sea. Maimonides, himself, became involved in conflict within the Jewish community — particularly with the Karaites.

After the death of his brother and a long period of mourning, Moses began to study medicine and before long his ability as a physician became well-known. Eventually (in 1185) he was employed as physician to Saladin's court, a position which was to demand much of his time and energy. The Jewish community also recognized his talents and chose him to be their unpaid but highly responsible leader. One wonders how, in the midst of his exhausting medical practice and his role as arbiter and representative of the Jewish community, he found time for intellectual pursuits. By his own admission, he scarcely had a moment to chat with a friend, to say nothing of engaging in extensive reading and writing. Nevertheless, despite a busy public career, he found occasion to produce extensive volumes which were to revolutionize the thought of Judaism.

Maimonides' major works, each impressive because of its originality, size, and abiding influence, are four: (1) *Perush Ha-Mishnah (Commentary on the Mishnah)*, (2) *Sefer Ha-Mitzvot (Book of the Commandments)*, (3) *Mishneh Torah*, and (4) *Moreh Nevukhim (Guide of the Perplexed)*. Although he is best known among Western philosophers for the last, it should be recognized that his fame among Jews was established by his earlier works long before he wrote the *Guide*. Indeed, it is probable that his more strictly philosophical work would have had considerably less influence had he not already been known as a master of the Talmud. Precisely because he had already established himself as a supreme teacher of the Jewish tradition, no one could regard his *Guide* as the work of an aberrant, heterodox Jew. Therefore, before we look at the *Guide of the Perplexed* we must first examine briefly his earlier writings.

Commentary on the Mishnah is unique if only because, unlike most preceding Talmudists, Maimonides lifts out the Mishnah for special scrutiny as a self-sufficient unit for study. Characteristically, he presents a rare blend of minute textual analysis and broad conceptual interpretation. That is, in this introduction to the Talmud he treats both philological and lexicographical questions and the much broader philosophical problems which disturbed his generation. Frequently, he uses the text as an occasion for discussing such questions as the role of reason in the formulation of the Oral Law, the Jewish conception of life-after-death, and the relation between psychology and ethics.

In the course of his analysis of life-after-death he formulates his famous thirteen principles of belief which he regarded as essential for all Jews. In brief, these principles affirm that God, who alone is to be worshipped, is characterized by existence, unity, incorporeality, and eternity; that God has revealed himself to the prophets, among whom Moses is the greatest; that the Torah, which was revealed at Sinai, is imutable; that God knows the actions of men and will reward or punish them according to their actions; that the Messiah will come; and that, at last, there will be the resurrection of the dead (see I.B).

What makes this list unusual is that throughout the long history of Judaism very few Jews have felt it necessary to write creeds or dogmatic statements about what all Jews are expected to accept. Judaism has been united by tradition, custom, and family, not by assent to intellectual doctrines. This statement by Maimonides, therefore, quite naturally engendered considerable discussion and debate. For some, his summary was a comprehensive and acceptable articulation of faith. For others, such intellectualizing was anathema. To this day, Jews remain divided concerning the question: Must a man think in a certain way to be a Jew?

The Book of Commandments is a smaller but nonetheless ponderous work which attempts to classify and interpret the 613 divine commandments found in the Torah. The first half deals with the positive commands; the last half deals with the negative ones. In the process of his work, Maimonides works out fourteen guiding principles according to which God's will for man may be best understood.

The final work in this monumental series is the *Mishneh Torah* in which the author completely reorganizes and reclassifies the Mishnah in order to make the whole legal corpus more intelligible and more useful pedagogically. Although basically a code and not a commentary, the work nevertheless includes bits of exegesis, lengthy explanations, and philosophical interpretations. As in all his other works, Maimonides places considerable emphasis upon the use of reason in interpreting the law and spelling out its ethical implications.

Sometime between 1185 and 1190 our author composed what most consider his *magnum opus, The Guide for the Perplexed.* Most other men, busy with the affairs of the world, would have been more than satisfied with the enormous Mishnaic studies already undertaken, but not Maimonides. Throughout his life, he had emphasized the importance of the life of the intellect. For him, this was of supreme religious importance. Until this point, however, he had only hinted at the preeminence of the use of reason in the life of a Jew. Now, in the *Guide,* he demonstrates more systematically and overtly not only that revelation and reason cohere but that the truly religious man is also rational to the core.

By this time, Aristotle, though still largely unknown in Western Europe, had become *the* philosopher in the Islamic world. Therefore, Maimonides saw as his task the synthesis of Aristotelianism and Judaism. Ibn Daud had already dealt with the "points of contact" between these two divergent modes of thought, but had frequently glossed over important areas of conflict. Maimonides was determined to resolve these apparent points of difficulty and thus to remove the perplexity which many intellectual Jews were experiencing.

Among those issues which he found most important were: (1) How is it legitimate for the Bible to attribute various anthropomorphic qualities to God when God, as necessarily existent being, transcends predication? (2) How can Aristotle's affirmation of the eternality of the world be reconciled with the Biblical account of creation? (3) What is the relation between the truth attained through philosophical reason and that revealed to the prophets? (4) If God is absolutely all-powerful and good, how can evil and human freedom be possible? and (5) How can the rational ethics of Aristotle be reconciled with the commandments of the Torah?

At first glance, it would appear that Maimonides' effort led to the fitting of Jewish tradition to the Procrustean bed of Aristotle. Throughout his work Maimonides extolls reason as the chief of the virtues and accepts most of Aristotle's arguments as conclusive. The God of Israel is transformed into the Unmoved Mover. The prophets are said to depend upon reason in their preparation for prophethood. Biblical language about God is regarded as not just loaded with metaphors but as actually homonymous in nature. That is, just as we use the term "dog" to refer to an animal and to the star Sirius, so we use words in radically different senses when speaking of man and God. The Bible may describe God as loving, but that love has little, if anything, in common with human love. Overall, it would appear that the whole Jewish faith has been intellectualized to a point where reason governs all.

Maimonides, however, is an amazingly subtle thinker, and, if one follows his arguments carefully, the triumph of Jewish tradition over rationalism becomes more and more apparent. Now it is Aristotle who lies upon the Procrustean bed of the prophets and is made to conform. One ends the book with the distinct impression that though Aristotle is affirmed there is always that penetrating "nevertheless" which recasts the whole matter.

It would be misleading, then, to set forth in brief summary, the central teachings of Maimonides, for the expositor must avoid the temptation to over-simplify. The genius of Maimonides is not in the overt argumentation, for that was largely adopted from predecessors, but in those subtle nuances which shed new light upon old questions. Perhaps the term "primrose path" is too pejorative a term to use in this connection; still, Maimonides provides such a path which leads, with various twistings and turnings, from the metaphysics of Aristotle to the Torah.

Many, however, have lost their way on this route and have concluded either that Maimonides had the mind of a Greek and hence destroyed much of the uniqueness of Judaism or that he was, at best, an obscuring Semite who only used Aristotle for his own apologetic purposes. Neither conclusion is quite accurate if only because the tension between the philosopher and the prophet is never quite resolved in the mind of the author.

In 1204, after having completed some treatises on medicine during his last years, Maimonides died, full of years and fame. With amazing alacrity the *Guide* found its way through the Islamic, Jewish, and Christian worlds, inspiring men everywhere to new discussion and debate about the issues which he raised. It is not an exaggeration to say that the *Guide* created a whole epoch in the history of Jewish thought. Nor is it too much to conclude that the whole movement of Christian Aristotelianism, so well represented by Thomas Aquinas, might never have taken the direction it did had it not been for Maimonides. Just as Philo Judaeus set the stage for such

Christian theologians as Clement of Alexandria and Origen, so Maimonides provided a philosophical vision for scholastic Europe which Aquinas was to acknowledge gratefully.

One should not infer from this, however, that the influence of Maimonides was not resisted. On the contrary, many of the leading Jewish thinkers in the thirteenth and fourteenth centuries took issue with much of what he had to say. Nahmanides (b. 1194) opposed, among other things, his depreciatory remarks about the body, arguing that sin corrupts rather than arises from the body. Hasdai Crescas (b. 1340) attacked several key Aristotelian arguments, acutely undercutting many features of the thought of Maimonides. For Crescas, man can reach God only through love, not through reason. Others, like Levi ben Gerson (1288-1344), however, generally followed Maimonides in his appropriation of Aristotle. Well into the fourteenth century, the battle raged. On several occasions, the *Guide* was consigned to the flames and even "excommunicated." Nevertheless, even the sturdiest opponents had to fight on the battleground laid out by Maimonides. In the end perhaps he educated most those who disagreed with him.

The Zohar

Not everyone, however, chose to worry specifically about the authority of Aristotle and the claims of pure reason. In 1275 a strange book suddenly appeared which was to have abiding influence for centuries to come. Written in a peculiar form of Aramaic which marks the work as a literary creation of the thirteenth century, it purports to have been composed by the famous second century teacher of Midrash, Rabbi Simeon ben Yohai. In fact, however, it was probably written by Moses de Leon, the Spanish Kabbalist who actually introduced it to the world.

The work, of course, was *Sefer Ha-Zohar, The Book of Splendor.* No two works could be more unlike than the *Guide* and the *Zohar;* yet each in its own way has found a place in the hearts of Jews around the world. While Maimonides appeals to reason, the author of the *Zohar* presents us with imaginative, occult exegesis, bizarre imagery, descriptions of ecstasy, and veiled allusions. One is reminded throughout of the ancient apocalypses, of Merkabah mysticism, of the *Sepher Yetzirah*. It is as though the burden of rationalism had become too offensive, too all-pervasive. Suddenly from the depths of Judaism the images of mystery erupted.

Perhaps "erupted" is too strong a term, however, for one should not infer that the *Zohar* represents something entirely new. On the contrary, it rather perpetuates and develops an already rich Kabbalistic tradition which had found exponents in the Rhineland, the Provence, and Italy as well as Spain before this time. One thinks of Jehudah the Hasid and Eleazar of Worms who taught in Germany early in the thirteenth century; of Abraham Abulafia (b. 1240), that prophetic mystic who not only wrote prolifically concerning a mystical interpretation of Judaism but actually developed various meditational techniques for achieving ecstasy; and of the *Bahir*, that compendium of ancient texts which appeared in the Provence in the twelfth century. Spain also knew its esoteric groups of mystics of which the author of the *Zohar* was doubtless a member. Thus the *Zohar* was a culmination of a long tradition of theosophic thought within Judaism which could trace its lineage back to the Hekhaloth books, the *Sepher Yetzirah*, and to the apocalypses.

The *Zohar* is, in form, an extended commentary upon the five books of Moses, written in a style which sometimes mirrors the Babylonia Talmud (*see* III.D). Only the well-versed student of Talmud will be able to catch the subtle and sometimes witty allusions to that authoritative work. Although the overall intent of the *Zohar* is sublimely serious, the reader is sometimes led to suspect that the author is offering what is meant to be a "take off" on Talmudic style.

From the outset, in any event, it is clear that this is no ordinary work of exegesis. Of the four levels of interpretation distinguished by Christian exegetes (i.e., the literal, the aggadic, the allegorical, and the mystical), the *Zohar* concentrates upon the last. Even the most apparently obvious sentence in Scripture becomes, in the hands of the mystical exegete, a symbol for something much higher and deeper. Each letter and combination of letters suggests to the author a mystic truth. For instance, the word *Elohim* (God) is seen to contain the consonants of *eleh* ("these": a symbol for the objective world) and *mi* ("who": a symbol for the personal and subjective). Thus God is interpreted as synthesizing in his very nature the subjective and the objective. Unlike the Aristotelians who regarded God as primarily an object of thought, the *Zohar* emphasizes that *mi* (who) is on a higher level than *mah* (what).

The author of the *Zohar* doesn't argue; he reveals. He could not care less about Unmoved Movers, infinite progressions, syllogisms, and inferences. He pulls back the curtain and, in a pastiche of compositions which defies analysis, sets forth the symbols of mystery which have haunted human religion since the beginning of recorded history. Maimonides had said that the mysterious doctrines of the Talmud called "Maase Bereshit" and "Maase Merkaba" denote none other than physics and metaphysics, respectively. The *Zohar*, however, is obviously discontented with such banalizing of the mysteries. At most, physics and metaphysics are but parables of those greater mysteries which transcend ordinary thought and language. The *Zohar* points far beyond the biology of this world to the inner mysteries of the life of God, himself.

Throughout the *Zohar* we find a reaffirmation of the central, theosophic mysteries of existence. Ethical calculation and rationalistic metaphysics are missing. Rather the reader is called to envision the ten *sephiroth,* those phases or spheres in which the Divinity manifests himself and, thereby, to contemplate God, Himself. Stylistically and intellectually Maimonides and the *Zohar* are miles apart, but they do agree on this: God, himself, — called by the esotericists *En-Sof* — is hidden and unknowable. Our words, when applied to him, take on a wholly different meaning. The *Zohar*, through symbol and vision, attempts to reveal how different that meaning is.

En-Sof is hidden, unknowable, and beyond words; yet somehow the Hidden One is also related to the world. The mystery of this relation is bound up in the ten *sephiroth* or spheres of divine manifestation. These *sephiroth* are named respectively: *Kether* (Crown), *Hokmah* (Wisdom), *Binah* (Intelligence), *Hesed* (Love), *Geburah* (Power), *Rahamin* (Compassion), *Netsah* (Endurance), *Hod* (Majesty), *Yesod* (Foundation), and *Malkuth* (Kingdom). Each word is used in common parlance to refer to things or relations in this world, but in order to understand the *sephiroth* one must recognize that earthly things and relations are mere shadows and reflections of the divine mystery. It is of man and the world that one must speak metaphorically; the *sephiroth* represent univocal reality.

Together these spheres form the Tree of Life or the Cosmic Man which, in effect, is to *En-Sof* as a man's body is to his soul. Traditionally, the interrelations among the *sephiroth* have been diagrammed in the following way:

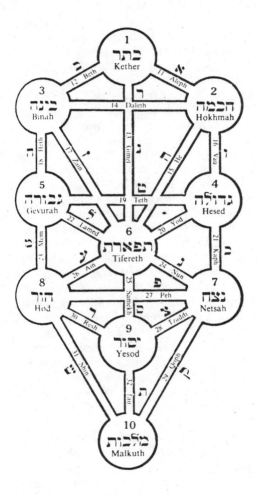

This diagram represents the "body" of God, its aspects, and their interrelations. Through all of them the hidden, divine life flows, enlivening them all. God is one; yet his appearances and hence his names are many.

In a sense, the *Zohar* does Christian, Trinitarian theology "one better." Like the Trinitarians, the author sees in God several, interacting principles; yet the relations among the ten are far more complex than those among the three. Through them the divine light is refracted and the created world comes into being.

Within the Godhead the *Zohar* also sees a duality which is reflected on earth in the relation between male and female. One of the most moving passages in the *Zohar* is found near the conclusion of Book III, in a section called *Terumah*. Rabbis Simeon, Eleazar, Abba, and Jose are pictured as sitting under a tree near the Lake of Genessareth (Galilee). Their discourse is meant to be a commentary on Exodus 25:1-27:19, but only an occasional reference reminds us of the text itself. Instead, the Rabbis, alluding frequently to the Song of Songs, discourse on the mystical meaning of Jewish worship.

When the truly pious pray together — there must be ten to make a *minion* — the *shekhinah* (the presence) descends upon them and unites them. The *shekhinah* is the divine presence and yet, at the same time, is the bride of the most High. In the course of the prayers, this bride unites with her heavenly bridegroom in divine love. In that moment, the traditional Jewish assertion that God is One takes on a deeper ecstatic meaning. The Oneness of God is the union of the Most High and his *Shekhinah* in divine love. In the prayer and praise of Israel, men become enwrapped in the love of God and are lifted out of themselves to a life of divine splendor. Much of the *Zohar* is devoted to describing that world of the *Hekhaloth* (palaces) to which man ascends in ecstasy.

Like the *Guide of the Perplexed*, the *Zohar* was to have lasting effects upon Judaism, particularly during the later Middle Ages. Both works were written for the few, for those "in the know"; yet ideas from both were to be popularized and adopted by Jews everywhere. Particularly during the Renaissance the *Zohar* and other Kabbalistic writings were discovered by small groups of Christians and eventually made their impact felt upon men such as Jacob Boehme and William Blake.

Judaism in the Christian West

While Judaism experienced several centuries of prosperity and intellectual brilliance in Islamic Spain, conditions in the rest of Western Europe were hardly so favorable for either political security or intellectual growth. Christendom, despite its many affinities with Judaism and its continued emphasis upon the virtues of forgiveness and love, seemed incapable of the type of tolerance manifest in Islamic countries. The history of Judaism in most of Europe was, therefore, largely one of tragic suffering.

Long before the barbarian invasions and the rise of Christianity as a political force, communities of Jews were to be found all over the European continent. When Paul carried his Christian gospel to the west, there were already synagogues in Greece, Rome, Spain, France, and even Germany. Nevertheless, Christendom normally seems to have regarded the Jew as an outsider, as an unredeemable "surd" in the midst of a faithful population.

From the beginning, of course, Jews and Christians had hotly disputed the interpretation of Hebrew Scriptures, which Christians had appropriated as their own, and many denunciations and anathemas were uttered from both sides. When, under Constantine, Christian convictions began to influence the law, debate was replaced with growing repression. Attempts to convert others to Judaism were forbidden by law as were attempts to restrain Jews tempted by conversion to Christianity. Judaism, as a proselytizing competitor, was publicly suppressed. From that time onward, Judaism had to be satisfied with its position as an ethnic minority.

The barbarian invasions, which shook the very foundations of Western culture, did little to help the Jews. Aside from occasional anecdotes, however, we know little of Judaism in the West until the time of Charlemagne. By that time, the Jews had generally lost even the rights of citizenship which had been granted to them in the Roman Empire by Caligula. In order to preserve themselves, they were forced to plead for direct protection from ruling monarchs and feudal lords who, in turn, defined their rights and duties. In a sense, the Jews became the "property" of whomever served as their protector. Each Jewry had its own internal laws, but there were few lands

(Portugal is the prime exception) where the various local communities were united under a common head.

Thus arose the ghetto, a separate, walled-in quarter close to the ruler's palace, which was populated by men and women who, in the outside world, had few rights or privileges. They were a separate nation, existing only by the authority of the ruler. His promise was to protect them, but it was also within his power to expel the whole community when it no longer served his purposes.

Within the ghetto the Jews largely governed themselves. They had their own courts to mete out punishment and most Jews assiduously avoided Gentile courts of justice whenever possible. Jewish tribunals could not inflict the death penalty and did not have jurisdiction over cases involving Gentiles, but in purely Jewish matters they ruled supreme. The consequences of excommunication from the synagogue and the ghetto were so harsh that, in effect, the courts did not need the death penalty in order to elicit fear. No Jew wished to be cast out defenseless into Christian society.

Jews also developed their own schools, guilds, and other social institutions and thus were radically segregated from their Christian neighbors. Even in tax collection they were separate. Rulers imposed a tax upon the Jewry as a whole and allowed Jewish leaders to collect that tax from individual members as they would.

Until the fifteenth century, Judaism had no paid clergy. The Rabbis were simply self-supporting scholars who served as religious and social leaders in their spare time. The learned Rabbis were highly respected but were not set apart from the congregation as were their Christian counterparts. Thus was preserved among Jews a democratic tradition which Christians have only slowly and partially recovered. A synagogue needs no ordained priest or other sacramental officer to survive. Ten men are all that is required to form a worshipping community.

Of course, the development of the ghetto was by no means uniform and not all Jews were so confined. The growth of feudalism meant, however, that Jews were, for all intents and purposes, driven off the land. No Jew was allowed to hold serfs, for serfs generally took the religion of their lord and Christians could not countenance the conversion of anyone to

Judaism. This meant, in effect, that Jews were by-and-large confined to the cities and hence had to relinquish their long-standing occupation as farmers. The fact that most medieval guilds were religiously oriented meant that Jews were also excluded from many trades and crafts.

According to popular caricature, many Jews during the Middle Ages became money-lenders, often charging exorbitant rates of interest and hence incurring the wrath of their Christian neighbors. A careful examination of the facts, however, belies the truth of this picture.

In the first place, during much of the Middle Ages, the Rabbis themselves often forbade engaging in what Christians termed usury. When the Christian Church, in turn, prohibited the lending of money at interest, some Jews did enter this type of business, but their interest rates were almost invariably set by the ruler who, himself, reaped the bulk of the profits. Furthermore, Christians themselves soon learned how to avoid the letter of the law and were no less rapacious than their Jewish counterparts. Over all, though some Jewish money-lenders may have exhibited heartlessness toward their debtors, they were in a distinct minority. Their sins surely ought not to be heaped upon Judaism as a whole.

In general, cultural life in European Jewry, like that in early Christian Europe, was much less developed than in Islamic Spain. Nevertheless, by the tenth century, intellectual activity did develop, though without the dominant influence of Greek philosophy. One of the greatest of the early leaders was Rabbenu Gershom (d. circa 1040) called "The Light of the Diaspora," who taught in the Rhineland. So great was the esteem for him that many of his legal opinions were taken as authoritative all over Western European Jewry. Perhaps his most important *takkanoth* (pronouncement) concerned monogamy. In neither the Bible nor the Talmud is polygamy forbidden. In fact, to this day Eastern (Sephardic) Judaism countenances the taking of more than one wife. Gershom reasoned, however, that in a monogamous society, Jews should practice monogamy and that judgment became law for Ashkenazic (Western) Jews.

Among the pupils of Rabbenu Gershom was a French Jew by the name of Rabbi Solomon Yizchaki (1040-1105). Almost universally known as Rashi, a name formed from his initials, he was to become perhaps the foremost medieval authority for

Ashkenazic Judaism. Living in Troyes, France, he was one of the outstanding Talmudists of his day, writing running commentaries on most of the Babylonian Talmud and the Torah. These commentaries are known, not for their philosophical interpretation or philological expertise but for their conciseness and lucidity. The commentaries of Rashi have been reprinted numerous times and even today are widely used by modern Jews (*see* III.E).

The mystical and occult traditions were not without their representatives in Western Europe either. Particularly in the Rhineland in the twelfth and thirteenth centuries there developed a school of mystics, called the *Hasidim*, who explored the ancient techniques of numerology, gematria, etc., to discover hidden mysteries in the Scriptures. Among the most famous of these men were Samuel the Hasid (twelfth century), Jehudah the Hasid (d. 1217), and Eleazar ben Jehudah of Worms (d. circa 1223). Drawing upon ancient lore already recovered and studied by Italian Jews of the eleventh century, these mystics produced esoteric tradition which was to complement, if not influence, the Zohar tradition which was to surface later in that century.

In this connection, mention should also be made again of Abraham Abulafia (b. 1240) who was active at about the time the *Zohar* was written. Unlike most of his fellow Kabbalists, he was more deeply interested in philosophy — particularly that of Maimonides — than he was in Talmudic studies. At first rather uninterested in Kabbalistic literature, he eventually became intrigued with the *Sepher Yetzirah* and subsequently developed his own form of Kabbalism which he himsef labelled "prophetic."

Abulafia believed himself to be prophetically inspired; in one of his moments of inspiration, indeed, he claimed to have been given the true name of God. So great was his assurance that his claims were correct that he even journeyed to Rome to convert the Pope. He was, as might be expected, thrown into prison, but, fortuitously, was not executed. He survived the ordeal of confinement and continued to write both Kabbalistic and prophetic works.

Not only did Abulafia consider himself inspired; he believed that he had developed techniques whereby any adept could "untie the tangles" which bind him to this world and hence attain prophetic vision. Central for his method was the contemplation and manipulation of Hebrew letters (which the Sepher Yetzirah so long before had said contain the mysteries of existence). He also employed breathing techniques and certain postures reminiscent of Yoga.

In all this, curiously enough, Abulafia was following Maimonides who had taught that prophecy does not just come as a "bolt from the blue" but is based upon adequate preparation of the intellect. Unfortunately for him, however, neither the philosophers nor the Kabbalists were enthusiastic about his message. Therefore, although several manuscripts by him still exist, little has been made available to the modern reader. Undoubtedly, one reason why his work has gone unheralded is the great danger to the faith which it entails. If anyone working diligently can become a prophet, there is a strong probability that prophets will arise who disagree with Moses and the tradition. Such a result could only lead to religious schism and ultimate disaster for the faith.

Anti-Jewish Persecutions

By the thirteenth century, Judaism was already under a cloud of persecution. Several of the mystical writings from the Rhineland Hasidim, in fact, seem to offer an escape from the brutal world through esotericism and piety. This is not surprising, for it was the Rhineland in particular which was to know the terror of mob violence for several centuries.

Curiously enough, this new age of fear was begun in far-away Palestine by Muslims during the eleventh century. Ever since the time of Constantine, Christian pilgrims had flocked to the Holy Land to see the great sites of their faith's birth and Muslims had generally allowed this practice to continue. The eleventh century, however, witnessed the murder of Christian pilgrims by the Seljuks and the virtual end of pilgrimages. As a result, Pope Urban II preached a crusade in 1095, calling upon Christian knights to recover this central place of holy veneration for Christendom. Many noblemen and their squires, interested in both piety and adventure, began to answer the call.

In Normandy, however, a band of disreputable, unrestrained rabblerousers, suddenly announced that there was no need to travel all the way to Palestine when the murderers of Jesus lived in great prosperity in their midst. Thus there began at Rouen a slaughter of Jews for which Western Europe was to be notorious for centuries. The original rationale may have been quasi-religious at the start but before long the murder of Jewish citizens in order to confiscate their property and negate debts became almost a popular pastime. It is true that many church and civic officials tried to stop these anti-Semitic outbursts, but each foreign crusade saw further domestic slaughter of the most savage kind. France, England, and Germany all witnessed angry mobs which burned, looted and murdered. Whatever good relations that had existed between Christians and Jews were now largely dissolved.

To the accusation that the Jews had murdered Jesus and thus deserved death were added even more preposterous claims. Jews, it was said, kidnapped Christians, killed them, and used their blood in secret ceremonies. Rumor also had it that Jews stole holy wafers from churches and profaned them by stabbing the living Christ within. Jews became responsible for all heresies within the Church and even, in the fourteenth century, for the Black Death. Popes and bishops might protest, but their own anti-Jewish polemics had born bitter fruit. It is perhaps significant that it was not until the second Vatican Council in the twentieth century that the Catholic Church officially repudiated the notion that the Jews were responsible for Jesus' death.

Furthermore, official Church legislation did little to aid the Jew in his plight. At the Third Lateran Council in 1179 all close intercourse between Jew and Christian was forbidden. In the Fourth Lateran Council of 1215, the Church declared that (1) no Jew could exercise authority over a Christian, (2) no crusader was under obligation to pay usury to a Jew, (3) all Jews would henceforth be required to wear a badge by which they could be identified (*see* V.D). [For a more modern and tolerant Catholic view, *see* V.H].

In the thirteenth century, the Dominican Order was founded to combat Christian heresy in southern France, but this preaching order of monks soon turned its attention to the Jews as well. Among those techniques used to convert Jews to Christianity were: the confiscating and burning of Jewish books, the forcing of Jews into open debates which Jewish scholars were never allowed to win, and the entering of ghetto synagogues to preach Christian sermons to unwilling congregations. The use of Jewish converts to perform this last degrading practice only made the situation that much worse. The whole idea of trying to convert anyone in this scurrilous way would appear ludicrous were it not so obviously tragic.

Not only were Jews harried by mobs and insulted by representatives of the Church; they were also often "bled dry" and then driven out by the national or local rulers who were presumably their protectors. The English Jewish community, which had only arrived in the British Isles at the time of the Norman Conquest, was used by the English kings to increase their wealth. When the Jews, having been made virtual paupers, proved to be of no more use, Edward I simply expelled them from England in 1290. It was not until the seventeenth century that they were allowed to return to England.

In France Jews were expelled and then recalled on numerous occasions between 1182 and the final expulsion in 1394. Each time the Jews were brought back the king believed he could make a profit from "his" Jewry. After its usefulness had been exploited to the full, expulsion again followed. In Germany (the Holy Roman Empire), no general expulsion occurred, but one city after another closed its doors to Jews until only a few sizable Jewries were left by the sixteenth century.

Where did all these exiled communities go? Although some Jews migrated to Italy and Spain and others traveled to the Near East, the general movement was eastward, to Poland. There, the kings of this "new nation" recognized their need for a middle class of merchants, bankers, and tradesmen and hence welcomed Jews gladly, granting them quite favorable charters. The ghetto was maintained, but Jews were allowed to become prosperous and even to play important roles in society.

This is not to say that there were no problems in Poland. The populace frequently expressed resentment against the Jews, if only because they tended to be the merchants, financiers, and tax-farmers. This antipathy was also certainly encouraged by the Catholic clergy who called repeatedly for enforcement of the decrees of the Lateran Councils and stirred up anti-Jewish feelings. Nevertheless, the situation in Poland was better than anywhere else in Europe and to that land thousands of immigrants came.

Because of the good will of Polish kings like King Boleslav the Pious, who issued a model charter of protection and liberties for Jews in 1264, and Casimir the Great, who extended the provisions of that Charter in 1354, the Jewish community prospered and gained more freedom than in any other Christian land. In fact, the Jews constituted a nation within a nation having their own government, the Council of the Four Lands, and a Chief Rabbi who was answerable only to the king. Great fairs were held several times annually and at them Jews met, not only to buy and sell, but to conduct communal affairs.

Intellectually, Polish Jews also reached new heights of accomplishment. Rabbi Jacob Pollak (d. 1541) and Shalom Shakna (d. 1559) both developed a unique, if obscurantist, method of reconciling divergent traditions called *pilpul*. More important than any individual teachers, however, was the general level of education maintained among the Jews. Not only were there local elementary schools, each city had its Yeshiva where young men pored over the Talmud and other traditional literature. At no time in the history of Judaism was the Talmud so widely and deeply studied as in Poland.

When the early immigrants came to Poland from Germany, attempting to escape persecution, they brought with them a Medieval German dialect. Because of both the ghetto and the rather uncultivated nature of the Polish language at the time, this language did not die but rather, through the addition of both Hebrew and Slavic words, developed into Yiddish. Since Poland became, over the years, the center for Judaism in Europe, Yiddish became the Jewish language *sine qua non*. Rich in both vocabulary and idiomatic expression it was to serve generations of Jews as a vehicle for religious and literary expression. It should be noted, however, that this was a unique phenomenon. Virtually everywhere else Jews adopted the language of the culture in which they lived.

Strangely enough, the other land where Jews could live in relative peace during the Middle Ages was Italy. Even in the Papal States Jews were accepted and enjoyed a modicum of freedom. Although Popes might make anti-Jewish pronouncements and might, sometimes, encourage persecution elsewhere, they were usually astute enough to realize that the Italian Jew contributed considerably to the economy of the Italian city-states and hence was worth retaining. By the same token, because Italian merchants and financiers were numerous, the Jews were not singled out by the populace as responsible for their economic woes. Not until the time of the Counter-Reformation of which we will speak in the next chapter did the Italian Jews suffer the indignities known in other, northern lands.

In the meantime, things had gone from bad to worse in Christian Spain. Although Christian rulers initially adopted the Islamic attitude of tolerance toward Jewish subjects, by the fourteenth century the religious climate had changed decidedly and there were bloody massacres all over the Iberian peninsula, even in Portugal. Particularly as a result of the wild and irresponsible preaching of Fernando Martinez in 1390, Jews were given the simple option: the baptismal font or death.

Quite understandably, many Jews under such conditions chose the former, but in private continued to observe their beloved Jewish traditions. Despised by the Christian dogmatists who realized that their conversion was only nominal, they were branded as *"Marranos"* (pigs) and were subjected to the most vicious forms of inquisition. The covert Jews were now classified as heretics and often were subjected to the most insidious types of examination and torture which the royally-controlled Spanish Inquisition could muster.

Still, Churchmen remained unsatisfied and, profoundly disturbed by the fact that not all Spaniards would conform absolutely to the faith of "Christian Spain," called for the expulsion of all Jews from the nation. In 1492, the same year that Christopher Columbus (himself perhaps a Jew) discovered the New World, Spain forced the last remnants of that once highly prestigious community to leave Iberia forever. So ended another chapter of that profoundly tragic epic called "The Jews in Western Europe." From a Jewish point of view, it is a tale of sorrow, suffering, and hate. From a Christian vantage point it well exemplifies the truth that the currents of sin run deeply through the lives of men, even (no, especially) through the lives of those supposedly redeemed.

As the medieval period began to wane, Christendom waxed more and more inflexible and intolerant. Those Jews who remained in Western Europe, either as nominal Christians or, illegally, as remnants who refused to depart their homeland, were generally impoverished and hence, in the eyes of many, despicable. Magic, superstition, and esoteric lore ran rampant; intellectuals were few. Christendom, through its own intolerance, had created an object of hate. The Jew was feared and despised as never before and the external observer might well have concluded, as the Cossacks began to massacre Jews in Poland, that the saga of Judaism had come to its final, bitter end.

Centuries before, Moses, standing on the slopes of Mt. Sinai, had seen a vision of a bush that burned but was not consumed. His vision of the mystery of Israel has proved to be far more accurate than that of the objective observer. Christendom sought to burn Judaism and destroy her, but without success. Out of the ashes of medieval Jewry arose a people who, despite new and brutal trials, were to prove once more their ability to endure.

Sukkos is the third of the festivals prescribed for Israel in the earliest strata of the Mosaic Law. (Exodus 23:16) It occurs in the fall, at the time of the full moon of the seventh month. Thus it serves as the culmination of a series of holy days which begins with Rosh hashana on the first day of the seventh month and continues with Yom Kippur, the day of atonement.

Sukkos, which originally was a festival celebrating the grape harvest and the coming of the fall rains, remains as a time of great joy and gladness. The repentance and soul searching of Yom Kippur is over. It is time to build booths covered with gourds and vines and to rejoice in them. Although officially Sukkos is meant to remind Israel of her years in the wilderness, the tone of the occasion is not that of the wasteland at all. Despite the persecution, the defamation, and the barrenness of much modern culture, Israel in her booths gives thanks and praise to God for his goodness.

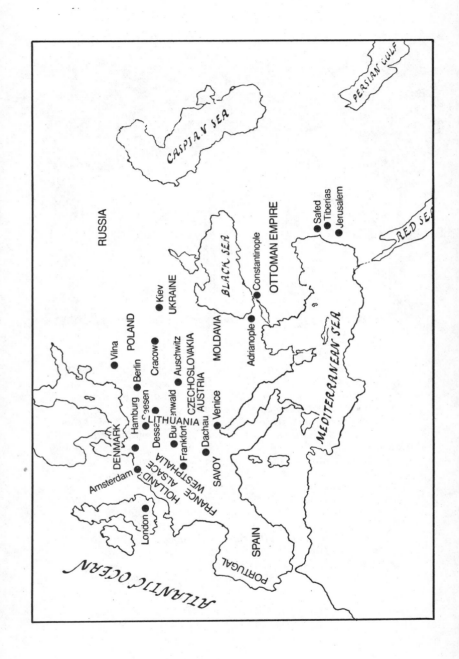

4

JUDAISM
IN THE MODERN WORLD

The era of the Renaissance and the Protestant Reformation, which came to full flower in the sixteenth century, was hardly an auspicious time for most Jews of Europe. Christian humanists like Pico Della Mirandola and Johanan Reuchlin may have learned much from Jewish Rabbis and may have spoken bravely in praise of the Jewish tradition, but Marranos were still being hunted down in Spain and throughout Christendom a mood of anti-Semitism seemed to prevail.

Martin Luther, early in his career, expressed an extraordinarily open attitude in his famous pamphlet, *Jesus Was Born a Jew* (*see* V.E), but as he grew older he became increasingly tolerant until, at last, he too joined the worst of the bigots by repeating many of the traditional accusations against the Jewish people. All of the major reformers — Luther, Calvin, Zwingli, and Hooker — envisioned a new Christian society united through faith in Jesus Christ. Obviously this was a society in which Jews could hardly be easily assimilated, for their very faith made them outsiders, permanent aliens in Christendom.

Judaism in the Ottoman Empire

Happily, however, there were some parts of the world which did welcome Jewish exiles. The Ottoman Empire, which had conquered nearly all of the Balkans by the fourteenth century and in 1453 had finally overpowered Christian Constantinople, was at the height of its glory. The usually tolerant sultans were quite willing to admit Jews and soon Constantinople boasted the largest Jewish community in Europe. As in the days of the early Middle Ages, before the noose of Islamic fanaticism had tightened and the lustre of Islamic culture was tarnished by poverty, Jews rose to positions of high prominence and wealth.

During the sixteenth century, Joseph Nasi, a Jewish financier, was compelled by the Inquisition to flee his native Portugal. Eventually, he made his way to Turkey where he soon gained the favor of the sultan, Suleiman II, and was given several high positions in the court. In this place of authority he worked to encourage the immigration of Jews, particularly to Palestine, and hence was instrumental in strengthening communities in Tiberias, Jerusalem, and Safed. Life in Palestine was far from idyllic for the new settlers, but before long the immigrant community had taken root and begun to develop an intellectual life of its own.

One of the most important new settlers was Joseph Karo, an eminent Talmudist who had, early in life, fled from the Spanish Inquisition and, after sojourns in Adrianople and Constantinople, finally arrived in Safed. There, working primarily within the Spanish Talmudic tradition, he prepared an extensive formulation of Jewish Law entitled *Bet Joseph* (House of Joseph). Since this work was too elaborate and ponderous for common use, he then offered an abridgement under the title *Shulchan Aruch* (Prepared Table). In so doing, he produced for world Jewry an easily used collection of "dos" and "don'ts" which was eventually, in "corrected form," to be one of the most authoritative works in the modern Jewish world.

The invention of printing, of course, greatly accelerated *Shulchan Aruch's* widespread use. When published in Venice in 1565, it was immediately hailed as epoch-making. Particularly attractive to the average Jew was the fact that it was much simpler to understand and use than the Talmud and the extensive literature surrounding it. In the past, only the learned could master the intricacies of Jewish Law. Now, even the relatively inexpert village Rabbi could understand. The problem, however, was and is that for the sake of simplicity and uniformity, the *Shulchan Aruch* tended to sacrifice the flexibility and subtlety of the Jewish legal tradition. Therefore, some would say that it threatened the whole of Jewish life with ossification by fixing the living law in sixteenth century form.

Furthermore, since Karo worked almost exclusively with Spanish authorities like Alfasi, Maimonides, and Asher, he often presented conclusions not wholly in accord with the somewhat divergent Ashkenazic traditions of Lithuania, Russia, and Poland. This deficiency, which led to resistance from many European Jews, was largely rectified by Moses Isserles of Cracow (c. 1520-1572) who added glosses which paid attention to the views of German and French authorities and to the *Minhag* (local customs and usages) of Eastern European Jewry. These glosses of Isserles have, since 1578, appeared within the text of *Shulchan Aruch* and have helped to make it the most authoritative code of Jewish law and practice available.

This legal compendium has often been attacked by modernists as stultifying and legalistic and, to be sure, there may be some truth to this characterization, but not as much as some critics would imply. Certainly, Talmudic studies did not end as with its appearance and Jewish law has continued to develop and grow according to the situation of the times. Furthermore, it gave to Judaism a sense of uniformity and unity which helped immensely during the dark days of persecution which lay ahead. The *Shulchan Aruch* may be anathema to many a secularized Jew today, but without it Judaism would have had much more difficulty persevering.

One feature of Karo's own life which bears mentioning in connection with his work is his own mystical experience. Although his legal code contains some exhortations and expressions of piety, one would scarcely guess that the author himself was a mystical Kabbalist very much caught up in the spiritual movement at Safed of which we will speak shortly. Far from being a dry-as-dust interpreter, he was a visionary who believed himself to be under the direct guidance of a heavenly mentor *(Maggid)* who gave him the impetus and certainty to decide hard points of the Law. In him, as in so many other Talmudists, therefore, we find a curious combination of concern for the outward fulfillment of the Law and an inwardness which radically transcends merely legalistic action.

The Safed to which Karo came was already fast becoming the center for Jewish mystical thought. Immigrants from Spain, Portugal, Germany, and elsewhere not only carried on the traditions of the German Hasidim and the Spanish Kabbalists; they added to that tradition their own unique ideas and emphases and in so doing reshaped the whole of the Kabbalistic movement.

Chief among the mystics of Safed were Moses ben Jacob Cordovero and Isaac Luria. Of the two, Cordovero was the more systematic thinker. His prolific works, many of which are still extant, develop the idea of the *Sephiroth* as the "organism" of *En-Sof* (The Hidden God) and explore the relation between God, who is All in All, and the world. His formulation of the relation between the divine and the cosmic in some ways foreshadows Spinoza, the great seventeenth century philosopher who also proclaimed that all things exist "in God."

Isaac Luria, on the other hand, was a true *"Zaddick,"* a saint whose life soon became legend. Although he wrote little or nothing, compendia of his thought by his disciples prove him to have been an original and creative thinker (*see* II.E). Like Cordovero, he was a mystic visionary who adopted the categories of the Kabbalistic tradition to explore the mysteries of creation and redemption.

For him the creation of the world was neither simply by divine fiat nor by emanation. The initial step for God was one of contraction and "exile" into himself *(tsimtsum)*. In this way, he "made room" for the world. Reflecting ancient gnostic speculation, Luria taught that creation must be understood in terms of both the contraction and emanation of God. He also introduced the figure of Adam Kadmon, that primordial man from whom emanated divine light. According to the speculation of Luria, when the vessels which caught the divine light from Adam Kadmon were broken, the divine sparks were plunged into the world of darkness. Still, had Adam, the first earthly man not fallen, the light would have been reunited at the time of his first Sabbath prayers. Because Adam fell, however, man's role as the reunifier of divine light has not been fulfilled.

This possibility, however, was never destroyed. Through mystical prayer, the divine sparks can be regathered, the primoridal man reunified, and the age of the Messiah brought about. Just as Jews live in exile away from the homelands, so the divine spark within man, which rightfully belongs in heaven is exiled in darkness. Through obedience to the 613 laws of the Torah and the use of *Kawwanah* (mystical-magical) prayer, the primordial, and hence the historical, exile can be overcome.

Luria also taught the doctrine of metempsychosis, believing that each spark is reincarnated until it achieves its heavenly freedom. Although quite at odds with the traditional doctrine of the resurrection, the idea of reincarnation became, at least for a time, quite popular among Jews through the influence of Luria and his school.

Luria, himself, taught orally, but his pupils put his teachings into writing and they spread with great rapidity throughout the Jewish world. His poems were incorporated in synagogue worship, legends about his great saintliness (*see* II.E) were retold from one end of the world to the other. Unlike earlier Kabbalistic movements, the influence of Luria was not confined to the esoteric elite. The common Jew became caught up in the grandeur of his gnostic vision and his practice of mystical prayer. Driven from his land, the Jew set forth now on a pilgrimage to his heavenly homeland. In his exile, he reflected the cosmic situation of both man and God. Just as God's exile into himself had preceded the creation of the cosmos, was it not logical to believe that the exile of the Jews from Spain would result in a new creation, perhaps the Messianic kingdom?

Earlier Kabbalists had drawn heavily from the apocalyptic imagery of the prophets and other early writers but had generally steered clear of Messianism. They looked to the mysteries of creation, not historical redemption. Luria and his school, however, combined cosmic speculation with both ecstatic experience and apocalyptic hope. This new synthesis was to lead to one of the most astonishing and perplexing movements ever to erupt out of the depths of Judaism: Sabbataism.

Nathan of Gaza (1644-1680) was a follower of Lurianic mysticism. Not only did he believe in Luria's doctrines and follow his practices, he was also an experiential mystic who on more than one occasion saw visions of the *Merkabah,* the chariot-throne of God. As fate (or was it destiny?) would have it, Nathan chanced to meet Sabbatai Zevi who had settled in Jerusalem in 1662. Zevi was a strange man by any standards, a manic-depressive perhaps, who during periods of peculiar mania would overtly break the Jewish Law. He had also occasionally announced to others that he was the Messiah, but virtually no one took him seriously. He came to Nathan in a moment of lucidity, not to proclaim his mission but because he believed Nathan could cure him of his psychic problems.

Nathan of Gaza, however, glimpsed in a vision Sabbatai's Messiahship and, his friend's intentions to the contrary, accepted his claims as the Lord's anointed. Combining the vigor of a John the Baptist and the zeal of a St. Paul, Nathan preached his message and gathered converts. Like a whirlwind the movement spread, appealing to the yearning of Jews everywhere for a better world in which they could find a home.

Even before the "moment of truth" arrived, Nathan had laid the groundwork for Sabbatai's apparent failure. The soul of the Messiah, he said, has been in bondage in the dark world ever since the breaking of the vessels and the scattering of the divine light in primordial times. Tempted by the serpents of darkness, he fights the fight of all men and takes upon himself their exile, their bondage.

Hundreds of Jews, eager to follow the incarnation of the Messiah, flocked to Jerusalem. From there many set forth for Constantinople with Sabbatai Zevi at their head. The sultan responded firmly but not without a fair portion of tolerance. The "Messiah" was imprisoned but the followers were allowed to visit him. Eventually, however, the sultan had enough and offered to the Messiah the simple option: conversion to Islam or death. When he chose the former, one can imagine the dismay which swept his large following.

Dismay, however, did not lead to the total destruction of the Sabbatian movement. On the contrary, followers argued that the apparent apostasy of the Messiah was actually a necessary part of his work, for by becoming a Muslim he went to release the hidden sparks within Islam itself. With that task accomplished he will return triumphant. This message was not without appeal, particularly among those Marranos who had themselves committed apostasy through forced conversion to Christianity. In his choice, the Messiah took upon himself their sins and hence gave to their tortured lives new justification.

Sabbatai Zevi apparently taught little or nothing and, unlike Jesus, left behind no sayings for disciples to remember. They did recall, however, his strange, antinomian actions which seemed to attack the very heart of Jewish Law. For his followers, these actions implied that the old Torah was to be transcended by a new one. Moderates within the movement continued to obey the Laws of Judaism but the more radical elements proclaimed that what had not been allowed was now permitted. Belief in the coming Kingdom implied throwing off the yoke of the Torah. This attitude led to wild excesses, particularly when Sabbatians were led by a charlatan like Jacob Frank in the eighteenth century.

There is considerable debate about just how extensive a movement Sabbatianism was during the hundred years which followed Nathan's proclamation. Jewish interpreters who favor normative, Torah-Talmud Judaism argue that it was a relatively small movement which never appealed to the great mass of Jews. There are indications, however, that Sabbatianism was by no means a tiny sect. Not only were there many able spokesmen for the movement but its influence seems to have spread everywhere. A "head count," however, is difficult, for many moderates seem to have preferred to espouse the new Messianism in secret. They continued to obey the Law and to attend orthodox synagogues even though Sabbatai's Messiahship was implicitly recognized by them.

If the vitality of a movement can be judged by the virulence of the opposition to it, eighteenth century Sabbatianism must have been more than a minor sect. The reaction to it led to an outpouring of vitriolic criticism and, eventually, to general contempt for the whole Kabbalistic movement. By the nineteenth century Jewish leaders were so concerned about the ill-effects of Kabbalism that the movement went under a cloud. Even today the great majority of the Kabbalistic writings remain untranslated and hence unavailable to the reading public.

Judaism in the Age of Reason

Meanwhile, in Europe, new currents of thought were moving through Christendom. As we have seen, neither the Protestant Reformers nor the Roman Catholics found much place for Jews in their vision of a Christian society. A culture united in common religious faith was the ideal of both sides. The failure of all attempts at reconciliation between Catholics and Protestants plus the proliferation of dissenting Protestant sects, however, made this ideal more and more unachievable. At the same time, the intelligentsia, repelled by the bloody squabbling among Christians, turned increasingly to the idea that reason rather than any particular brand of the Christian religion ought to be the unifying factor of society anyway.

In a word, Western Europe was becoming pluralistic and secular. Under these conditions, tolerance for all religious groups, including the Jews, appeared an ever-more reasonable alternative. This is not to say that anti-Jewish prejudices were quickly dissolved. Theologically, many Christians still found the presence of Jews in "their" society difficult to bear. Furthermore, the fact that those struggling Jewish communities which did remain tended to be impoverished and hence both dirty and superstitious did not aid in the growth of toleration. Most Christians simply never considered the obvious fact that Jews were impoverished and bitter because they had endured long years of Christian persecution.

Despite these theological and emotional anti-Jewish feelings, doors began to open to Jews in Europe. In the late sixteenth century Holland won its freedom from Hapsburg Spain. The Protestant leadership of the new country was Calvinistic and hence not enthusiastic about a great influx of Jews but permitted their settlement as long as they didn't cause trouble. Soon the Netherlands became the home of a thriving community of both Spanish Marranos and Central European Jews.

Actually, one should say "communities," for the Sephardic Jews of Spain had little love for their northern brethren. By this time, each branch of Judaism had developed its own customs and legal traditions and even pronounced Hebrew quite differently. The Sephardic Jews, as heirs of Judaism's golden age in Spain, looked down upon their Ashkenazic brethren as uncouth and uneducated. The Ashkenazic, in turn, looked askance, particularly at those who had committed apostasy by posing as new converts to Christianity. Today, many of the rough edges of dispute have been worn smooth, but major areas of difference still exist.

In any event, the Jews, no matter what stripe, soon found the burgeoning economy of Holland most propitious for their own financial and mercantile enterprises and many Jewish families became wealthy. The contributions of Jews to the economic prosperity of the whole nation, in turn, attracted the attention of other countries. In 1622 the king of Denmark invited Jews to settle in his country, promising them every privilege. The Duke of Savoy and the Duke of Modena followed suit. In 1650, Dutch Jews petitioned Cromwell, the Lord Protector of the British Isles, for the right to settle in his domain. Although Cromwell met with objections from the merchants of London and the Clergy, he rode roughshod over the opposition and consented to Jewish settlement. The rights of Jews in England were not clarified and the permanence of their immigration remained in doubt but at least, after centuries of banishment, a beginning was made.

Undoubtedly the most famous thinker of Jewish descent to emerge in the midst of this "new birth of freedom" was Benedict de Spinoza (1632-1677). Whether or not he can be termed a "Jewish thinker," however, is a matter of some debate, for he was excommunicated from the Jewish community fairly early in his career and spent the rest of his life outside the fold, grinding lenses and writing philosophy.

Despite Spinoza's overt alienation from his people, it is clear that his early education in the traditions of Judaism left a profound impression upon him. To the end of his life he remained a "God-intoxicated" man who sought to reconcile his belief in the oneness of God and the newly emerging science. In his *Ethics,* which reflects the current fascination with mathematics by its format — his whole argument is spelled out through a series of geometric "proofs" — God is identified as the one substance of the universe. Spinoza's God is, to be sure, non-anthropomorphic in the extreme, his (its) two known attributes being space and time, but in this the philosopher went no further than many earlier Jewish thinkers who also sought to circumvent the apparent naivete of Biblical descriptions of God. Furthermore, his insistence that the chief end of man ought to be the contemplation and love of God has a profoundly religious, even mystical ring to it. Like Maimonides before him Spinoza attempted to reconcile his own religious passions and contemporary science. Had he not been excommunicated from the synagogue so early, his own Judaism might have played a much larger role in his final formulation.

The occasion for his excommunication was not so much his implicit metaphysical position, which had not yet come to fruition at the time of his severance from the synagogue, but his insistent, critical analysis of Scripture itself. Like Abraham ben Ezra, he was unwilling to accept the tradition that Moses wrote the whole Torah. If we are to take Scripture literally, he argued in his *Theologico-Politico Tractatus,* we must approach it as literature, raising the critical questions about authorship and style which Renaissance scholars had asked about so many other documents (*see* III.F). In taking this position he disturbed both his fellow Jews and many contemporary Christians who believed him to be shaking the very basis of the faith. Despite his strong insistence upon the centrality of God, the terms "Spinozist" and "atheist" came to be used almost interchangeably. Eventually, both philosophers and Biblical scholars came to see the importance of his views; today Spinoza is often heralded as one of the founders of modern Biblical criticism and as one of the greatest philosophers the seventeenth century was to produce. At the time, however, Spinoza was considered, by Jew and non-Jew alike, a dangerous thinker.

Perhaps in more stable times Spinoza might have been allowed to continue his work within the fold of the faithful. Surely he was no more radical in his philosophical formulations than Gabirol or Luria. But the Jews of Holland in no way wished to "rock the boat" in which they were sailing. Unity was important to them as was reasonable peace with their Christian neighbors. They certainly did not wish to risk expulsion from Holland because some dissident taught ideas which Christians regarded as dangerous. So Judaism lost one of its most gifted sons, a man of supreme intelligence and loving gentleness. This loss, however, was the world's gain, for Spinoza remains one of the pivotal thinkers in the history of Western thought.

The leaders of Judaism in Holland may have deeply suspected the free thinking of men like Spinoza for very good reason, but they also were to benefit enormously from the freedom of thought which characterized the Age of Reason. After so many years of dominance, the Church suddenly found itself on the defensive, unable to cope with the claims of reason put forward by the philosophers. By and large, men like Locke, Leibnitz, and Voltaire were not particularly concerned about the plight of the Jews, but their call for reasonableness and toleration had lasting effects upon Western society. Once the ideal of a society united by a common, specifically Christian faith was eroded by their efforts, there seemed, at least theoretically, no good reason why Jews should be excluded from society as a whole.

Nevertheless, old prejudices die hard and it took decades before the Jewish people were emancipated from the confines of the ghetto. It is true that particularly in the various states of Germany *Hofjuden* (court Jews) were employed because of their financial expertise, but it is equally true that their good fortune, which depended entirely upon the good will of the ruler, scarcely improved the lot of the people as a whole. Jews might be used by the state, but they were hardly accepted as of equal status in the Holy Roman Empire. As late as 1745 the Jews of Bavaria were threatened with banishment. Only the intervention of Jewries in England and Holland prevented the actual expulsion.

One of the few who found recognition in secular society was the famous philosopher and apologist for Judaism, Moses Mendelssohn (1729-1786). Mendelssohn was born in Dressau, Germany, the son of a poor scribe who, despite his humble means, succeeded in providing his son with a good Jewish education. Moses proved to be worthy of his father's sacrifices, though perhaps not in the way his father anticipated.

When only fourteen years of age Mendelssohn made his way to Berlin, a city still forbidden to Jews, and there, with much privation and suffering, gained for himself a secular education. In 1754 he chanced to meet the famous critic and dramatist, Gotthold Lessing, who was enormously impressed by Mendelssohn's intellect. The two became fast friends and through Lessing's influence one door after another was opened.

Mendelssohn did not initially make his mark as a Jewish thinker but rather as a literary critic and philosopher. For all intents and purposes, he was a Deist who could, in *Phaedon* (1767), argue for the immortality of the soul and, in *Morgenstunden* (1785), establish philosophically the existence of God without an appeal to either Torah or Talmud. Throughout his life, in fact, he maintained that the essence of religious faith is founded upon reason and hence is, at least theoretically, universal among all men. Only ignorance, laziness, and confusion prevent men from acknowledging the God of reason.

As the result of a prize essay on the philosophy of the beautiful published in 1755, Mendelssohn received public acclaim and was accorded the privileges of a *Schutzjude*, which released him from the usual burdens placed upon Jews. Nevertheless, he remained a Jew both in practice and in faith. When his Jewishness was challenged by a would-be converter to Christianity, he began to respond more positively about his own religious tradition in public (*see* I.C).

For Mendelssohn, all religions are at root the same, for all are based upon the truths of reason. What the Hebrew Scriptures provide are not demonstrations of God's existence, but a revealed law by which to live. This law assumes the truths which reason provides but offers to the Jew a way of life through which he can express his love for God. While Spinoza had argued that the law of Moses was meant as a political law for the ancient nation of Israel and hence is no longer applicable, Mendelssohn believed contemporary observance of it to be of value and hence remained much closer to his Jewish tradition than did Spinoza.

Beside his strictly philosophical works, Mendelssohn wrote prolifically in favor of the freedom of conscience and the toleration of various religious groups, including the Jews. In so doing he set the stage for the age which was to follow. Moreover, he translated the Torah into excellent German, thus giving to his fellow Jews a sense of their own Germanness. Some of the stricter conservatives in the Jewish community resisted his work, but he was too well respected to be silenced. Before long his translation was being widely read by German-speaking Jews.

Mendelssohn like Spinoza was, however, unique. A comparison of his writings with the work of, say, Moses Hayyim Luzzato (1707-1747) whose ethical treatise *Mesillat Yeshaiim* was enormously popular during the eighteenth century, reveals that Mendelssohn was scarcely a part of the main stream of Judaism at all. Jews in the ghetto continued to live a medieval life and to think in a medieval way. They still had to pay a special poll tax levied upon Jews each time they crossed a border and were frequently subject to other penalties and humiliations imposed by "Christian" governments. Mendelssohn may have helped to bring toleration to Judaism, but he scarcely understood the ghetto better than many of his Christian brethren. It is significant that his own children, cut adrift from their own Jewish past, felt compelled to convert to Christianity in order to find for themselves a place in society.

It was not until the French Revolution and the rise of Napoleon that a radical change took place in the life of European Jewry itself. The great revolution of 1789 which overthrew the *ancien regime* was strongly influenced by the French philosophers — men like Voltaire, Diderot, and Rousseau — who had long called for freedom of conscience and toleration. "The Declaration of the Rights of Man" pronounced all men equal, regardless of race or religion. True, it took some time before theory became fact but by 1791 all Jews had been granted the rights of full citizenship. The ghetto in France was at an end. Marranos living in Bordeaux and Bayonne could now publicly proclaim what they had practiced in secret for centuries. The Alsatian Jews, impoverished by years of persecution, could begin to flee the ghetto.

Although in many respects propitious, this emancipation from the ghetto was not without problems. Throughout the Middle Ages the Jews, despite persecution and harassment, had enjoyed a modicum of self-government. They had their own schools, courts, and social system. They even paid their taxes as a corporate group. The end of the ghetto meant, therefore, that the cohesive unity of Jewish life was threatened. Many Jews were neither ready nor totally willing to give up their old institutions.

Furthermore, emancipation did not mean the end of anti-Semitic feelings or the total acceptance of Jews within society. The ghetto, though cramped and confining, had meant security. As Jews moved out of the ghetto, they found new social responsibilities thrust upon them but not full acceptance by their neighbors. It was not clear at all that emancipation was a move for the better.

As Napoleon took over control of France and began his struggle to "liberate" and unite the whole of Europe, he carried the idea of emancipation wherever he went. When his forces conquered Italy the gates of ghettos were literally torn down and the Jews, by Napoleonic fiat, were granted equal rights before the law. In the German states the same practice was followed even though Germans in many areas accepted the innovation very grudgingly.

Actually, the Holy Roman Empire, under Joseph II, had already taken a few first steps toward greater equality for Jews before Napoleon's onslaught. The Edict of Toleration of 1782 removed some restrictions on the travel and occupations of Jews, but nevertheless also involved a price; the Jews were required to reform both their educational and social institutions. They were also required to take surnames — but not the surnames common among Christians. When a Jewish father could not think of a name for his family, an official simply gave him one. Often the name selected was of a derogatory nature, to say the least.

Neither the Jews nor the Christians were happy about these measures, though obviously for quite different reasons. With the death of Joseph II the reform died and emancipation was not furthered until Napoleon's victory. Even then resistance to any amelioration of the Empire's restrictive laws proved to be so great that emancipation did not become a reality for several generations.

Napoleon, as one might suspect, was no lover of the Jews but rather used them, as he used virtually everyone else, to further his own ambitions. Although the story may be apocryphal, it has been alleged that when Napoleon's campaign in Africa and Asia floundered, he promised to give Palestine back to the Jews if they would rise up and help him. They did not and he returned to France something less than triumphant.

At home the French Emperor, beset by irate countrymen who despised the Alsatian Jews and hence resisted emancipation, decided to "make the Jews more respectable" by giving them an organizational structure. With a flourish of imperial majesty and a total disregard for history, he recreated in France the Sanhedrin, a judicial body which had not existed for centuries. Rabbis were called together to serve in this august body and many dutifully responded. The Sanhedrin, however, had little to do and soon died of inactivity.

Though the Sanhedrin was a failure, Napoleon was instrumental in creating a national Jewish organization for France which to this day retains, to a large extent, the form which he invented. The chief legacy of the era, however, was the end of the ghetto as a legal body and the development of a new official status for the Jew. Henceforth, each Jew was to be regarded as an individual under the law, not a member of a separate nation living within the boundaries of France. The problems which this new status produced have already been alluded to. The answers to these problems which Jews formulated will have to wait until we have looked briefly at two other areas of major importance: Eastern Europe and the New World.

Judaism in Eastern Europe in the Seventeenth and Eighteenth Centuries

From the eleventh century onward, Jews, seeking to escape the horrors of the West, tended to migrate eastward. Particularly in Poland, the Baltic States, and Roumania, Jews found a more or less cordial welcome and eventually put down roots. Although the ghetto remained, many of them were able to attain a relatively high level of prosperity. All this was to change radically in the seventeenth century.

In 1648 the Cossacks of the Ukraine, led by Bogdan Chmielnicki, rose up against their Polish oppressors. Since the Jews had frequently acted as tax collectors and agents for the Polish crown they were singled out for special brutality by the Cossack forces. The massacre was enormous, especially after the Czar of Russia took the Cossacks under his protection and invaded Poland himself. It is estimated that as many as 100,000 Jews died during the bloody period between 1648 and 1658.

This period of out-and-out bloodshed was followed by persecution and harassment on a local level until the Polish Jewish community, once known for its Talmudic scholarship and distinctive mode of life, was but a shadow of its former self. Now the pendulum of immigration swung westward as thousands fled persecution. Penniless and broken, they made their way to Germany, Holland, and anywhere else that they could find a home. The ghettos of Western Europe, much to the annoyance of both civil officials and many local Jews who were having enough troubles of their own, soon became bloated by the influx of Yiddish-speaking Jews.

Many of the Jews of Eastern Europe, of course, were unwilling to risk uprooting and thus remained in their homeland, now more than likely under the hegemony of Holy Russia. This political change was of no minor importance. Russia had, for centuries, sought to keep Jews out of her domain and officially took a particularly vigorous anti-Jewish stance. As late as 1742 Catherine the Great prohibited free travel by Jews in her empire, even by those who had lived in Russia for generations.

Nevertheless, with the partition of Poland, Russia found within her territory at least a million Jews. These were allowed to remain within "The Pale," that strip of conquered territory where most Jews lived, but were not allowed to travel elsewhere. Somehow the Czars believed that by so confining the Jews and by making their life absolutely miserable, they could convert their non-Christian subjects to the orthodox faith. The Age of Enlightenment never really penetrated the eastern giant and the ideal of a religiously uniform society prevailed. During the eighteenth, nineteenth, and twentieth centuries, Russian Jews were to experience perhaps the most vicious forms of persecution known during Judaism's long history — and that's saying a great deal.

In the midst of this era of woe a new religious movement emerged which was to transform radically the style of Eastern Jewry. The man who was to initiate this cataclysmic change was a poor, simple lime digger, Israel of Moldavia (1700-1760), better known to the world as Ba'al Shem Tov ("Master of the Good Name"). Unlike most other great leaders of Judaism, Israel received only a minimal education in Torah and Talmud, deriving his inspiration not from the hair-splitting, scholastic techniques of the schools but from the beauties of nature in the Carpathian mountains. There he lived a life of poverty for several years, digging lime and praising God from his heart.

When Israel returned to a more civilized life he brought to the world a mystical awareness of the presence of God which he began to communicate to others. Unlike his more scholastic contemporaries who prized the intricate *pilpul* of the schools and looked down on the uneducated laboring class, he taught that communion with God is available to all. Although he respected learning for what it is, he believed, and believed deeply, that God is present for scholar and peasant alike (*see* IV.E.).

Gershom Scholem has demonstrated quite convincingly that Israel and his followers were influenced by certain Sabbatian writings which carried on the tradition of Lurianic mysticism and there is no reason to dispute this fact.* Nevertheless, it is also clear that Israel's central vision was his own, derived through his own life of prayer and praise. He did not learn about God from the Sabbatians or anyone else. By his own admission, he learned about God from God himself.

Israel and his disciples followed a life of enthusiastic devotion to God unmarred by scholastic quibbling and noxious ascetic practices. Theirs was a life of optimism, of singing and dancing in praise of the Blessed One, of religious ecstasy. So infectious was their devotion that the movement quickly spread to south Russia, Poland, the Baltic States — all over Eastern Europe.

As the new Hasidism spread it is not surprising that disdain for learning grew among the adherents until they found true piety and the scholastic tradition virtually antithetical. Their life was one of ecstatic devotion, revolving around a *zaddik*, a supremely pious man of whom Ba'al Shem Tov was the prototype and who received their almost idolatrous devotion. Eventually each *zaddik* became the founder of a line of holy men, son following father to the holy office. Legends about the *zeddikim* grew and a luminous folk tradition was elaborated. Soon much of Eastern European Jewry was singing, dancing, and praying in praise of God.

This new Hasidic movement, of course, also had its severe critics, particularly among the learned who believed the Hasidim to be threatening the very basis of Jewish law and thought. But it was not only the members of the old scholastic, *pilpul* tradition who were critical. One of the leaders of the fight against the hair-splitting of the schools was Elijah, the Gaon of Vilna, (1720-1796), who worked diligently to bring Jewish scholars back to the study of the simple text of Torah and Talmud. He, like Ba'al Shem Tov, was radically opposed to academic obscurantism, but he was equally opposed to the excesses of the Hasidim, especially when some of the more degenerate forms of their teaching came to his attention. An acrid dispute broke out and eventually Elijah excommunicated the whole Hasidic movement. Even an authority like Elijah,

---

*Gershom G. Scholem, *Major Trends in Jewish Mysticism* (New York: Schocken Books, 1961), p. 327ff.

however, could not stem the tide and Hasidism continued to dominate Judaism in Eastern Europe, producing both new vitality and new aberrations. Despite the problems which an hereditary spiritual office might produce, Hasidism flourished, for it offered to the faithful a religion filled with awe and delight and physical exuberance.

Judaism in America During the Seventeenth and Eighteenth Centuries

While persecution raged in the East and Western Europe was cautiously opening the ghetto door, a whole new world of possibility blossomed across the Atlantic in America. If Columbus himself was not a Jew — and there is great debate about that issue — several of his crewmen certainly were. These men were followed by other Spanish Jews who sought to escape the Inquisition, founding communities of Marranos in the New World. America, however, proved no safe haven for the Marrano; the Inquisition soon followed, attacking and burning presumed heretics with considerable gusto.

Nor were the English settlements in Massachusetts Bay initially much more open to Jewish immigrants. The Puritans had come to found a new and Christian Jerusalem and saw little advantage in accepting anyone who did not conform to their Christian ideals. Again, however, Christian noncomformity came to the aid of the Jews. Roger Williams, reacting against the narrowness of the Puritan ideal, established a colony in Providence which was founded upon the principle of religious liberty. In it Jews were welcome and a small settlement was made.

Even before this time Jews had also immigrated to New Amsterdam, a Dutch colony. When they found Peter Stuyvesant reluctant to grant them full rights, they appealed successfully to the Dutch East India Company. Still, Stuyvesant and his successors put obstacles in their path and for many years Jews were discriminated against in a variety of ways under both Dutch and English rule.

Thus, in one sense, nothing changed in the New World. Old World prejudices traveled the seas just like the men who held them. American Jews, like their European counterparts, were still not accepted as full members of society. Nevertheless, in the New World all was transformed. There were no ghetto walls to break down or hide behind for there was no ghetto. American life was rough-hewn and full of possibilities which no Old World attitudes could deny the Jew. In America a man could be judged as an individual rather than as a member of a group and, despite old cliches, the courage and intelligence of the Jew shown through.

The American Revolution, like that in France, was strongly influenced by the Age of Reason. Hence, despite the initial quest for religious uniformity which characterized colonizing Christians, the constitution of the new nation expressed in simple but powerful terms the principles of religious freedom. Although anti-Semitism in the New World was not unknown, the Jew was free to immigrate, to express his religion in word and action, and to compete on equal terms with his fellow Americans.

His fellow Americans! After reviewing the whole history of Judaism in Christendom, what a strange but wonderful sound that has! And it is as accurate as it is unique. Jews, with Christians, discovered the New World. They worked to colonize America and to develop her industries. They fought in the revolution and helped to shape the new nation. Despite the innuendoes of the bigots who have not yet learned what America is all about, Judaism is as American as Catholicism or Protestantism. It is no wonder that over the years America has appeared to Jews in many lands as a safe haven in the midst of stormy seas and that to her shores have come literally millions of Jews seeking a better life.

European Jews in the Nineteenth Century

Meanwhile, in Western Europe the cause of toleration and the freedom of conscience was suffering a setback. The defeat of Napoleon led to a reversal of the trend which so many of the enlightened thought inevitable. Monarchies were restored, neo-Gothic architecture was erected, a fading Catholicism was revitalized. This great swing back to tradition implied to many non-Jews that a return to the ghetto was in order. In Italy the ghetto gates were again set up and the badge was even reintroduced. In Germany, the cities of Bremen and Lubeck expelled all Jews who had settled there in recent years.

Return to the old age, however, was not as easy as the conservatives imagined. Once out of the ghetto the eyes of many Jews had been opened. The Jewish folk, so long confined, had tasted freedom and were no longer so easily made subservient. One of the extraordinary features of this new age was the tremendous burst of intellectual, social, and commercial activity of Jews all over Europe. It was as though a mighty flood which had been dammed up for years had suddenly broken through. No longer did Jewish intellectuals confine their interest to the study of the Talmud but now entered virtually every field of human endeavor. Before the nineteenth century had closed there were prominent Jewish writers, actors, musicians, scientists, playwrights, philosophers, scholars, and statesmen in virtually every Western European country.

Quite naturally many Jewish intellectuals tried to relate their own Jewish tradition to current philosophizing. Samuel Hirsch (1815-1889) was a Jewish Hegelian who sought to correct Hegel's estimation of Judaism and to affirm, far more than Hegel did, the unique nature of Jewish monotheism. Solomon Formstecher (1808-1889) employed the ideas of the prolific Schelling in order to restate the meaning of Judaism. Solomon Ludwig Steinheim (1789-1886) emphasized the limitations of reason pointed out by Immanuel Kant, thus attempting to secure a place for divine revelation. Nachman Krochmal (1785-1840) developed a Jewish philosophy of history based upon German idealism, especially Hegel. Finally, Hermann Cohen (1842-1918), an academic philosopher who founded the Marburg school of Neo-Kantianism, argued that the concept of God is necessary for both science and ethics. In his later years, he was to speak much more directly about his own religion, arguing for a religion of reason as a basis for Judaism.

In the realm of commerce and finance, Jews of the nineteenth century were to play an even larger role, serving as international bankers and merchants. The power of the House of Rothschild is well known, though one must add that it never became — as critics would have it — the hidden government of Western Europe, determining public policy by the granting or withholding of loans to governments. Nevertheless, the Rothschilds, the Pereires, the Goldsmids, and the Sassons wielded great economic power and, in effect, made the return to the ghetto impossible.

Still, it is shocking to remember how long it took for the Jews of Europe to attain full and equal rights of citizenship. Such did not occur in England until 1866 and in some parts of the German Empire until 1871. Switzerland, a country long known for its "exemplary" democracy, only truly emancipated the Jews in 1874. It is no wonder, then, that in those turbulent years, when political revolution was often in the wind, Jews aligned themselves with the liberals and radicals against their conservative oppressors. Jews played an exceptional role in Italy, siding with Mazzini and Garibaldi against the status quo and eventually regaining their freedom from the ghetto walls. The abortive revolutions of 1848 which swept Europe also had their Jewish supporters who fought valiantly to turn back the tide of reactionism. Perhaps it is not surprising that Karl Marx, a descendant from a long line of illustrious Jewish Rabbis, should enter the lists against the repressive forces of society.

Marx's urbane father, in order to acquire a "passport" into European society, had converted to Protestant Christianity and Marx himself was not brought up a Jew. In fact, virulent anti-Semitic comments are to be found in many of his writings, as though he wished to prove to all that he "belonged" to Western society too. Nevertheless, his diatribes echo with the moral indignation of the Hebrew prophets while his vision of history as proceeding toward a utopia of the proletariat appears to be a very secularized form of Messianism. Judaism, however, should be neither praised nor blamed for Marx. He was his own man, an individualist to the core who tragically and ironically was to foster a system where individuals frequently do not count for much.

It is not surprising that in this post-ghetto age many Jews began to question the relevance of their venerable ghetto traditions. Laws and customs once quite acceptable within the ghetto walls seemed anachronistic and stifling in the heady years of emancipation. The old institutions had been badly shaken. New vistas had opened up. It was in this situation that Reform Judaism was born.

Pioneering in the process of reform was Israel Jacobson (1768-1828) who, as president of the Westphalian consistory, introduced several liturgical changes in his synagogue at Seesen. His concern was that services had become both unaesthetic and unintelligible and hence hardly appropriate in the enlightened atmosphere in which Jews now lived. In 1801 he established a boarding school where both Jewish and Christian boys might learn mutual toleration and understanding. Then, after some experimentation at the school, he opened a synagogue in 1810 where German as well as Hebrew prayers were heard, where an organ was introduced, and where confirmation of both sexes was practiced.

When the Kingdom of Westphalia fell in 1813, the experiment came to a momentary end, but Jacobson continued his reforms in private in Berlin. Although harassed by the Prussian government which opposed all liberal tendencies, the movement spread. In 1818 a Reform synagogue was opened in Hamburg.

What began as a modest revision of worship soon became a general revolt against traditional forms as Reform leaders came to an increasing awareness that the old style and many of the traditional ideas were no longer relevant for nineteenth century Germany. One of the foremost leaders in this fight against fixed and immovable Judaism was the able scholar and critic, Abraham Geiger (1810-1874). Geiger emphasized with much acumen that Judaism had, since its inception, been a continuously developing religion. He was not againt tradition *per se* but believed that traditions can outlive their usefulness and must be abandoned for the sake of the spirit of tradition. Not very interested in dietary laws and phylacteries, Geiger emphasized the ethical side of Judaism, expressing deep concern for social justice. The destiny of Israel was conceived in terms of striving to fulfill the ethical teachings of the prophets rather than in hoping for the Messiah and the Promised Land.

Even before the time of Geiger, several educated Jews had begun to explore Jewish history with open eyes. In 1819 a group of keen-minded young men organized a society for the scientific study of Judaism. One of the chief leaders was Leopold Zunz who believed that an objective study of Jewish history and tradition would facilitate the separation of the wheat and the chaff within Jewish life. He himself contributed greatly to that end by his studies of Jewish liturgy and synagogal poetry. Moritz Steinschneider, another member of the movement, explored the libraries of Europe for Jewish manuscripts, while Isaac Marcus Jost published the first real history of the Jews to be written by a Jew since Biblical times. Within a short time his work was surpassed by the monumental achievement of Heinrich Graetz whose history of the Jews still makes profitable reading today.

These reforming tendencies which sought to answer many of the questions raised by emancipation, produced repercussions throughout the Jewish world. Even in Russia there was a movement to reproduce in Hebrew translation works of contemporary importance so that the Jew there might also become enlightened. This movement, called *Haskalah* was to meet with considerable opposition from both the Hasidim and their rivals, the scholastic Rabbis, but it was also to encourage a far more open and questioning attitude, particularly among the young adults.

It was also predictable that Reform would produce a counter reaction from more conservative elements within the Jewish community of Germany. Leading the opposition was Samson Raphael Hirsch, Rabbi at Frankfort, who formulated a defense of strictly traditional Judaism and who argued that neither emancipation nor the growing influence of secular culture legitimized the forsaking of traditional Jewish belief and practice. In many areas the struggle between reformers and the traditionalists was intense and polarization of the Jewish community occurred.

By the 1840s a moderate party, led by Zechariah Frankel (1801-1875) had also developed. This movement, which eventually became a source of what is today called Conservative Judaism, was willing to adopt certain modest changes but quite adamant in its defense of the Talmudic tradition with its dietary laws, etc. Although this current within Judaism grew slowly, it came to attract a large number of Jews, particularly in America, who were repelled by both the radicalness of Reform and the apparent obscurantism of Orthodox Judaism.

After the revolution of 1848, Reform Judaism waned in influence in Germany but became evermore firmly established in America. During the early part of the nineteenth century the great majority of Jewish immigrants to America were German. With them they brought their reforming ideas. The American situation, with its emphasis upon freedom and modernity, encouraged their optimistic hopes for social reform and made the more traditional attitudes which tended to isolate the Jewish community seem quite irrelevant. Thus, while Reform virtually perished in the land of its birth, it found new life and hope in the New World.

Eastern Europe in the Nineteenth Century

While Judaism breathed the fresh air of emancipation in Western Europe and America, the situation in Czarist Russia and its territories was merciless beyond belief. Particularly under Nicholas I (1825-55) the Russians used every conceivable method to unJew the Jews. Jewish boys were taken from their families at the age of twelve and forced to serve in the army for twenty-five years. The Jewish community was compelled to supply the number of boys required and the selection of who should serve produced great bitterness. In 1835 Jews were expelled from Kiev and other expulsions were threatened elsewhere. Censorship of Hebrew literature was introduced and, since the censors themselves were not able to read the language, they felt themselves perfectly free to concoct fanciful stories about the anti-social ideas they discovered. The *Kahal* or ghetto organization was deprived of its legal basis; schools for Jews were established, but were staffed by Christians and apostate Jews. It is no wonder that Jews heaved a sigh of relief when Nicholas died.

Alexander II (1855-81) promised and initiated reforms, ameliorating some of the worst excesses of his predecessor, but overall the situation of the Jews improved only slightly under his rule. Toward the end of his reign monumentally libellous charges were leveled at the Jews by an apostate from Judaism, Jacob Brafman, and this led to anti-Jewish riots which the government did little to stop. When Alexander was assassinated in 1881 rumor spread that the Jews were to blame and that the new government would not look askance upon further "spontaneous" anti-Jewish outbursts.

During the reigns of Alexander III (1881-94) and Nicholas II (1894-1917) pogroms became numerous and thousands of Jews were forced to flee as best they could. Police brutality, the repressive "May Laws," and general harassment made life in Russia a living hell. It is no wonder that during this period thousands of emigrants fled to the Americas to escape the torture of their own land. It is also not surprising that many Jews supported the revolutionaries who eventually overthrew the Czarist government in 1917 and established the world's first Marxist state. Many of these men, like Leon Trotsky, were scarcely Jewish in their attitudes and beliefs, but one can imagine that the long era of Jewish persecution under the Czars did little to sweeten their attitude toward the government.

Unfortunately for the Jews, the Bolsheviks were no more willing to accept the non-conformist than were the Czars. The quest for Christian unity was simply replaced by the dogmatic assertion of dialectical materialism and the latter soon became an equally ready reason for the expression of popular anti-Semitic feelings. The combination of popular prejudice and governmental insistence upon conformity proved as lethal under Communism as it did under the Czars.

Anti-Semitism

Unfortunately, anti-Semitic ideas were by no means confined to Czarist Russia and the Soviet Union. During the middle decades of the nineteenth century Jews were granted the rights of citizenship in European countries but were immediately met with a new wave of scurrilous propaganda. The causes for this anti-Jewish campaign are too complex and sometimes too debatable to summarize briefly. Certainly, the jealousy aroused by successful and powerful Jews contributed to the movement. So too did the antagonism of Protestants and Catholics engendered by Jewish efforts to free school and government of Church control. The strong sense of national unity felt in newly emerging nations like Italy and Germany also produced greater allegiance to "race" and cultural homogeneity. Perhaps most important, however, was that long-standing human need for a scapegoat upon whom all the problems and failures of a changing society can be blamed. As usual the Jews were forced once more to carry the sins of the world on their backs.

Despite the notable contributions made by Jews in the nineteenth century to nearly every branch of human culture, "Jew" again became a despicable word, one which was freely applied to almost anyone a propagandist didn't like. Politicians like Bismarck found anti-Jewish slogans a useful device for catalyzing political support; clergy, needing some evil to attack, found the Jew a ready-made target. All the old accusations were dredged up and even intellectuals who should have known better were caught in the vortex. The Dreyfuss Affair, in which a loyal French soldier who happened to be Jewish was court-martialed and sent off to Devil's Island for a crime he never committed, is an outstanding example of how otherwise intelligent men can be blinded to the obvious by prejudice.

Ironically, this outburts of anti-Jewish feelings occurred precisely at a time when Western European Jewry was becoming more and more secularized and hence less and less "Jewish." With the withering of Reform Judaism in Germany the Jew seemingly was left with the choice: Orthodoxy or the secular world. Even those who chose the former discovered that somehow life had gone out of the synagogue and that only dull and lifeless "dry bones" were left.

This was the situation to which Franz Rosenzweig (1886-1929) addressed himself. From his youth Rosenzweig sensed the barrenness of middle class Judaism, but unlike many of his contemporaries wished neither to abandon the tradition completely for the secular world nor to convert to Christianity. Both his correspondence with Eugene Rosenstock, an articulate Christian convert, and his famous *Star of Redemption* reveal the depth of Rosenzweig's perception as he attempted to wrestle with the question: How can one be truly and religiously Jewish in a "Christian" society?

Unlike most earlier apologists for Judaism (or Christianity, for that matter) Rosenzweig argued that Judaism and its offspring, Christianity, are both authentic manifestations of one religious truth. While Christianity's aim is to bring the Gentiles to the Father through faith, Judaism lives with the Father and does not need to be introduced to him. Judaism, then, is not a missionary religion but witnesses to the Truth through organic, natural growth and through the preservation of ancient tradition.

This latter function, the preservation of tradition, represented for Rosenzweig one of his most difficult problems. Reared in a very secular fashion, he initially looked at Judaism with the eyes of an outsider and hence felt little innate compulsion to obey the law in all detail. At the same time, he was not disposed to adopt some new, liberal "orthodoxy" like Reform which only replaced old laws by modern innovations. On the one hand, he emphasized that Judaism is an organic, changing religion which will die if it becomes crystallized, as in the *Shulchan Aruch.* On the other, he showed repeatedly a sensitivity to tradition and a capacity to learn its meaning.

In a sense, Rosenzweig's contribution to Judaism is not found in the answers which he gave but in the struggle in which he engaged. Those who read his writings receive from him few final answers but rather derive a much deeper sense of what it means to be a Jew — an honest, modern, religious Jew — in the twentieth century. What a tragedy it was that such a thoughtful and creative person should have been afflicted with a paralysis which left him totally helpless and then took his life at the age of forty-two. And what a greater tragedy it was that throughout his life anti-Semitism continued to flourish and expand its diatribes.

Perhaps the reader, aware that anti-Semitism was not one of Rosenzweig's major themes, will think it strange that a discussion of him has taken place under this particular heading. In a sense, however, Rosenzweig's thought offers one of the best responses to the anti-Semites which Judaism has expressed. The perennial criticism of Judaism in Christendom has been that it is legalistic, insensitive, and atavistic — the religion of the Pharisees. Rosenzweig is willing to admit some truth in this accusation, but he also demonstrates that it need not be so at all. Through his very life he reveals to the world that Judaism and narrow, unthinking legalism are by no means synonymous. Beneath the surface of the law beats the fervent heart of faith.

Zionism

For the Jew the obviously fallacious propaganda of the anti-Semites only confirmed once more his long-standing opinion of Western culture. It is no wonder that Reform Judaism, with its more positive attitude toward Christendom and the future, lost ground in Germany. Jews around the world began to see that hope for the recovery of a homeland was not simply an ideal which could be discarded as the Reformers wanted. In the face of such virulent criticism, a return to Zion began to appear as an attractive, though obviously still difficult, possibility.

This is not to say that most Jews, overnight, became ardent Zionists. On the contrary, the pioneers of Zionism, like Theodore Herzl (1860-1904) found little enthusiasm for their vision of a Jewish state among either the governments of Europe or the Jews. Reform Jews had consciously repudiated hopes for a rebirth of the Jewish nation, replacing such dreams with a concern for the social betterment of society. They looked to an active role for Judaism within Western culture, not to a separate Jewish state. Many Orthodox Jews, on the other hand, theoretically hoped for a return to Zion but linked such a return to the coming of the Messiah and "the last days." It is up to God, not us, to refound the nation in the promised land, they said.

Curiously enough, the cause of Zionism was initiated, not by the pious leaders of Judaism but by secularized Jews who had little connection with the traditions of their own people. Moses Hess, a sometime compatriot of Karl Marx, was one of the first to speak seriously of "practical Zionism." In his *Rome and Jerusalem* (1862), he criticized those who placed their hopes in political emancipation and called instead for a return to Palestine. Others, like Hirsch Kalischer, Henri Dumont, and Leo Pinsker, also urged the creation of a national homeland but received little popular support. A few immigrants made their way to Palestine, but the new settlers found even survival extremely difficult in the land supposedly flowing with milk and honey.

Above all, it was Theodore Herzl who really got Zionism under way. He was, to say the least, a strange leader for the movement, for he began his career as an Austrian journalist, quite ungrounded in Jewish tradition. The Dreyfuss Affair, however, stirred his indignation and imagination. Largely unaware of the efforts of earlier Zionists, he began a one-man movement to found a Jewish state in Palestine. The rest of his life was devoted to pressing the idea among his fellow Jews and attempting to gain political support among the ruling heads of Europe. Eventually, he even gained an audience with the sultan of Turkey, but that potentate, like all the others, simply nodded his head and promised nothing.

Herzl was a man of undying optimism. Repeatedly, he met with apathy, hostility, and diplomatic double-talk, but he never gave up. He organized a series of Zionist conferences, a Jewish Colonial Trust, and the Jewish National Fund. Like a man possessed, he proceeded as though all of Judaism were behind him, badgering diplomats, wooing Prime Ministers, arguing with fellow Jews (*see* IV.F).

When Herzl died suddenly in his forty-fourth year, however, it appeared that his monumental efforts had produced little. The British Government had asked the Jews to consider settling in Uganda, but that, for the Zionists, would hardly do. No other very concrete advances were made. Even Herzl's most loyal supporters must have thought their cause but a visionary dream.

World War I, however, was to transform that dream into at least a modest possibility. In many respects, that international conflict was disastrous for Judaism. At the outbreak of the war, the greatest concentration of European Jews was located in those borderlands between Germany and Russia and hence was caught in the withering struggle on the Eastern Front. Thousands died as both armies devastated their settlements in the ebb and flow of war. Furthermore, anti-Semites on both sides used the war as an opportunity to carry out a full-scale slaughter of those Jews which the pogroms had left behind. Even before the rise of Hitler, therefore, Eastern Jewry had already been decimated.

One event did occur which was of positive benefit. Germany's ally, the Ottoman Empire, crumbled before the British army and its Arab guerrilla allies and Palestine, for the first time since the crusades, fell into Western hands. Almost immediately after the defeat of the Turks, as a result of diplomatic negotiations between Zionists and the British Government, the British Foreign Secretary (later dubbed Lord Balfour) had issued a declaration favoring the creation of a Jewish homeland. This famous Balfour Declaration of 1917 became the basis of Jewish aspirations from that time onward (*see* V.G). It should be noted, however, that in the heat of the war Britain, to curry the favor of various parties — the Jews, the Arabs, her allies — made a number of conflicting promises concerning Palestine which could not all be kept. When the war ended, Britain was accorded Palestine by League of Nations mandate, but it was not at all clear which promises she would choose to honor. Until the very end of the mandate, Her Majesty's Government vacillated, attempting to placate everyone but succeeding in pleasing no one (*see* IV.F).

For the Zionists, at any rate, a promise was a promise and, with a tenacity worthy of Herzl's memory, they called upon Britain to fulfill the specifics of the Declaration. The story of how, in spite of herself Britain finally, quite grudgingly, gave in, must wait until we have reviewed other development in the twentieth century which have contributed to the fulfillment of Zionist dreams.

The Jews after World War I

The situation of world Jewry after the Great War was by no means a happy one. The largest concentration of Jews remained in Eastern Europe and there the anti-Semites were having a field day. The whole post-war settlement in Europe was based upon Wilson's idea of "self-determination," a notion which predictably emphasized racial and ethnic differences. The new nations which were carved out of the holdings of the Austro-Hungarian Empire and Czarist Russia were understandably proud of their own ethnic peculiarities and hence had even less toleration for those who did not fit into the new national homogeneity. In Poland, Hungary, and Roumania, in particular, the governments themselves took an almost official anti-Semitic stance. Only in Czechoslovakia were Jews allowed to live in peace as a highly respected, middle-class community.

The new Soviet Union officially adopted a policy of just treatment for all the many minorities within its boundaries, but the Jews constituted a special case because of their religion. With the triumph of Communism, Russia had become officially anti-religious and considered Judaism, in particular, as an affront to dialectical materialism. The Jew who was willing to give up his religious tradition found a place in society and some, like Leon Trotsky, rose to positions of power, but the religious Jew was abused, harassed, and persecuted as much as before; he did not conform and the watchword in the Soviet Union was conformity. Furthermore, because many Jews in pre-Soviet Russia had been shopkeepers and merchants, they were a part of the bourgeois class which the Communists sought to destroy. Communism meant that vast numbers of Jews were driven out of business and impoverished permanently.

In Germany, too, the situation rapidly became impossible for Jews. Both Germany and Austria had been left economically shattered and politically unstable by the war and by the Treaty of Versailles. Unemployment was dangerously high; inflation was disastrous. The Germanic people seethed with resentment and found in the Jews a ready scapegoat for all their problems. Adolph Hitler, himself, reared on a diet of anti-Semitic propaganda in Austria, played upon the feelings of desperation known by the struggling Germans and voiced the most vicious form of anti-Semitism imaginable (*see* V.F). The Jews were blamed for everything, from the threat of communism to unemployment to Germany's humiliation. All those romantic notions about racial superiority, the will to power, and Teutonic greatness which had been voiced in the nineteenth century by men like Count de Gobineau and Friederick Nietzsche were twisted out of context and made the ideological basis for the Third Reich. When Hitler was elected Chancellor in 1933 a highly civilized and cultured nation was plunged into the most vicious anti-Jewish purge the world has ever known. No longer was the question of Jewish religion predominant. Any person in whom could be found a drop of "Jewish blood" was subjected to the agonies of the Reich.

The days of horror which followed were so unspeakably brutal that they almost defy description. Hitler was intent upon solving the Jewish problem once and for all, through mass murder, and this he almost immediately set out to accomplish. Many German Jews, realizing the danger, fled as best they could to more hospitable climes, but because immigration laws in the United States and elsewhere had become more stringent, flight was by no means so easy. Many were trapped in Germany or fled only to a nearby nation where the German army eventually overtook them.

The community of German Jews was relatively small, but when Hitler's armies moved eastward they came to control large Jewish populations in Poland, Hungary, Czechoslovakia, Roumania, and Western Russia. The plan of persecution and extermination established originally for Germany alone was now implemented with savage fury among a people who had no defense and little means for escape. Estimates of the number murdered in the gas chambers and by other forms of execution vary, but somewhere between four and six million Jews died in the wholesale slaughter which made medieval barbarities look like child's play.

Hitler virtually accomplished what he set out to do: in Western and Eastern Europe today only a remnant of a once vital Jewish community remains. The civilization which had so benefitted from men like Kafka, Buber, Einstein, and a whole host of other prominent Jews was now bereaved of Jewish influence. All that was left by the end of World War II were smoldering ruins, tales of heroic resistance, and a burning sense of shame on the part of many Europeans.

Judaism in America

While Europe moved from emancipation to anti-Semitism to bloody catastrophe, quite a different process was taking place in America. Before 1880 most Jewish immigrants to America had been German. Although a few of the older congregations clung to orthodoxy, the German immigrants of the 1830s and 40s brought with them ideas of reform which quickly took root in America. Under the leadership of Isaac Mayer Wise, who arrived in 1846 and David Einhorn, who came in 1855, Reform became by far the most popular and influential form of Judaism in America. Under the influence of German rationalism and the freedom of American culture, American Judaism began to look increasingly like a form of very liberal Protestantism. Organs, mixed choirs, services and sermons in English all became popular while observance of the laws of the *Shulchan Aruch* was largely neglected.

Wise, the perennial organizer, helped to found the Union of American Hebrew Congregations, Hebrew Union College in Cincinnati, and an organ of Reform opinion, the *American Israelite*. He also produced the *Minhag America*, a Jewish prayerbook which incorporated many of the reforms of American Jewry. David Einhorn, a far more theologically-minded Rabbi, developed the theoretical side of Reform. When in 1885 the Pittsburgh Platform was adopted by an unofficial conference it appeared that Reform Judaism was to be forever triumphant in America (*see* I.D).

In that radical statement of belief, the authors accepted modern Biblical criticism, rejected the binding nature of ceremonial and dietary laws found in the Bible, described Judaism as a religious community but not as a nation, and rejected the doctrine of the resurrection of the dead in favor of a belief in the immortality of the soul. At the time it was not inconceivable to believe that eventually Judaism and liberal religious movements like Unitarianism and Universalism might unite. Judaism in America had become very American.

In reaction to the extremes of Reform, more conservative Jews united to found their own center for rabbinical education, the Jewish Theological Seminary, but support was only modest and it was not at all clear that the more conservative tradition would survive. Then, just at the time when Reform appeared forever triumphant, everything changed. The 1880s suddenly brought a flood of new, usually orthodox Jewish immigrants to the American shores from Eastern Europe. For these new Americans, the Reformed synagogues seemed unaccountably strange and heretical. Conservative Judaism, though still more radical than the religion of the ghetto, began to attract substantial numbers to its movement. Instead of withering away, Conservative Judaism began to prosper.

This change, however, did not occur immediately. Even the more conservative congregations were both dismayed and afraid of their Eastern European brethren. On the one hand, the new immigrants were often far more pious and more knowledgeable about Jewish lore than their American coreligionists. Often, they didn't need to "join" an American congregation; they could found their own. On the other hand, among the new immigrants were men with far more radical political and social ideas than their middle-class American counterparts. Freed from the ghetto, many of these immigrants became thoroughly secularized and politicized.

Solomon Schecter (1847-1915), who was called from England to become president of the newly revived Jewish Theological Seminary in New York, was instrumental in winning over many Eastern Europeans to a Judaism which was relatively orthodox in form and yet which was open to modern scholarship and some innovation. While Reform Judaism experienced only "natural growth" in the first decades following the turn of the century, Conservative Judaism increased much more rapidly.

Not all of the new immigrants who remained faithful to Judaism found the essentially American Conservative tradition to their liking. Hence they worked to found their own Orthodox synagogues. Yeshiva University in New York City was established as the primary Orthodox institution of higher education. By the 1920s, when immigration was largely halted by new federal legislation, American Judaism was divided into three quite different traditions: Reform, Conservative, and Orthodox. Of these Reform and Conservative are distinctly American and really do not exist in any numbers outside the Western Hemisphere. Thus, in many respects, American Judaism is decidedly unique.

In 1927, shortly after the end of mass immigration, 80% of the Jews in America were Eastern Europeans living in a few big cities. Initially, they were largely manual laborers and artisans but, due to a strong emphasis upon education and self-betterment, this picture changed quickly. By 1947, few Jewish laborers were left; by this time most Jews in America had entered the professions, business, or other white collar positions. As Jews moved up the social and economic ladder they tended to leave the Orthodox synagogue which still reflected the style of the Old World and to join Conservative or Reform synagogues. At the same time, Reform Judaism witnessed a swing back to tradition marked by the introduction of customs and symbols once despised by Reform. Overall, then, the direction of development has been toward upper middle class homogeneity rather than diversity.

During the 1930s and 40s an equally strong tendency was toward a far more secular, areligious life. Many Jews left the synagogue entirely. They might live in a relatively Jewish community, eat Jewish food, and support Jewish causes and charities, but did not find the synagogue personally important. This situation led Mordecai Kaplan, in *Judaism as a Civilization* (b. 1934) to reassess the nature of Judaism. He concluded that it is a mistake to think of Judaism as just a "religion." Rather it is a whole civilization in which both the religious and the non-religious Jew play a part. Kaplan's ideas led to the foundation of the Reconstructionist Movement within Judaism. Although as intellectual a movement as Reform it emphasized the preservation, rather than the rejection, of Jewish customs and symbols. Kaplan and Reconstructionism, like Reform, abrogate traditional Jewish Law in so far as it stifles "Jewish civilization." Nevertheless, custom and tradition are frequently preserved as important elements in the life of Jews together.

Thus, while European Jews were experiencing the worst catastrophe in their long history, American Jews, prosperous and more or less accepted by society as a whole, became more homogeneous and, at the same time, more secularized. Since World War II this trend has been reversed somewhat. Both the Nazi persecution and the subsequent foundation of the State of Israel have greatly enhanced Jewish consciousness. Many Jews who once sought for absorption into American culture have come to delight in things specifically Jewish. Synagogue attendance, though still not high, has increased and there is renewed interest in Jewish studies among college-age Jews.

From the beginning, American Judaism depended heavily upon Europeans for intellectual leadership. Isaac Mayer Wise, David Einhorn, Solomon Schechter, Abraham Heschel, and even Mordecai Kaplan were all European-born. Of these, only Kaplan was educated in America. Even today, the most widely read "American" theologian is Abraham Heschel who draws heavily upon his European education and experience. Still, in the twentieth century American Jewish scholarship, after years of reliance upon European immigrants, has come into its own. Such diverse figures as Louis Finkelstein (b. 1895), Nelson Glueck (b. 1900), Judah Goldin (b. 1914), Robert Gordis (b. 1908), Will Herberg (b. 1909), and Jacob Neusner (b. 1932), have all achieved international fame as scholars in the field of Judaism. It is to be expected that in the future American Jewry, the large community of Jews in the world, will contribute increasingly to the reassessment and interpretation of Jewish history, life, and thought.

The Birth and Growth of Israel

Under British mandate between the two World Wars Jewish immigration to Palestine increased enormously. By 1931 there were 175,000 Jews settled in the land and Zionism no longer appeared as only an idealistic dream. The rising percentage of

Jews in Palestine, however, disturbed the Arabs and, though much was done by the new settlers which benefited all inhabitants, local Muslims were adamant that a Jewish takeover should not occur. By 1929, bloody anti-Jewish riots had broken out as a result of radical, nationalistic propaganda. Arab nations also put pressure on the British, through acts of terrorism and diplomacy, to prevent the emergence of a Jewish State.

The British, seeking the good will of the Arabs, took a frustratingly neutral role in regard to the riots and became less and less enthusiastic about a Jewish homeland. Despite the Balfour Declaration and many other tokens of good will, the British began to back down. The Arab tactics were working. In 1939 the Chamberlain government, intent upon appeasement on all fronts, scrapped the Balfour Declaration and limited Jewish immigration to 75,000 over the next five years. The tragedy was that it was at just this time that thousands of Jews were attempting to flee Germany and its neighbors. This new decision left many of them with literally no place to go.

Even during the Second World War, when millions of Jews sought asylum from the terror of Hitler's henchmen, the British would not ease the restrictions. Ships loaded with immigrants were refused permission to dock in Palestine. Some of these, over-loaded and ancient, sank in the Mediterranean before reaching another port. After the war, the British continued their adamant policy. On one occasion, a ship called ironically the "Exodus" was sent back to Germany with passengers for whom return meant only reinterment in the D.P. camps from which they had come.

Despite firm measures by the British, many immigrants, however, illegally slipped into Israel and took up residence. The Jews organized themselves militarily and fought back against the terrorists. What amounted to civil war developed. British plans for the foundation of a new state which would be two-thirds Arab and one-third Jewish were frustrated, not only by the covert growth of the Jewish community but by increasing Arab resistance which made one unified Arab-Jewish state impossible to conceive.

Nevertheless, the British doggedly clung to their policy for some time. Finally, in 1947, the Labor Government, fed up with increasing violence and bloodshed, decided to end the mandate. Ernest Bevan, the Prime Minister, dumped the whole matter into the lap of the United Nations, refusing to decide on a final settlement himself. A United Nations Commission was formed to study the matter and, despite strong Arab pressure, recommended the partition of Palestine into a Jewish and an Arab state.

Hopes for an acceptance of the Commission's report were dimmed by the diplomatic pressures exerted by the oil-rich Arabic states. As the vote by the General Assembly approached, no one was sure what the outcome would be. Strong Jewish pressure in the United States encouraged President Truman to back the plan and the United States worked hard to secure its acceptance. When the votes were cast, the plan of partition was approved by a slim margin of three votes.

On May 15th, 1948, the twenty-eight-year old British mandate came to an end and a new Jewish state, the first since the victory of Pompey in 63 B.C., was born. Prospects for the new state, however, were dim. Arab nations massed armies on its borders, prepared to wipe out the intruders and the Jews, officially left unarmed by the British, appeared to be at their mercy. Long experience in fighting Arab terrorists, however, had toughened Jewish military might enormously. With almost superhuman determination and skill, the Jewish settlers fought back, routing the huge forces from Egypt, Jordan, Iraq, Syria, and Lebanon which surrounded the tiny country. Against all hope, they secured what their people had dreamed of for centuries: the nation, Israel.

After the truce settlements had been signed in early 1949 on the island of Rhodes, the future of Israel remained in doubt. The Arab nations, smarting under their humiliating defeat, refused to recognize or accept the new nation but continued to draw maps of the Near East as though Israel did not exist. Terrorist attacks and virulent propaganda from Radio Cairo and Radio Damascus were common. Furthermore, though Israelis had already done much to improve agriculture and other industries, the country, long poor and neglected, was hardly in a sound economic condition. Had it not been for massive financial support from the American government, the new nation might soon have collapsed.

During the 1950s and particularly after Gamal Abdul Nasser took over the leadership of Egypt terrorist attacks upon Israel increased. Finally, in 1956 Israel, to protect herself, struck against terrorist bases in the Sinai, driving deep into Egyptian territory. Unfortunately for Israel, France and Britain joined forces and landed near the Suez Canal to assert their own power in the area. As a consequence, both Israel and the European allies were condemned by the United Nations and forced to withdraw. Still, the consequent placement of United Nations troops on the borders meant a lessening of terrorist attacks; Israel also now was able to enjoy free shipping through the Gulf of Aqaba.

A new threat to Israel developed in the early 1960s when Egypt's Nasser again sought to unite Arab forces under his leadership to remove what Arabs saw (and see) as a distressing pocket of Western colonialism in the keystone of the fertile crescent. In 1967 Nasser, after winning the support of Jordan, Syria, and Iraq, asked the United Nations peace-keeping force to leave, closed the Red Sea to Israeli shipping, and massed a huge but ill-prepared army in the Sinai.

Israel responded quickly and effectively. In a lightning fast, six-day war Israel virtually destroyed Egypt's military might, seizing the Sinai up to the Suez Canal. The Jordanians were driven back across the Jordan and the Syrians from the Golan Heights. In a stroke, Israel came to possess the Old City of Jerusalem and the heartland of the ancient Israelite kingdom. Once more the Arabs retreated in humiliation and resentment. Militarily, Israel appeared as supreme in the Near East. Once more the abundant confidence of Israel in her own ability to defend herself was supported.

One wonders how long, however, Israel can continue to perform such feats of military magic. The so-called Yom Kippur War of 1973 was a sign that Israel must in the future take Arab power more seriously. Israel did not exactly lose that military encounter, but she did not overwhelm the Arabs either. The result in Israel has been the loss of momentum, galloping inflation, and a sense of malaise about the future.

Moreover, it has become increasingly clear that a far more potent threat than force of arms or acts of terrorism comes from the Arab control of huge oil reserves. Oil diplomacy has proved to be an effective arm-twisting weapon through which Israel's allies can be forced to reevaluate their commitment to the Jewish state. Even Americans must now ask what price they are willing to pay for the continuation of Israel. Israel remains tough and determined; yet she also has come to recognize both the power of her enemies and the precariousness of her own position.

During this whole period of settlement, growth, and independence, Israel also developed both culturally and socially. Significantly, one of the first actions taken under British mandate was the creation of the Hebrew University in Jerusalem. To that institution, which opened in 1925, were attracted some of the best minds of European Jewry. Soon it became the foremost university in the Near East. Although its initial emphasis was scientific and technological, it has also been represented by outstanding scholars and thinkers of a more specifically religious nature.

One thinks, for instance, of Judah Leib Magnes, the founder of the university, who wrestled deeply in his writings with the problem of evil; of Gershom Scholem, the leading world authority on Jewish mysticism; and of Martin Buber, the famous philosopher of dialogue. One also thinks of outstanding Biblical scholars like Yezekiel Kaufmann and of Biblical archaelogists such as Yigael Yadin and Johanan Aharoni. Outside the university itself, but contributing greatly to the development of Jewish thought were A. D. Gordon and, above all, Rav Kook.

Perhaps a few words ought to be said particularly about Buber and Kook. Martin Buber (b. 1878) is undoubtedly the best known Jewish thinker of the modern world, though it must be noted that he has had far more theological influence among Christians than among Jews. In his famous work, *Ich und Du (I and Thou)* he developed, in a highly poetic yet philosophical way, his belief that religious faith is rooted in man's primordial capacity for saying "Thou" as well as "It." Modern civilization may be dominated by the objectivizing tendency of the sciences; human culture may seem to reflect the callous belief that the world is there simply to be used. Yet the expression "I-Thou" remains as the key to man's humanity and as a line pointing to God. For Buber, all true religion is grounded in man's primordial penchant to say "Thou." Without "I-Thou" man is merely an automaton.

Buber, however, was more than just a philosopher of religion. In his *Moses and the Covenant* and in *The Prophetic Faith* he revealed himself to be an acute interpreter of Scripture. His works on Eastern European Hasidism must be credited with the fostering of a major revival of interest in that form of spirituality, while *Paths in Utopia* spells out his ideas about Israeli experiments in socialism. In many respects, he was a renaissance man, the complete Jewish scholar. To the end of his days he labored valiantly to express the meaning of Judaism in the twentieth century and to promote Jewish-Christian and Jewish-Arab understanding.

Unlike Buber, Abraham Isaac Kook, Chief Rabbi of Jerusalem and then Ashkenazic Chief Rabbi for all Palestine (1919-35), is little known in America. Many of his works have not been translated and even his basic ideas unheralded. For all that, he remains an important, seminal thinker who is due to be discovered.

Kook's works are a rare combination of mystical Jewish piety, scientific insight, and Zionistic fervor. Essentially, he believed, like many mystics before him, that all exists "in God." The whole evolutionary process is God's kingdom if man would but recognize it as such. Evil may appear to exist in this world, but it is ultimately an illusion, the fruit of Adam's fall. There is no evil; rather there is an unfinished process which moves forward under the direction of God. Reminiscent in some ways of the thought of Teilhard de Chardin, Kook's works combine in an unusual way the evolutionary perspective of science and the deep inner ecstasy of the Hasidim.

Throughout his life in Palestine, Kook labored to reconcile the pious old men who had come to the land to die and the secular young men who were attempting to create a vital Jewish state. In his own day, he was particularly successful in interpreting each to the other, but the problem for Israel remains.

Religiously, Israel is something of a paradox. Officially, the faith of the nation is Orthodox; little interest is found in the American Reform tradition. Although there are small communities of truly orthodox practitioners, however, the great mass of modern Israelis is quite secularized. Enthusiastic interest in ancient Israel and in the archaeological discoveries which have been made is exhibited. The modern Israeli (the Sabra) identifies naturally and easily with Abraham, David, and Judas Maccabeus. But he frequently finds little relevance in the whole legal and ethnic tradition of the diaspora.

Many an American Jew has been shocked by the rather cavalier attitude with which diaspora traditions have simply been abandoned in Israel itself. Problems of desalinization, quantum mechanics, and military deployment seem much closer to the heart of modern Israel than the minutiae of Talmudic study. In a word, Judaism as a traditional religion has largely been replaced by Israel, the nation.

One can, of course, overgeneralize about what Israel is like. Differences of opinion are as common among Israelis as among any other group of people. Nevertheless, it is significant that what is emerging in Israel is religiously as distant from the Polish ghetto or the upper middle class American synagogue as the sands of Negeb are from the sidewalks of New York. But only time will tell into precisely what form the Israeli experiment will crystallize.

Conclusions

Aside from relatively small communities of Jews remaining in Europe, South and Central America, and the Arabic Near East, the largest Jewish populations are to be found today in the United States (over five million), the Soviet Union (about three million) and Israel (over two million). Each community has its own special problems which raise questions for the future; yet the answers to these questions seem profoundly interrelated.

In the United States, Judaism has been experiencing something of a revival due, in part, to the emergence of the state of Israel, and, in part, to a search by many younger Jews for "their roots." The question remains, however, whether this revival will continue or whether Judaism, freed from persecution and the ghetto and no longer infused with new blood by mass immigration, will not be so assimilated into American culture that it will lose its reason for existence.

This may seem a radical, even an absurd, possibility to consider. Has not Judaism, in spite of all odds, persisted for more than two and one half millennia? The answer to that question, of course, must be "Most Certainly!" But it must also be noted that persistence is often encouraged by hardship, persecution, and threat. The American Jew must ask himself seriously today, "Is persistence so easy in the face of affluence, indifference, and brotherhood?"

In the Soviet Union the problem is somewhat different, for the government there has been far less happy about the overt expression of the Jewish faith. Already many Jews have been thoroughly secularized and politicized and hence alienated from their religious traditions. If the door for immigration is opened further, however, and many of the more religious Jews are allowed to leave for Israel, what sort of community will be left? Is it not possible that Judaism could very well disappear as a religious community in the Soviet Union?

The problems of Israel are even more crucial. Israel has won many battles against the Arabs, but not the war. Danger continues to exist that the Arabs, who vastly outnumber the Israelis, will win at length a decisive military victory. An even greater danger exists that oil diplomacy with the West will wean allies away from Israel and shift the balance of power. Even today only the United States remains as a truly staunch ally. Given America's need for oil and her own energy crisis, how long can her pro-Israel attitude be expected to continue?

Conversely, let us suppose that eventually an accommodation with the Arabs is reached and Israel settles down to dwell in peace in the Islamic world. Will Israel be able to retain the cohesive unity and strength thus far impressed upon her by Arab pressure? And how long will it be before the Arabs come to outnumber the Jews in Israel itself?

In a sense, all these questions hang together. As long as Israel exists as a threatened bastion in the Near East and Jews are threatened with persecution in the Soviet Union, American Judaism will remain vigorous. The very existence of Israel has awakened new interest and pride in being Jewish and has slowed demonstrably the process of assimilation. By the same token, the reality of Israel has also kept the hopes and faith of Soviet Jewry alive by providing at least a possible haven in the face of persecution. In the other hand, as long as American Jews remain prosperous, politically strong, and religiously faithful, Israel's future looks secure and promising.

Predicting the future about anything is difficult; predicting the future of Judaism seems well-nigh impossible. Perhaps in the midst of all the imponderables of history it is well to remember that the secret of Israel is the secret of the bush which is burned but which is not consumed. Repeatedly, as we have seen, a decimated Israel has risen from the ashes of disaster to new life and hope. Despite the problems which world Judaism faces today — the problems of persecution, military threat, and loss of identity through assimilation — history would seem to indicate that the future will make room for the most resilient and enduring people the world has ever known: the Jews.

Chanukkah preserves the very ancient custom of lighting lights during the dark season of the year. The festival, which falls on the 25th of the lunar month of Kislev, frequently occurs fairly close to Christmas. In fact, it must be admitted that were it not for Christmas Chanukkah would probably not be celebrated as heartily as it is.

Still, Chanukkah preserves important ancient memories. According to an old Jewish tradition, during the persecution of the Jews by Antiochus Epiphanes in the second century B.C. the temple light remained miraculously lit. When the Maccabees drove out the hated enemy, the temple was purified and the menorah light restored. (See I Maccabees, chapt. IV; II Maccabees, chapt. X.) Chanukkah celebrates this and every victory of the Jews over the darkness of persecution. The menorah lights pictured here are a symbol of that triumph. In the midst of a darkened world Judaism, though gravely threatened, survives.

DOCUMENTATION

This collection of documents draws together, in brief compass, quotations and excerpts from a wide variety of sources. Its aim is to illustrate the history of Judaism with concrete examples and then expand upon certain points made during the course of our examination of Judaism's history.

Although many important men and movements could not be included in this collection, it is to be hoped that a picture of both the Jewish faith and its critics will be made more evident herein.

The collection of documents is arranged topically and it is hoped that this will make references easier to locate.

In the text, when these documents are cited, the Roman numeral refers to one of the following Parts as listed below. The capital letter then refers to the particular document in that Part. So *See* IV.F directs the reader to Part IV (Jewish Sects and Movements); document F refers to Judaism in the twentieth century, *see* listed below.

PART I: AFFIRMATIONS OF THE JEWISH FAITH
  A. Eighteen Benedictions or the *Shemoneh 'Esreh*
  B. Maimonides' Thirteen Principles of Faith
  C. Moses Mendelssohn, The Principles of Judaism
     — A Credo
  D. The Pittsburgh Platform of 1885, Reform Judaism

PART II: FAITH IN POETRY
  A. Three Poems of the Merkabah Mystics
  B. Eleazar Kalir, *The Lord is King*
  C. Solomon ibn Gabirol, *The Royal Crown*
  D. Judah Halevi, *Lord, where shall I find thee?*
     and *Longing for Jerusalem*
  E. Isaac Luria, *Zemira*

PART III: THE INTERPRETATION OF SCRIPTURE
    A. From the Book of Enoch
    B. Philo Judaeus interprets Genesis 12:1-3
    C. Chapter XXXIX, Lech Lecha, from the Midrash Rabbah
    D. The Zohar, Mystic Explanation of Genesis 1:1
    E. Solomon ben Isaac ("Rashi") Interprets Genesis 1
    F. Baruch de Spinoza, "Of the Interpretation of Scripture" from his *Theologico-Political Treatise*

PART IV: JEWISH SECTS AND MOVEMENTS
    A. From Flavius Josephus' *Antiquities of the Jews* (37-100 A.D.)
    B. *Manual of Discipline of the Essenes* (from Dead Sea Scrolls)
    C. Early Jewish Monasticism from Philo's *On the Contemplative Life*
    D. Anan ben David, 8th Century Kairite, from *Book of Precepts*
    E. Beginnings of Hasidic Movement, *In Praise of the Baal Shem Tov*
    F. Judaism in the Twentieth Century — Zionism, Theodore Herzl's *The Jewish State*

PART V: JUDAISM AND THE WORLD
    A. The New Testament Speaks of Jews
    B. The Emperor Justinian — Novella 146
    C. Jews in the Quran, Revelations of Mohammed from angel Gabriel (Seventh Century)
    D. Provisions set forth at Fourth Lateran Council, 1215 A.D.
    E. Martin Luther, from "That Jesus was Born a Jew," 1512
    F. Hitler's *Mein Kampf,* Selections from Chapter IX
    G. The Balfour Declaration, 1917
    H. 1965 Vatican II Council: The Church's Attitude toward Non-Christian Religions

PART 1

AFFIRMATIONS OF FAITH

A.

One of the oldest formulated expressions of the Jewish faith coming from the post-Biblical period are the Eighteen Benedictions or the *Shemoneh 'Esreh.* Derived, perhaps from the Second Temple period, they remain the epitome of Jewish prayer and praise. Curiously, today there are actually nineteen blessings offered, though when the extra words were added is unclear.

1 "Blessed be Thou, O Lord, our God and God of our fathers, God of Abraham, God of Isaac, and God of Jacob, the great, the mighty, and the fearful God — God Most High — who bestowest goodly kindnesses, and art the Creator ["Koneb," which signifies primarily "Creator" and then "Owner"] of all, and rememberest the love of [or for] the Fathers and bringest a redeemer for their children's children for the sake of [His] Thy name in love. King, Helper, Savior, and Shield; blessed be Thou, Shield of Abraham" (*see* Dembitz, "Jewish Services in the Synagogue and Home," pp. 112 *et seq.*).

2 "Thou are mighty forever, O Lord ["Adonai," not the Tetragrammaton]: Thou resurrectest the dead; art great to save. Sustaining the living in loving-kindness, resurrecting the dead in abundant mercies, Thou supportest the falling, and healest the sick, and settest free the captives, and keepest [fulfillest] Thy [His] faith to them that sleep in the dust. Who is like Thee, master of mighty deeds [= owner of

the powers over life and death], and who may be compared unto Thee? King sending death and reviving again and causing salvation to sprout forth. Thou are surely believed to resurrect the dead. Blessed be Thou, O Lord, who revivest the dead."

3 "Thou are holy and Thy name is holy, and the holy ones praise Thee every day. Selah. Blessed be Thou, O Lord, the holy God."

4 "Thou graciously vouchsafest knowledge to man and teachest mortals understanding: vouchsafe unto us from Thee knowledge, understanding, and intelligence. Blessed be Thou, O Lord, who vouchsafest knowledge."

5 "Lead us back, our Father, to Thy Torah; bring us near, our King, to Thy service, and cause us to return in perfect repentance before Thee. Blessed be Thou, O Lord, who acceptest repentance."

6 "Forgive us, our Father, for we have sinned; pardon us, our King, for we have transgressed: for Thou pardonest and forgivest. Blessed be Thou, O Gracious One, who mul ipliest forgiveness."

7 "Look but upon our affliction and fight our fight and redeem us speedily for the sake of Thy name: for Thou art a strong redeemer. Blessed art Thou, O Lord, the Redeemer of Israel."

8 "Heal us and we shall be healed; help us and we shall be helped: for Thou art our joy. Cause Thou to rise up full healings for all our wounds: for Thou, God King, art a true and merciful physician: blessed be Thou, O Lord, who healest the sick of His people Israel."

9 "Bless for us, O Lord our God, this year and all kinds of its yield for [our] good; and shower down [in winter, "dew and rain for"] a blessing upon the face of the earth: fulfil us of Thy bounty and bless this our year that it be as the good years. Blessed be Thou, O Lord, who blessest the years."

10 "Blow the great trumpet [*see* SHOFAR] for our liberation, and lift a banner to gather our exiles, and gather us into one body from the four corners of the earth; blessed be Thou, O Lord, who gatherest the dispersed of Thy [His] people Israel."

11 "Restore our judges as of yore, and our counselors as in the beginning, and remove from us grief and sighing. Reign Thou over us, O Lord, alone in loving-kindness and mercy, and establish our innocence by the judgment. Blessed be Thou, O Lord the King, who lovest righteousness and justice."

12 "May no hope be left to the slanderers; but may wickedness perish as in a moment: may all Thine enemies be soon cut off, and do Thou speedily uproot the haughty and shatter and humble them speedily in our days. Blessed be Thou, O Lord, who strikest down enemies and humblest the haughty" (Dembitz. *l.c.* p. 132).

13 "May Thy mercies, O Lord our God, be stirred over the righteous and over the pious and over the elders of Thy people, the House of Israel, and over the remnant of their scribes, and over the righteous proselytes, and over us, and bestow a goodly reward upon them who truly confide in Thy name; and assign us our portion with them forever; and may we not come to shame for that we have trusted in Thee. Blessed be Thou, O Lord, support and reliance for the righteous."

14 "To Jerusalem Thy city return Thou in mercy and dwell in her midst as Thou hast spoken, and build her speedily in our days as an everlasting structure and soon establish there the throne of David. Blessed be Thou, O Lord, the builder of Jerusalem."

15 "The sprout of David Thy servant speedily cause Thou to sprout up; and his horn do Thou uplift through Thy victorious salvation; for Thy salvation we are hoping every day. Blessed be Thou, O Lord, who causest the horn of salvation to sprout forth."

16 "Hear our voice, O Lord our God, spare and have mercy on us, and accept in mercy and favor our prayer. For a God that heareth prayers and supplications art Thou. From before Thee, O our King, do not turn us away empty-handed. For Thou hearest the prayer of Thy people Israel in mercy. Blessed be Thou, O Lord, who hearest prayer."

17 "Be pleased, O Lord our God, with Thy people Israel and their prayer, and return [*i.e.*, reestablish] the sacrificial service to the altar of Thy House, and the fire-offerings of Israel and their prayer [offered] in love accept Thou with favor, and

may the sacrificial service of Israel Thy people be ever acceptable to Thee. And may our eyes behold Thy merciful return
to Zion. Blessed be Thou who restorest Thy [His] Shekinah to
Zion."

18 "We acknowledge to Thee, O Lord, that Thou art our God
as Thou wast the God of our fathers, forever and ever. Rock
of our life, Shield of our help, Thou art immutable from age to
age. We thank Thee and utter Thy praise, for our lives that
are [delivered over] into Thy hands and for our souls that are
entrusted to Thee; and for Thy miracles that are [wrought]
with us every day and for Thy marvelously [marvels and]
kind deeds that are of every time; evening and morning and
noontide. Thou art [the] good, for Thy mercies are endless:
Thou art [the] merciful, for Thy kindnesses never are complete: from everlasting we have hoped in Thee. And for all
these things may Thy name be blessed and exalted always
and forevermore. And all the living will give thanks unto
Thee and praise Thy great name in truth, God, our salvation
and help. Selah. Blessed be Thou, O Lord, Thy name is good,
and to Thee it is meet to give thanks."

19 "Bestow peace, happiness, and blessing, grace, loving-
kindness, and mercy upon us and upon all Israel Thy people:
bless us, our Father, even all of us, by the light of Thy
countenance, for by this light of Thy countenance Thou
gavest us, O Lord our God, the law of life, loving-kindness,
and righteousness, and blessing and mercy, life and peace.
May it be good in Thine eyes to bless Thy people Israel in
every time and at every hour with Thy peace. Blessed be
Thou, O Lord, who blessest Thy [His] people Israel, with
peace."

B.

Judaism, unlike Christianity, generally has avoided enumera-
tions of beliefs in creeds. Moses Maimonides (1135-1204),
however, came close to providing a standard creed for his people when he formulated his Thirteen Principles of Faith.

1. I firmly believe that the Creator, blessed be his name, is
the Creator and Ruler of all created beings, and that he alone
has made, does make, and ever will make all things.
2. I firmly believe that the Creator, blessed be his name, is
One; that there is no oneness in any form like his; and that he
alone was, is, and ever will be our God.

3. I firmly believe that the Creator, blessed be his name, is not corporeal; that no bodily accidents apply to him; and that there exists nothing whatever that resembles him.

4. I firmly believe that the Creator, blessed be his name, was the first and will be the last.

5. I firmly believe that the Creator, blessed be his name, is the only one to whom it is proper to address our prayers, and that we must not pray to anyone else.

6. I firmly believe that all the words of the Propets are true.

7. I firmly believe that the prophecy of Moses our teacher, may he rest in peace, was true; and that he was the chief of the prophets, both of those who preceded and of those that followed him.

8. I firmly believe that the whole Torah which we now possess is the same which was given to Moses our teacher, may he rest in peace.

9. I firmly believe that this Torah will not be changed, and that there will be no other Torah given by the Creator, blessed be his name. Etc., etc.

C.

Moses Mendelssohn (1729-1786), undoubtedly the greatest Jewish thinker of the European Enlightenment of the eighteenth century, expressed his understanding of Judaism in the following way in a work entitled *Bonnet's Palingenesis: A counter inquiry:*

THE PRINCIPLES OF
JUDAISM — A CREDO

As far as its major tenets are concerned, the religion of my fathers knows no mysteries which we have to accept on faith rather than comprehend. Our intellect can quite comfortably start out from the well-established primary principles of human cognition and be sure that it will eventually encounter religion on the same road. Here is no conflict between religion and reason, no rebellion of our natural cognitive faculty against the stifling authority of faith. "Its ways are ways of pleasantness, and all its paths are peace."

Essentially, the religion of the Israelites encompasses only three central principles: *God, Providence,* and *legislation.* These principles were expanded by our religious leaders along the following lines:

(a) God, the Author and absolute Sovereign of all things, is one and simple [single] (in His person as well as His nature).

(b) This God is aware of all that happens in His creation. He rewards good and punishes evil by natural and, at times, by supranatural means.

(c) This God has made known His laws to the children of Israel through Moses, the son of Amram. We still possess these laws in writing.

We believe that man was created in the image of God but that he was, nevertheless, also meant to be man — inclined to sin. We recognize no original sin. Adam and Eve sinned because they were human. They died because they had sinned. This is the condition of all their descendants . . . .

However, they die only physically. I recognize no death of the soul. True, Maimonides,[64] writing on repentance, makes the assumption that the soul of the godless must perish, and he rightfully considers this the harshest punishment that is possible.[65] I, however, agree with Nachmanides,[66] who rejects this doctrine in his tractate on retribution and denies that the soul can perish and that punishment can be everlasting . . . .

> God punishes the sinner not according to His own infinity but according to the sinner's frailty. We know of no less majesty which wants or has to be avenged. We know of no criminal judgment that must be executed — if not against the guilty party, then against the innocent person who voluntarily takes this suffering upon himself. While, according to our views, it is unjust to spare the guilty, it is even more unjust to let the innocent suffer. Even though he may wish to take suffering upon himself out of compassion, supreme wisdom cannot approve of it, and justice (that is, all-wise grace) cannot be satisfied by such self-imposed suffering . . . .
>
> We believe the laws of Moses are strictly binding upon us as long as God does not revoke them explicitly and with the same public solemnity with which He has given them. Is their purpose no longer completely known to us? Granted. But where did the Legislator declare that they should be binding only as long as we know their purpose? And what mortal would be presumptuous enough to limit their validity without such a divine declaration? Human laws can be changed by men in response to changing times and circumstances. But divine laws remain unalterable until we can be utterly sure that God himself has announced a change.
>
> Will God ever change these laws? On this point, our scholars are of divided opinion. Some consider them absolutely immutable and insist that this position represents one of Judaism's central doctrines. Others do not consider it unlikely that the supreme Legislator may plan a second public giving of the law in connection with some future miraculous restoration of the Jewish nation. In this case, many of our present ceremonial laws might undergo changes. My views in this matter are based on the following considerations:

I have said repeatedly that, in the opinion of all our rabbis, the Mosaic laws are binding only upon the Jewish people and that all other peoples are merely required to abide by the law of nature and the religion of the patriarchs. However, most peoples have deviated from the simplicity of this first religion and, to the detriment of truth, have evolved false notions of God and His sovereignty. Therefore, it seems that the ceremonial laws of the Jews have, among other unfathomable reasons, the additional purpose of making this people stand out from among all other nations and reminding it, through a variety of religious acts, perpetually of the sacred truths that none of us should ever forget. This is undoubtedly the purpose of most religious customs. Clear and explicit evidence for this view can be found in our Holy Scriptures. These customs are to remind us that God is one; that He has created the world and reigns over it in wisdom; that He is the absolute Lord over all of nature; that He has liberated this people by extraordinary deeds from Egyptian oppression; that He has given them laws, etc. This is the purpose of all the customs that we observe, though they must necessarily seem superfluous, cumbersome, and ludicrous to all who do not understand their meaning.

Now, all prophets of the Old Testament are agreed, and reason fully concurs in this hope, that the difference between religions will not last forever, that ultimately there will be one shepherd and one flock, and that the acknowledgment of the true God will cover the earth as the waters cover the sea. Xt that time, divine wisdom may no longer find it necessary to set us apart from other peoples by special ceremonial laws. In fact, it might choose a second public manifestation to introduce ritual observances that will link the hearts of *all* men in adoration of their Creator and in mutual love and benevolence.

From *Bonnet's Palingenesis:*
A Counterinquiry.

D.

The Pittsburgh Platform of 1885 is a clear statement of Reform Judaism's faith as it developed in America in the late nineteenth century.

First — We recognize in every religion an attempt to grasp the Infinite One, and in every mode, source or book of revelation held sacred in any religious system the consciousness of the indwelling of God in man. We hold that Judaism presents the highest conception of the God-idea as taught in our holy

Scriptures and developed and spiritualized by the Jewish teachers in accordance with the moral and philosophical progress of their respective ages. We maintain that Judaism preserved and defended amid continual struggles and trials and under enforced isolation this God-idea as the central religious truth for the human race.

Second — We recognize in the Bible the record of the consecration of the Jewish people to its mission as the priest of the One God, and value it as the most potent instrument of religious and moral instruction. We hold that the modern discoveries of scientific researches in the domains of nature and history are not antagonistic to the doctrines of Judaism, the Bible reflecting the primitive ideas of its own age and at times clothing its conception of divine providence and justice dealing with man in miraculous narratives.

Third — We recognize in the Mosaic legislation a system of training the Jewish people for its mission during its national life in Palestine, and today we accept as binding only its moral laws and maintain only such ceremonials as elevate and sanctify our lives, but reject all such as are not adapted to the views and habits of modern civilization.

Fourth — We hold that all such Mosaic and Rabbinical laws as regulate diet, priestly purity and dress originated in ages and under the influence of ideas altogether foreign to our present mental and spiritual state. They fail to impress the modern Jew with a spirit of priestly holiness; their observance in our day is apt rather to obstruct than to further modern spiritual elevation.

Fifth — We recognize in the modern era of universal culture of heart and intellect the approach of the realization of Israel's great Messianic hope for the establishment of the Kingdom of truth, justice and peace among all men. We consider ourselves no longer a nation but a religious community, and therefore expect neither a return to Palestine, nor a sacrificial worship under the administration of the sons of Aaron, nor the restoration of any of the laws concerning the Jewish state.

Sixth — We recognize in Judaism a progressive religion, ever striving to be in accord with the postulates of reason. We are convinced of the utmost necessity of preserving the historical identity with our great past. Christianity and Islam being daughter religions of Judaism, we appreciate their mission to aid in the spreading of monotheistic and moral truth. We acknowledge that the spirit of broad humanity of our age is our ally in the fulfillment of our mission, and therefore we extend the hand of fellowship to all who co-operate with us in the establishment of the reign of truth and righteousness among men.

Seventh — We reassert the doctrine of Judaism, that the soul of man is immortal, grounding this belief on the divine nature of the human spirit, which forever finds bliss in righteousness and misery in wickedness. We reject as ideas not rooted in Judaism the belief both in bodily resurrection and in Gehenna and Eden [hell and paradise], as abodes for everlasting punishment or reward.

Eighth — In full accordance with the spirit of Mosaic legislation which strives to regulate the relation between rich and poor, we deem it our duty to participate in the great task of modern times, to solve on the basis of justice and righteousness the problems presented by the contrasts and evils of the present organization of society.[9]

PART 2

FAITH IN POETRY

Since earliest times, Jews have expressed their faith through poetry. No book has been more influential in the worship and praise of all Western religions than the book of Psalms. Although less well-known to the non-Jew, poetry in post-Biblical Judaism has continued to serve as an important vehicle for expressing the faith. In this collection the following five selections will have to serve as an indicator of the very rich heritage of which they are a part.

A.

Three short poems express the deep spirituality of the Merkabah mystics. As Gershom Scholem says, "Their immense solemnity of style is unsurpassed in Hebrew hymnology. In the strangely vacuous sublimity and august repetitiousness of their diction they reflect marvelously the religious mood of those who conceived them. They are, indeed, outstanding paradigms of what Rudolf Otto has called 'Numinous Hymns'."

1. From the praise and song of each day,
   From the jubilation and exultation of each hour,
   And from the utterances which proceed out of the mouth of
       the holy ones,
   And from the melody which welleth out of the mouth of the
       servants,
   Mountains of fire and hills of flame
   Are piled up and hidden and poured out each day.

2. O wreathed in splendor, crowned with crowns,
   O chorister of Him on high,
   Extol the Lord enthroned in flames
   For in the presence of the Presence.
       In the inmost glory
       Of the inmost chambers
       You set up your posts.
   Your name He distinguished from His servant's name,
   From the Chariot's servants He set you apart.
   Him who the name of one of you mentions
       The flame surrounds, a leaping fire,
       Around him burning, glowing coals.*

3. O you
   Who
   Annul the decree, undo the oath,
   Remove the wrath, avert the ire,
   Recall the love, in order to set it
   Before the splendor of the Temple of our Awe:
   What is it with you that you fear
   While there are times when you rejoice?
   What is it with you that you sing
   While there are times when you're aghast?
       They said:
   When the Ofanim of Might the Chariot overcast
   In fearful dread we stand;
   But when the sparks of Shekhinah the Chariot set in light
   We're gay, O very gay.

B.

Eleazar Kalir (seventh century A.D.) composed a large number
of poems for virtually every celebration of the Jewish liturgical
year. Many of his works are still chanted by orthodox Jews.

*The Lord Is King, the Lord Was King,
the Lord Shall Be King for Ever and Ever*

(Abridged)

The terrible sons of the mighty race
  Shout in thunder the Lord is King,
The angels whose figure the lightnings trace
  Flame to the world that the Lord was King,

    And seraphs whose stature is one with space,
    Proclaim that the Lord shall be King for ever.
The Lord is King, the Lord was King, the Lord shall be
    King for ever and ever.

    The bards who remember the songs of yore
      Sing aloud that the Lord is King,
    The sages enshrouded in mystic lore
      Find and proclaim that the Lord was King,
    And rulers of spans of the heavenly floor
      Cry that the Lord shall be King for ever.
The Lord is King, the Lord was King, the Lord shall be
    King for ever and ever.

    The heirs of the Torah, Thy rich bequest,
      Chant in joy that the Lord is King,
    The lordly warriors with crown and crest
      Crown Thee, declaring the Lord was King,
    And angels in fiery garments drest
    Repeat that the Lord shall be King for ever.
the Lord is King, the Lord was King, the Lord shall be
    King for ever and ever.

    Thy people in passionate worship cry
      One to another the Lord is King.
    In awe of the marvels beneath the sky
      Each explains that the Lord was King.
    One sound from Thy pastures ascends on High:
    One chant that the Lord shall be King for ever.
The Lord is King, the Lord was King, the Lord shall be
    King for ever and ever.

    The universe throbs with Thy pauseless praise,
      Chorus eternal, the Lord is King.
    Thy glory is cried from the dawn of days,
      Worshippers calling the Lord was King.
    And ever the Saints who shall witness Thy ways
    Shall cry that the Lord shall be King for ever.
The Lord is King, the Lord was King, the Lord shall be
    King for ever and ever.

                Eleazar Kalir
         (Translated by Israel Zangwill)

C.

Solomon ibn Gabirol (1021-1058) is perhaps best known for
"The Royal Crown", a poem widely used in Sephardic circles.
The emphasis upon man's lostness and his need for God is
typical of him.

THE ROYAL CROWN

Man entereth the world,
And knoweth not why;
He rejoiceth
And knoweth not wherefore;
He liveth,
And knoweth not for how long.
In his childhood he walketh in his own stubbornness,
And when the spirit of lust beginneth in its season
To stir him up to gather power and wealth,
Then he journeyeth from his place
To ride in ships
And to tread in the deserts,
And to carry his life to dens of lions,
Adventuring in among wild beasts;
And when he imagineth that great is his glory
And that mighty is the spoil of his hand,
Quietly stealeth the spoiler upon him,
And his eyes are opened and there is naught.

At every moment he is destined to troubles
That pass and return,
At every hour evils,
At every moment chances,
On every day terrors.
If for an instant he stand in security,
Suddenly disaster will come upon him,
Either war shall come and the sword will smite him,
Or the bow of brass transpierce him,
Or the sorrows will overpower him,
Or the presumptuous billows flow over him,
Or sickness and steadfast evils shall find him,
Till he become a burden on his own soul,
And shall find the gall of serpents in his honey.

When his pain increaseth
His glory decreaseth,
And youth make mock of him,
And infants rule him,
And he becometh a burden to the issue of his loins,
And all who know him become estranged from him.
When his hour hath come, he passeth from the courts of his
 house to the court of Death,
And from the shadow of his chambers to the shadow of
 Death.
He shall strip off his broidery and his scarlet
And shall put on corruption and the worm,
And lie down in the dust
And return to the foundation from which he came.

O man, whom these things befall,
When shall he find a time for repentance
To scour away the rust of his perversion?
For the day is short and the work manifold,
And the task-masters irate,
Hurrying and scurrying,
And Time laughs at him,
And the Master of the House presses.

Therefore I beseech Thee, O my God,
Remember the distresses that come upon man,
And if I have done evil
Do Thou me good at my latter end,
Nor requite measure for measure
To man whose sins are measureless,
And whose death is a joyless departure.

D.

Judah Halevi (1085-1140) wrote innumerable poems long
prized within Jewish circles. The first, "Lord, where shall I
find thee?" is used in some versions of the morning service.
The second, "Longing for Jerusalem," is particularly poignant
because the poet was killed on pilgrimage outside the walls of
the Holy City.

1.   LORD, WHERE SHALL I FIND THEE?

Lord, where shall I find Thee?
High and hidden is Thy place!
And where shall I not find Thee?
The world is full of thy glory!

Found in the innermost being,
He set up the ends of the earth:
The refuge of the near,
The trust of those far off.
Thou dwellest amid the Cherubim.
Thou abidest in the clouds,
Yet art raised above their praise.
The (celestial) sphere cannot contain Thee;
How then the chambers of a temple?

And though Thou be uplifted over them
Upon a throne high and exalted,
Yet art Thou near to them,
Of their very spirit and their flesh.
Their own mouth testifieth for them,
That thou alone art their creator.
Who shall not fear Thee,
Since the yoke of Thy kingdom is their yoke?
Or who shall not call to Thee
Since Thou givest them their food?

I have sought Thy nearness;
With all my heart have I called Thee;
And going out to meet Thee
I found Thee coming toward me.
Even as in the wonder of Thy might
In the sanctuary I have beheld Thee.
Who shall say he hath not seen Thee? —
Lo the heavens and their hosts
Declare the fear of Thee
Though their voice be not heard.

Doth then, in very truth,
God dwell with man?
What can he think — every one that thinketh,
Whose foundation is in the dust?
Since Thou art holy, dwelling
Amid their praises and their glory,
Angels adore Thy wonder,
Standing in the everlasting height;
Over their heads is Thy throne,
And Thou upholdest them all!

2.
LONGING FOR JERUSALEM

O city of the world, with sacred
  splendor blest,
My spirit yearns to thee from out the
  far-off West,
A stream of love wells forth when I
  recall thy day,
Now is thy temple waste, thy glory
  passed away.
Had I an eagle's wings, straight would
  I fly to thee,
Moisten thy holy dust with wet cheeks
  streaming free.

— Translated from the Hebrew
by Emma Lazarus

E.

Isaac Luria (1534-1572) was one of the leading Kabbalists of the sixteenth Century. Living with a community of like-minded men in Safed, Israel, he influenced literally millions through his holy life and teachings. The following is a *Zemira* or table-hymn written by Luria for the Sabbath noon meal.

A SABBATH OF REST

This day is for Israel light and
  rejoicing,
A Sabbath of rest.

Thou badest us, standing assembled at
  Sinai,
That all the years through we should
  keep Thy behest —
To set out a table full-laden, to honor
The Sabbath of rest.

This day is for Israel light and
  rejoicing,
A Sabbath of rest.

Treasure of heart for the broken
  people,
Gift of new soul for the souls distrest,
Soother of sighs for the prisoned
  spirit —
The Sabbath of rest.

This day is for Israel light and
  rejoicing,
A Sabbath of rest.

When the work of the worlds in their
  wonder was finished,
Thou madest this day to be holy and
  blest,
And those heavy-laden found safety
  and stillness,
A Sabbath of rest.

This day is for Israel light and
  rejoicing,
A Sabbath of rest.

If I keep Thy command I inherit a
  kingdom,
If I treasure the Sabbath I bring Thee
  the best —
The noblest of offerings, the sweetest
  of incense —
A Sabbath of rest.

This day is for Israel light and
  rejoicing,
A Sabbath of rest.

Restore us our shrine — O remember our
  ruin
And save now and comfort the sorely
  opprest
Now sitting at Sabbath, all singing and
  praising
The Sabbath of rest.

This day is for Israel light and
  rejoicing,
A Sabbath of rest.

— Translated from the Hebrew
by Nina Davis Salaman

PART 3

THE INTERPRETATION OF SCRIPTURE

Central to the faith and life of Judaism is the Torah, the five books of Moses, which has been interpreted and reinterpreted by each generation of scholars. Here are some representative examples of the variety of appraoch taken.

A.

The apocalyptic book of Enoch is not normally considered an exegetical work, for the emphasis is upon visions of God's will and judgment. Nevertheless, in his visions Enoch neatly resolves difficult problems of interpretation. Here, his vision provides a key to the understanding both the enigmatic words of Genesis 6:1 ff which seem to indicate that God has a number of sons and the reference to Azazel in Leviticus 16:08ff.

> VI. 1. And it came to pass when the children of men had multiplied that in those days were born unto them beautiful and comely daughters. 2. And the angels, the children of heaven, saw and lusted after them, and said to one another: 'Come, let us choose us wives from among the children of men and beget us children.' 3. And Semjâzâ, who was their leader, said unto them: 'I fear ye will not indeed agree to do this deed, and I alone shall have to pay the penalty of a great sin.' 4. And they all answered him and said: 'Let us all swear

an oath, and all bind ourselves by mutual imprecations not to abandon this plan but to do this thing.' 5. Then sware they all together and bound themselves by mutual imprecations upon it. 6. And they were in all two hundred; who descended [in the days] of Jared on the summit of Mount Hermon, and they called it Mount Hermon, because they had sworn and bound themselves by mutual imprecations upon it. 7. And these are the names of their leaders: Sêmîazâz, their leader, Arâkîba, Râmêêl, Kôkâbîêl, Tâmîêl, Râmîêl, Dânêl, Ezêqêêl, Bâraqîjâl, Asâêl, Armârôs, Batârêl, Anânêl, Zaqîel, Samsâpêêl, Satarêl, Tûrêl, Jômjâêl, Sariêl. 8. These are their chiefs of tens.

VII. 1. And all the others together with them took unto themselves wives, and each chose for himself one, and they began to go in unto them and to defile themselves with them, and they taught them charms and enchantments, and the cutting of roots, and made them acquainted with plants. 2. And they became pregnant, and they bare great giants, whose height was three thousand ells: 3. Who consumed all the acquisitions of men. And when men could no longer sustain them, 4. The giants turned against them and devoured mankind. 5. And they began to sin against birds, and beasts, and reptiles, and fish, and to devour one another's flesh, and drink the blood. 6. Then the earth laid accusation against the lawless ones.

VIII. 1. And Azâzel taught men to make swords, and knives, and shields, and breastplates, and made known to them the metals (of the earth) and the art of working them, and bracelets, and ornaments, and the use of antimony, and the beautifying of the eyelids, and all kinds of costly stones, and all colouring tinctures. 2. And there arose much godlessness, and they committed fornication, and they were led astray, and became corrupt in all their ways. 3. Semjâzâ taught enchantments, and root-cuttings, Armârôs the resolving of enchantments, Barâqîjâl, (taught) astrology, Kôkabêl the constellations, Ezêqêêl the knowledge of the clouds, (Araqiêl the signs of the earth, Shamsiêl the signs of the sun), and Sariêl the course of the moon. 4. And as men perished, they cried, and their cry went up to heaven . . . .

IX. 1. And then Michael, Uriel, Raphael, and Gabriel looked down from heaven and saw much blood being shed upon the earth, and all lawlessness being wrought upon the earth. 2. And they said one to another: 'The earth, made †without inhabitant, cries the voice of their crying† up to the gates of heaven. 3. "And now to you, the holy ones of heaven," the soul of men make their suit, saying, "Bring our cause before the Most High".' 4. And they said to the Lord of the ages: 'Lord of lords, God of gods, King of kings (and God of the ages), the throne of Thy glory (standeth) unto all the generations of the ages, and Thy name holy and glorious and blessed unto all the ages. 5. Thou hast made all things, and power over all things has Thou: and all things are naked and open in Thy sight, and all things Thou seest, and nothing can hide itself from Thee. 6. Thou seest what Azâzêl hath done, who hath taught all unrighteousness on earth and revealed the eternal secrets which were (preserved) in heaven, which men were striving to learn: 7. And Semjâzâ, to whom Thou has given authority to bear rule over his associates. 8. And they have gone to the daughters of men upon the earth, and have slept with the women, and have defiled themselves, and revealed to them all kinds of sins. 9. And the women have borne giants, and the whole earth has thereby been filled with blood and unrighteousness. 10. And now, behold, the souls of those who have died are crying and making their suit to the gates of heaven, and their lamentations have ascended: and cannot cease because of the lawless deeds which are wrought on the earth. 11. And Thou knowest all things before they come to pass, and Thou seest these things and Thou dost suffer them, and Thou dost not say to us what we are to do to them in regard to these.'

X. 1. Then said the Most High, the Holy and Great One spake, and sent Uriel to the son of Lamech, and said to him: 2. '(Go to Noah and) tell him in my name "Hide thyself!", and reveal to him the end that is approaching: that the whole earth will be destroyed, and a deluge is about to come upon the whole earth, and will destroy all that is on it. 3. And now instruct him that he may escape and his seed may be preserved for all the generations of the world.' 4. And again the Lord said to Raphael: 'Bind Azâzêl hand and foot, and cast him into the darkness: and make an opening in the desert, which is in Dûdâêl, and cast him therein. 5. And place upon him rough and jagged rocks, and cover him with darkness, and let him abide there for ever, and cover his face that he may not see light. 6. And on the day of the great judgement he shall be cast into the fire. 7. And heal the earth which the angels have corrupted, and proclaim the healing of the earth, that they may heal the plague, and that all the children of men may not perish through all the secret things that the Watchers have disclosed and have taught their sons. 8. And the whole earth has been corrupted through the works that were taught by Azâzêl: to him ascribe all sin.' 9. And to Gabriel said the Lord: 'Proceed against the bastards and the reprobates, and

against the children of fornication: and destroy [the children of fornication and] the children of the Watchers from amongst men: [and cause them to go forth]: send them one against the other that they may destroy each other in battle: for length of days shall they not have. 10. And no request that they (*i.e.* their fathers) make of thee shall be granted into their fathers on their behalf; for they hope to live an eternal life, and that each one of them will live five hundred years.'
11. And the Lord said unto Michael: 'Go, bind Semjâzâ and his associates who have united themselves with women so as to have defiled themselves with them in all their uncleanness. 12. And, when their sons have slain one another, and they have seen the destruction of their beloved ones, bind them fast for seventy generations in the valleys of the earth, till the day of their judgement and of their consummation, till the judgement that is for ever and ever is consummated. 13. In those days they shall be led off to the abyss of fire: (and) to the torment and the prison in which they shall be confined for ever. 14. And whosoever shall be condemned and destroyed will from thenceforth be bound together with them to the end of all generations. 15. And destroy all the spirits of the reprobate, and the children of the Watchers, because they have wronged mankind. 16. Destroy all wrong from the face of the earth, and let every evil work come to an end: and let the plant of righteousness and truth appear: [and it shall prove a blessing: the works of righteousness and truth] shall be planted in truth and joy for evermore.
17. And then shall all the righteous escape,
    And shall live till they beget thousands of
        children,
    And all the days of their youth and their old
        age shall they complete in peace.
18. And then shall the whole earth be tilled in righteousness, and shall all be planted with trees and be full of blessing. 19. And all desirable trees shall be planted on it, and they shall plant vines on it: and the vine which they plant thereon shall yield wine in abundance, and as for all the seed which is sown thereon each measure (of it) shall bear a thousand, and each measure of olives shall yield ten presses of oil. 20. And cleanse thou the earth from all oppression, and from all unrighteousness, and from all sin, and from all godlessness: and all the uncleanness that is wrought upon the earth destroy from off the earth. 21. [And all the children of men shall become righteous], and all nations shall offer adoration and shall praise Me, and all shall worship Me. 22. And the earth shall be cleansed from all defilement, and from all sin, and from all punishment, and from all torment, and I will

never again send (them) upon it from generation to generation and for ever.

.XI. 1. And in those days I will open the store chambers of blessing which are in the heaven, so as to send them down [upon the earth] over the work and labour of the children of men. 2. And truth and peace shall be associated together throughout all the days of the world and throughout all the generations of men.'

B.

Philo Judaeus (circa 42 B.C. - 50 A.D.) is best known for his allegorical interpretation of Scripture. Little concerned about the historical facts of the Bible, he sees in virtually every feature of the Genesis story indications of a truth which is very similar in nature to that taught by Plato and other Greco-Roman philosophers. This is how he interprets Genesis 12:1-3:

A TREATISE
ON
THE MIGRATION OF ABRAHAM

I. And the Lord said to Abraham, "Depart from thy land, and from thy kindred, and from thy father's house, to a land which I will show thee; and I will make thee into a great nation. And I will bless thee, and I will magnify thy name, and thou shalt be blessed. And I will bless them that bless thee, and I will curse them that curse thee; and in thy name shall all the nations of the earth be blessed."   Genesis xii 1-3

God, wishing to purify the soul of man, first of all gives it an impulse towards complete salvation, namely, a change of abode, so as to quit the three regions of the body, the outward sense and speech according to utterance; for his country is the emblem of the body, and his kindred are the symbol of the outward sense, and his father's house of speech. Why so? Because the body derives its composition from the earth, and is again dissolved into earth; and Moses is a witness of this when he says, "Dust thou art, and unto dust shalt thou return." (Genesis iii. 19.) For he says, that man was compounded by God fashioning a lump of clay into the form of a man; and it follows a necessity that, a composite being, when dissolved, must be dissolved into its componext parts. But the outward sense is nearly connected with and akin to the mind, the irrational part to the rational, since they are both parts of one soul: but speech is the abode of the father, because our father is the mind, which implants in each of its parts its own powers, and distributes its energies among them, undertaking the care and superintendence of them all; and the abode in which it dwells is speech, a dwelling separated from all the rest of the house; for as the hearth is the abode of a man, so is speech of the mind: at all events, it displays itself, and all the notions which it conceives, arranging them and setting them in order in speech, as if in a house.

And you must not wonder that Moses has called speech in man the abode of the mind, for he also says, that the mind of the universe, that is to say, God, has for his abode his own word. And the practiser of virtue, Jacob, seizing on this apprehension, confesses in express words that, "This is no other than the house of God," (Genesis xxviii. 17), an expression equivalent to, The house of God is not this thing, or anything which can be made the subject of ocular demonstration, or, in short, anything which comes under the province of the outward senses, but is invisible, destitute of all specific form, only to be comprehended by the soul as soul. What, then, can it be except the Word, which is more ancient than all the things which were the objects of creation, and by means of which it is that the Ruler of the universe, taking hold of it as a rudder, governs all things. And when he was fashioning the world, he used this as his instrument for the blameless arrangement of all the things which he was completing.

II. That he means by Abraham's country the body, and by his kindred the outward senses, and by his father's house uttered speech, we have now shown. But the command, "Depart from them," is not like or equivalent to. Be separated from them according to your essence, since that would be the injunction of one who was pronouncing sentence of death. But it is the same as saying, Be alienated from them in your mind, allowing none of them to cling to you, standing above them all; they are your subjects, use them not as your rulers; since you are a king, learn to govern and not to be governed; know yourself all your life, as Moses teaches us in many passages where he says, "Take heed to thyself." (Exodus xxxiv. 12.) For thus you will perceive what you ought to be obedient to, and what you ought to be the master of. Depart therefore from the earthly parts which envelop you, O my friend, fleeing from that base and polluted prison house the body, and from the keepers as it were of the prison, its pleasures and appetites, putting forth all your strength and all your power so as to suffer none of thy good things to come to harm, but improving all your good faculties together and unitedly. Depart also from thy kindred, outward senses; for now indeed you have given yourself up to each of them to be made use of as it will, and you have become a good, the property of others who have borrowed you, having lost your own power over yourself. But you know that, even though all men are silent on the subject, your eyes lead you, and so do your ears, and all the rest of the multitude of that kindred connection, towards those objects which are pleasing to themselves. But if you choose to collect again those portions of yourself which you have lent away, and to invest yourself with the possession of yourself, without separating off or alienating any part of it, you will have a happy life, enjoying for ever and ever the fruit of good things which belong not to strangers but to yourself.

But now rise up also and quit speech according to utterance, which Moses here represents God as calling your father's house, that you may not be deceived by the specious beauty of words and names, and so be separated from that real beauty which exists in the things themselves which are intended by these names. For it is absurd for a shadow to be looked upon as of more importance than the bodies themselves, or for an imitation to carry off the palm from the model. Now the interpretation resembles a shadow and an imitation, but the natures of things signified under these expressions, thus interpreted, resemble the bodies and original models which the man who aims at being such and such rather than at appearing so must cling to, removing to a distance from the other things.

III. When therefore the mind begins to become acquainted with itself, and to dwell among the speculations which come under the province of the intellect, all the inclinations of the soul for the species which is comprehensible by the intellect will be repelled, which inclination is called by the Hebrews, Lot; for which reason the wise man is represented as distinctly saying," Depart, and separate yourself from me;" (Genesis xiii. 9) for it is impossible for a man who is overwhelmed with the love of incorporeal and imperishable objects to dwell with one, whose every inclination is towards the mortal objects of the outward senses.

Very beautifully therefore has the sacred interpreter of God's will entitled one entire holy volume of the giving of the law, the Exodus, having thus found out an appropriate name for the oracles contained therein. For being a man desirous of giving instruction and exceedingly ready to admonish and correct, he desires to remove the whole of the people of the soul as a multitude capable of receiving admonition and correction from the country of Egypt, that is to say, the body, and to take them out from among its inhabitants, thinking it a most terrible and grievous burden that the mind which is endowed with the faculty of sight should be oppressed by the pleasures of the flesh, and should obey whatever commands the relentless desires choose to impose upon it.

Therefore, after the merciful God has instructed this people, groaning and bitterly weeping for the abundance of the things concerning the body, and the exceeding supply of external things (for it is said, "The children of Israel groaned by reason of the works") when, God, I say, had instructed them about their going out, the prophet himself led them forth in safety.

But there are some persons who have made a treaty with the body to last till the day of their death, and who have buried themselves in it as in a chest or coffin or whatever else you like to call it, of whom all the parts which are devoted to the slavery of the body and of the passions are consigned to oblivion and buried. But if anything well affected towards virtue has shot up by the side of it, that is preserved in the recollection, by means of which good things are naturally destined to be kept alive.

C.

The Talmud itself deals primarily with the legal portions of the Torah (Halacha) and has less to say about the narrative passages. A good example of Tannaitic interpretation, however, can be found in the Midrash Rabbah, a work which was finally redacted in the sixth century A.D. but which contains traditional material of great antiquity. Here is the Midrash Rabbah dealing with the same passage about which Philo wrote:

CHAPTER XXXIX
LECH LECHA

1. NOW THE LORD SAID UNTO ABRAM: GET THEE OUT OF THY COUNTRY, etc. (XII, I). R. Isaac commenced his discourse with, *Hearken, O daughter, and consider, and incline thine ear; forget also thine own people, and thy father's house* (Ps. XLV, II). Said R. Isaac: This may be compared to a man who was travelling from place to place when he saw a building in flames.[1] Is it possible that the building lacks a person to look after it? he wondered. The owner of the building looked out and said, 'I am the owner of the building.' Similarly, because

Abraham our father said, 'Is it conceivable that the world is without a guide?' the Holy One, blessed be He, looked out and said to him, 'I am the Guide, the Sovereign of the Universe.' *So shall the king desire thy beauty (ib.* 12*):* i.e. to make thee glorious in the world. *For he is thy Lord, and do homage unto him (ib.):* hence, THE LORD SAID UNTO ABRAHAM: GET THEE, etc.

2. R. Berekiah commenced: *Thine ointments have a goodly fragrance* (S.S. I, 3). Said R. Berekiah: What did Abraham resemble? A phial of myrrh closed with a tight-fitting lid and lying in a corner, so that its fragrance was not disseminated; as soon as it was taken up, however, its fragrance was disseminated. Similarly, the Holy One, blessed be He, said to Abraham: 'Travel from place to place, and thy name will become great in the world': hence, GET THEE, etc.

3. R. Berekiah commenced: *We have a little sister —* ahoth (*ib.* VIII, 8): this refers to Abraham, who united *(ihah)* the whole world for us.[2] Bar Kappara observed: Like a person who sews a rent together. '*Little*': even while young he stored up pious acts and good deeds. *And she hath no breasts (ib.):* no breasts suckled him[1] in piety or good deeds. *What shall we do for our sister in the day when she shall be spoken for (ib.)?* i.e. on the day when the wicked Nimrod ordered him to be cast into the fiery furnace. *If she be a wall, we will build upon her (ib.* 9*):* if he resists [Nimrod] like a wall, He [God][2] will build up [a defence] for him.[3] *And if she be a door* (deleth), *we will enclose* (nazur) *her with boards of cedar (ib.):* if he is poor *(dal)* in piety and noble deeds, '*We will enclose* (nazur) *her with boards of cedar*': and just as a drawing *(zurah)* [on boards] is only temporary,[4] so will I protect him only for a time. Said he [Abraham] to Him: 'Sovereign of the Universe! *I am a wall (ib.* 10*):* I stand as firm as a wall; *And my breasts like the towers thereof (ib.):* my sons are Hananiah, Mishael, and Azariah.' *Then was I in his eyes as one that found peace (ib.):* he entered [the fiery furnace] in peace and left it unscathed: hence, NOW THE LORD SAID UNTO ABRAM: GET THEE.

4. *Wisdom maketh a wise man stronger than ten rulers* (Eccl. VII, 19)[5]: this refers to Abraham, [whom wisdom made stronger] than the ten generations from Noah to Abraham; out of all of them I spoke to thee alone, as it is written, NOW THE LORD SAID UNTO ABRAHAM.[6]

5. R. :Azariah commenced: *We would have healed Babylon, but she was not healed* (Jer. LI, 9). '*We would have healed Babylon*' — in the generation of Enosh; '*But she was not healed*' — in the generation of the Flood; *Forsake her, and let us go every one into his country (ib.),* as it is written, NOW THE LORD SAID UNTO ABRAM: GET THEE.[7]

6. R. ʿAzariah commenced in R. Aha's name thus: *Thou hast loved righteousness, and hated wickedness*, etc. (Ps. XLV, 8). R. ʿAzariah in R. Aha's name referred the verse to our father Abraham. When Abraham our father stood to plead for mercy for the Sodomites, what is written there? *That be far from Thee to do after this manner* (Gen. XVIII, 25). R. Aha explained this: Thou hast sworn not to bring a deluge upon the world. Wouldst Thou evade Thine oath! Not a deluge of water wilt Thou bring but a deluge of fire? Then Thou has not been true to Thine oath. R. Levi commented: *Shalt not the Judge of all the earth do justly (ib.)?* If thou desirest the world to endure, there can be no absolute justice,[1] while if Thou desirest absolute justice the world cannot endure, yet Thou wouldst hold the cord by both ends, desiring both the world and absolute justice. Unless Thou forgoest a little, the world cannot endure. Said the Holy One, blessed be He, to Abraham: '*Thou has loved righteousness, and hated wickedness*[2]; *therefore God, thy God, hath anointed thee with the oil of gladness above thy fellows (ib.)*: from Noah until thee were ten generations, and out of all of them I spoke with thee alone'; hence, NOW THE LORD SAID UNTO ABRAHAM.

7. Now what precedes this passage? *And Terah died in Haran (ib.* XI, 32*)*, [which is followed by] NOW THE LORD SAID UNTO ABRAM: GET THEE (LEK LEKA). R. Isaac said: From the point of view of chronology a period of sixty-five years is still required.[3] But first you may learn that the wicked, even during their lifetime, are called dead.[4] For Abraham was afraid, saying, 'Shall I go out and bring dishonour upon the Divine Name, as people will say, "He left his father in his old age and departed"?'[1] Therefore the Holy One, blessed be He, reassured him: 'I exempt thee *(leka)* from the duty of honouring thy parents, though I exempt no one else from this duty.[2] Moreover, I will record his death before thy departure.' Hence, '*And Terah died in Haran*' is stated first, and then, NOW THE LORD SAID UNTO ABRAM, etc.

D.

The Zohar, that medieval work of great mystical splendor, is the best example of a Kabbalistic interpretation of Scripture. The whole work is an extensive Midrashic treatment of the Torah. In this excerpt, the author, who was probably Moses of Leon (d. 1305), interprets Genesis 1:1, the opening words of the Bible.

BERESHITH[1]
Gen. I, I-VI, 8

At the outset the decision of the King made a tracing in the
supernal effulgence, a lamp of scintillation,[2] and there issued
within the impenetrable recesses of the mysterious limitless
a shapeless nucleus[3] enclosed in a ring, neither white nor
black nor red nor green nor of any colour at all. When he took
measurements, he fashioned colours to show within, and
within the lamp there issued a certain effluence from which
colours were imprinted below. The most mysterious Power
enshrouded in the limitless clave, as it were, without cleaving
its void, remaining wholly unknowable until from the force of
the strokes there shone forth a supernal and mysterious
point. Beyond that point there is no knowable, and therefore
it is called *Reshith* (beginning), the creative utterance which
is the starting-point of all.

It is written: *And the intelligent shall shine like the
brightness of the firmament, and they that turn many to
righteousness like the stars for ever and ever* (Dan. XII, 3).
There was indeed a "brightness" *(Zohar)*. The Most
Mysterious struck its void, and caused this point to shine.
This "beginning" then extended, and made for itself a palace
for its honour and glory. There it sowed a sacred seed which
was to generate for the benefit of the universe, and to which
may be applied the Scriptural words "the holy seed is the
stock thereof" (Is. VI, 13). Again there was *Zohar,* in that it
sowed a seed for its glory, just as the silkworm encloses
itself, as it were, in a palace of its own production which is
both useful and beautiful. Thus by means of this
"beginning" the Mysterious Unknown made this palace.
This palace is called *Elohim,* and this doctrine is contained in
the words, "By means of a beginning (it) created *Elohim.*"
The *Zohar* is that from which were created all the creative utterances through the extension of the point of this mysterious brightness. Nor need we be surprised at the use of the
word "created" in this connection, seeing that we read further on, "And God created man in his image" (Gen. I, 27). A
further esoteric interpretation of the word *bereshith* is as
follows. The name of the starting-point of all is *Ehyeh* (I shall
be). The holy name when inscribed at its side is *Elohim,* but

---

[1] *v. Appendix I.*

[2] *al. 'darkness'; al. 'measurement'.*

[3] *al. 'vapour'.*

when inscribed by circumscription[1] is *Asher,* the hidden and recondite temple, the source of that which is mystically called *Reshith.* The word *Asher* (i.e. the letters, *Aleph, Shin, Resh* from the word *bereshith*) is anagrammatically *Rosh* (head), the beginning which issues from *Reshith.* So when [15b] the point and the temple were firmly established together, then *bereshith* combined the supernal Beginning with Wisdom. Afterwards the character of that temple was changed, and it was called "house" *(bayith).* The combination of this with the supernal point which is called *rosh* gives *bereshith,* which is the name used so long as the house was uninhabited. When, however, it was sown with seed to make it habitable, it was called *Elohim,* hidden and mysterious. The *Zohar* was hidden and withdrawn so long as the building was within and yet to bring forth, and the house was extended only so far as to find room for the holy seed. Before it had conceived and had extended sufficiently to be habitable, it was not called *Elohim,* but all was still included in the term *Bereshith.* After it had acquired the name of *Elohim,* it brought forth offspring from the seed that had been implanted in it.

What is this seed? It consists of the graven letters, the secret source of the Torah, which issued from the first point. That point sowed in the palace certain three vowel-points, *holem, shureq,* and *hireq,* which combined with one another and formed one entity, to wit, the Voice which issued through their union. When this Voice issued, there issued with it its mate which comprises all the letters; hence it is written *Eth hashammaim* (the heavens), to wit, the Voice and its mate. This voice, indicated by the word "heaven", is the second *Ehyeh* of the sacred name, the *Zohar* which includes all letters and colours, in this manner. Up to this point the words "The Lord our God the Lord" *(Yhvh Eluhenu Yhvh)* represent three grades corresponding to this deep mystery of *bereshith bara Elohim. Bereshith* represents the primordial mystery. *Bara* represents the mysterious source from which the whole expanded. *Elohim* represents the force which sustains all below. The words *eth hashammaim* indicate that the two latter are on no account to be separated, and are male and female together. The word *eth* consists of the letters *aleph* and *tau,* which include between them all the letters, as being the first and last of the alphabet. Afterwards *he* was added, so that all the letters should be attached to *he,* and this gave the name *attah* (Thou); hence we read "and Thou *(ve-attah)* keepest all of them alive" (Neh. IX, 6). *Eth* again alludes to *Adonai* (Lord), who is so called. *Hashammaim* is

[1] i.e., between the *Ehyeh's.* v. Ex. III, 14.

Yhvh in its higher signification. The next word, *ve-eth*, indicates the firm union of male and female; it also alludes to the appellation *ve-Yhvh* (and the Lord), both explanations coming to the same thing. *Ha-aretz* (the earth) designates an *Elohim* corresponding to the higher form, to bring forth fruit and produce. This name is here found in three applications, and thence the same name branches out to various sides.

Up to this point only extend the allusions to the Most Mysterious who carves out and builds and vivifies in mysterious ways, through the esoteric explanation of one verse. From this point onwards *bara shith*, "he created six", from the end of heaven to the end thereof, six sides which extend from the supernal mystic essence, through the expansion of creative force from a primal point. Here has been inscribed the mystery of the name of forty-two letters.

And the intelligent shall shine (Dan. XII, 3). This "shining" corresponds to the movement given by the accents and notes to the letters and vowel-points which pay obeisance to them and march after them like troops behind their kings. The letters being the body and the vowel-points the animating spirit, together they keep step with the notes and come to a halt with them. When the chanting of the notes marches forward, the letters with their vowel-points march behind them, and when it stops they also stop. So here: "the intelligent" correspond to the letters and the vowel-points; "the brightness" to the notes; "the firmament" to the flow of the chant through the succession of notes; while "they that turn to righteousness" correspond to the pausal notes, which stop the march of the words and bring out clearly the sense. These "cause to shine" letters and vowels, so that they all flow together in their own mystical manner through secret paths. From this impetus the whole was extended. Again, the words "and the intelligent shall shine as the brightness of the firmament" may be referred to the pillars and sockets of the "celestial palanquin" *(apiryon).*[1] The "wise and intelligent" as the supernal pillars and sockets, since they ponder with understanding all things needful for the upholding of the palace. This use of the term "intelligent" *(maskilim)* has its parallel in the passage: "Blessed is he that considereth *(maskil)* the poor" (Ps. XLI, 2). "They will shine", for if they do not shine and give light, they cannot well consider and ponder the needs of the palace. "As the brightness of the firmament", [16a] namely, of that firmament which rests upon those "intelligent" we have mentioned, and of which it is written, "And over the head of the *Hayyah* there was the likeness of a firmament, like the colour of the terrible ice" (Ezek. I, 22). "The brightness" is that which illumines the Torah, and which illumines also the heads of the *Hayyah*, those heads being the "intelligent", who shine continually and ever contemplate the "firmament" and the light which issues therefrom, to wit, the light of the Torah which radiates perpetually without cease.

E.

Perhaps the greatest of all the medieval commentators was Solomon ben Isaac, commonly known as Rashi. Today, he is still read by many Jews as *the* interpreter of Scripture. Noteworthy is his interest in rational explanation and understanding rather than allegorical symbolism. Here is the way in which he comments upon the first words of Genesis:

(1) *In the beginning God created the heaven and the earth.*

Strictly speaking, the Torah should have commenced with the verse: "This month shall be to you the beginning of months" (Exodus 12:1), which is the very first commandment given to Israel. Why, then, did the Torah begin with the account of the Creation? In order to illustrate that God the Creator owns the whole world. So, if the peoples of the world shall say to Israel: "You are robbers in conquering the territory of the seven Canaanite nations," Israel can answer them: "All the earth belongs to God — He created it, so He can give it to whomsoever He wills. When He wished He gave it to them, then when He wished He took it from them and gave it to us."

In the beginning God created

This verse calls out to be explained in the same way that the sages have expounded it, viz.: "For the sake of the Torah which is called *reshit*, i.e., 'the beginning' " (Jeremiah 2:3). But if you want to explain it according to its obvious meaning, then translate it thus: "At the beginning of the Creation of heaven and earth, when the earth was desolate and void and there was darkness, then God said let there be light." The verse does not appear in order to show the order of Creation and tell us that the heaven and earth were created first. Because wherever the word *reshit* appears in Scripture, it is in the construct; so too here, "In the beginning God created the heaven and the earth" should be translated as "In the beginning of God's creating of the heaven and the earth." There are several Biblical examples which support this translation. Should you insist, however, that the verse does intend to give the actual order of Creation, and that the

meaning is that in the beginning of everything God created
the heaven and the earth, then you should be surprised to
find that the waters were really created first, since it is written that "The spirit of God hovered over the face of the
waters" (1:2), and that this appears before Scripture had yet
stated when the waters were created — or that anything else
had as yet been created. Consequently, you are compelled to
conclude that the verse teaches nothing about the sequence
in the Creation.

F.

Baruch de Spinoza (1632-1677) did not offer to the world a full
blown commentary on Scripture. What he did do was to set
forth an attitude toward the study of Scripture which
foreshadowed the whole history of modern Biblical criticism.
In this passage drawn from his *Theologico-Political Treatise,*
he sets forth his central, germinal ideas.

OF THE INTERPRETATION OF SCRIPTURE.

When people declare, as all are ready to do, that the Bible is
the Word of God teaching man true blessedness and the way
of salvation, they evidently do not mean what they say; for
the masses take no pains at all to live accordingly to Scripture, and we see most people endeavouring to hawk about
their own commentaries as the word of God, and giving their
best efforts, under the guise of religion, to compelling others
to think as they do: we generally see, I say, theologians anxious to learn how to wring their inventions and sayings out of
the sacred text, and to fortify them with Divine authority.
Such persons never display less scruple or more zeal than
when they are interpreting Scripture or the mind of the Holy
Ghost; if we ever see them perturbed, it is not that they fear
to attribute some error to the Holy Spirit, and to stray from
the right path, but that they are afraid to be convicted of error by others, and thus to overthrow and bring into com-
tempt their own authority. But if men really believed what
they verbally testify of Scripture, they would adopt quite a
different plan of life: their minds would not be agitated by so
many contentions, nor so many hatreds, and they would
cease to be excited by such a blind and rash passion for interpreting the sacred writings, and excogitating novelties in
religion. On the contrary, they would not dare to adopt, as
the teaching of Scripture, anything which they could not

plainly deduce therefrom: lastly, those sacrilegious persons who have dared, in several passages, to interpolate the Bible, would have shrunk from so great a crime, and would have stayed their sacrilegious hands.

Ambition and unscrupulousness have waxed so powerful, that religion is thought to consist, not so much in respecting the writings of the Holy Ghost, as in defending human commentaries, so that religion is no longer identified with charity, but with spreading discord and propagating insensate hatred disguised under the name of zeal for the Lord, and eager ardour.

To these evils we must add superstition, which teaches men to despise reason and nature, and only to admire and venerate that which is repugnant to both: whence it is not wonderful that for the sake of increasing the admiration and veneration felt for Scripture, men strive to explain it so as to make it appear to contradict, as far as possible, both one and the other: thus they dream that most profound mysteries lie hid in the Bible, and weary themselves out in the investigation of these absurdities, to the neglect of what is useful. Every result of their diseased imagination they attribute to the Holy Ghost, and strive to defend with the utmost zeal and passion; for it is an observed fact that men employ their reason to defend conclusions arrived at by reason, but conclusions arrived at by the passions are defended by the passions.

If we would separate ourselves from the crowd and escape from theological prejudices, instead of rashly accepting human commentaries for Divine documents, we must consider the true method of interpreting Scripture and dwell upon it at some length: for if we remain in ignorance of this we cannot know, certainly, what the Bible and the Holy Spirit wish to teach.

I may sum up the matter by saying that the method of interpreting Scripture does not widely differ from the method of interpreting nature — in fact, it is almost the same. For as the interpretation of nature consists in the examination of the history of nature, and therefrom deducing definitions of natural phenomena on certain fixed axioms, so Scriptural interpretation proceeds by the examination of Scripture, and inferring the intention of its authors as a legitimate conclusion from its fundamental principles. By working in this manner everyone will always advance without danger of error — that is, if they admit no principles for interpreting Scripture, and discussing its contents save such as they find in Scripture itself — and will be able with equal security to discuss what surpasses our understanding, and what is known by the natural light of reason.

In order to make clear that such a method is not only correct, but is also the only one advisable, and that it agrees with that employed in interpreting nature, I must remark that Scripture very often treats of matters which cannot be deduced from principles known to reason: for it is chiefly made up of narratives and revelation: the narratives generally contain miracles — that is, as we have shown in the last chapter, relations of extraordinary natural occurrences adapted to the opinions and judgment of the historians who recorded them: the revelations also were adapted to the opinions of the prophets, as we showed in Chap. II, and in themselves surpassed human comprehension. Therefore the knowledge of all these — that is, of nearly the whole contents of Scripture, must be sought from Scripture alone, even as the knowledge of nature is sought from nature. As for the moral doctrines which are also contained in the Bible, they may be demonstrated from received axioms, but we cannot prove in the same manner that Scripture intended to teach them, this can only be learned from Scripture itself.

If we would bear unprejudiced witness to the Divine origin of Scripture, we must prove solely on its own authority that it teaches true moral doctrines, for by such means alone can its Divine origin be demonstrated: we have shown that the certitude of the prophets depended chiefly on their having minds turned towards what is just and good, therefore we ought to have proof of their possessing this quality before we repose faith in them. From miracles God's divinity cannot be proved, as I have already shown, and need not now repeat, for miracles could be wrought by false prophets. Wherefore the Divine origin of Scripture must consist solely in its teaching true virtue. But we must come to our conclusion simply on Scriptural grounds, for if we were unable to do so we could not, unless strongly prejudiced, accept the Bible and bear witness to its Divine origin.

Our knowledge of Scripture must then be looked for in Scripture only.

Lastly, Scripture does not give us definitions of things any more than nature does: therefore, such definitions must be sought in the latter case from the diverse workings of nature; in the former case, from the various narratives about the given subject which occur in the Bible.

The universal rule, then, in interpreting Scripture is to accept nothing as an authoritative Scriptural statement which we do not perceive very clearly when we examine it in the light of its history. What I mean by its history, and what should be the chief points elucidated, I will now explain.

The history of a Scriptural statement comprises —

I. The nature and properties of the language in which the books of the Bible were written, and in which their authors were accustomed to speak. We shall thus be able to investigate every expression by comparison with common conversational usages.

Now all the writers both of the Old Testament and the New were Hebrews: therefore, a knowledge of the Hebrew language is before all things necessary, not only for the comprehenion of the Old Testament, which was written in that tongue, but also of the New: for although the latter was published in other languages, yet its characteristics are Hebrew.

II. An analysis of each book and arrangement of its contents under heads; so that we may have at hand the various texts which treat of a given subject. Lastly, a note of all the passages which are ambiguous or obscure, or which seem mutually contradictory.

I call passages clear or obscure according as their meaning is inferred easily or with difficulty in relation to the context, not according as their truth is perceived easily or the reverse by reason. We are at work not on the truth of passages, but solely on their meaning. We must take especial care, when we are in search of the meaning of a text, not to be led away by our reason in so far as it is founded on principles of natural knowledge (to say nothing of prejudices): in order not to confound the meaning of a passage with its truth, we must examine it solely by means of the signification of the words, or by a reason acknowledging no foundation but Scripture.

PART 4

JEWISH SECTS
AND MOVEMENTS

Although Judaism has, throughout its history, manifested a unity of faith and practice unknown by many other traditions, it has also experienced the development of sects and movements which have sometimes challenged the authority of the official leadership and have frequently reshaped the nature of Jewish life.

A.

In this passage taken from *Antiquities of the Jews*, Flavius Josephus (37-100 A.D.) describes the various Jewish parties which existed during the first century of our era. Since he was an eyewitness to life at that time, the testimony of Josephus is invaluable, but one must always remember that he writes to inform (and please) Roman readers.

2. The Jews had for a great while had three sects of philosophy peculiar to themselves, the sect of the Essenes, and the sect of the Sadducees, and the third sort of opinions was that of those called Pharisees; of which sects, although I have already spoken in the second book of the Jewish war, yet will I a little touch upon them now.

3. Now, for the Pharisees, they live meanly, and despise delicacies in diet, and they follow the conduct of reason; and

what that prescribes to them as good for them, they do; and they think they ought earnestly to strive to observe reason's dictates for practice. They also pay a respect to such as are in years; nor are they so bold as to contradict them in any thing which they have introduced; and when they determine that all things are done by fate, they do not take away the freedom from men of acting as they think fit; since their notion is, that it hath pleased God to make a temperament, whereby what he wills is done, but so that the will of man can act virtuously or viciously. They also believe, that souls have an immortal vigour in them, and that under the earth there will be rewards or punishments, according as they have lived virtuously or viciously in this life; and the latter are to be detained in an everlasting prison, but that the former shall have power to revive, and live again, on account of which doctrines, they are able greatly to persuade the body of the people, and whatsoever they do about divine worship, prayers, and sacrifices, they perform them according to their direction; insomuch that the cities give great attestatious to them on account of their entire virtuous conduct, both in the actions of their lives, and their discourses also.

4. But the doctrine of the Sadducees is this, that souls die with the bodies; nor do they regard the observation of any thing besides what the law enjoins them; for they think it an instance of virtue to dispute with those teachers of philosophy whom they frequent; but this doctrine is received but by a few, yet by those still of the greatest dignity. But they are able to do almost nothing of themselves; for when they become magistrates, as they are unwillingly and by force sometimes obliged to be, they addict themselves to the notions of the Pharisees, because the multitude would not otherwise bear them.

5. The doctrine of the Essenes is this, that all things are best ascribed to God. They teach the immortality of souls, and esteem that the rewards of righteousness are to be earnestly striven for; and when they send what they have dedicated to God into the temple, they do not offer sacrifices, because they have more pure lustrations of their own; on which account they are excluded from the common court of the temple, but offer their sacrifices themselves; yet is their course of life better than that of other men; and they entirely addict themselves to husbandry. It also deserves our admiration, how much they exceed all other men that addict themselves to virtue, and this in righteousness; and indeed to such a degree, that as it hath never appeared among any other men, neither Greeks nor barbarians, no, not for a little time, so hath it endured for a long while among them. This is demonstrated by that institution of theirs, which will not

suffer any thing to hinder them from having all things in common; so that a rich man enjoys no more of his own wealth than he who hath nothing at all. There are about four thousand men that live in this way; and neither marry wives, nor are desirous to keep servants; as thinking the latter tempts men to be unjust, and the former gives the handle to domestic quarrels, but as they live by themselves, they minister one to another. They also appoint certain stewards to receive the incomes of their revenues, and of the fruits of the ground; such as are good men and priests; who are to get their corn and their food ready for them. They none of them differ from others of the Essenes in their way of living, but do the most resemble those Dacæ, who are called Polistæ, [dwellers in cities].

B.

Although there is still some debate, most scholars would identify the monastic group from which the Dead Sea Scrolls came as Essene. Among those documents found in the vicinity of Qumran was the *Manual of Discipline,* apparently an authoritative book used in the ordering of the community.

THE MANUAL OF DISCIPLINE

Of the Commitment   (i, 1-15)

Everyone who wishes to join the community must pledge himself to respect God and man; to live according to the communal rule; to seek God [   ]; to do what is good and upright in His sight, in accordance with what He has commanded through Moses and through His servants the prophets; to love all that He has chosen and hate all that He has rejected; to keep far from all evil and to cling to all good works; to act truthfully and righteously and justly on earth and to walk no more in the stubbornness of a guilty heart and of lustful eyes, doing all manner of evil; to bring into a bond of mutual love all who have declared their willingness to carry out the statutes of God; to join the formal community of God; to walk blamelessly before Him in conformity with all that has been revealed as relevant to the several periods during which they are to bear witness (to Him); to love all the children of light, each according to his stake in the formal community of God; and to hate all the children of darkness, each according to the measure of his guilt, which God will ultimately requite.

All who declare their willingness to serve God's truth must bring all of their mind, all of their strength, and all of their wealth into the community of God, so that their minds may be purified by the truth of His precepts, their strength controlled by His perfect ways, and their wealth disposed in accordance with His just design. They must not deviate by a single step from carrying out the orders of God at the times appointed for them; they must neither advance the statutory times nor postpone the prescribed seasons. They must not turn aside from the ordinances of God's truth either to the right or to the left.

Of those who are (ii,25-iii, 12)
to be excluded

Anyone who refuses to enter the (ideal) society of God and persists in walking in the stubbornness of his heart shall not be admitted to this community of God's truth. For inasmuch as his soul has revolted at the discipline entailed in a knowledge of God's righteous judgments, he has shown no real strength in amending his way of life, and therefore cannot be reckoned with the upright. The mental, physical and material resources of such a man are not to be introduced into the stock of the community, for such a man 'plows in the slime of wickedness' and 'there are stains on his repentance.' He is not honest in resolving the stubbornness of his heart. On paths of light he sees but darkness. Such a man cannot be reckoned as among those essentially blameless. He cannot be cleared by mere ceremonies of atonement, nor cleansed by any waters of ablution, nor sanctified by immersion in lakes or rivers, nor purified by any bath. Unclean, unclean he remains so long as he rejects the government of God and refuses the discipline of communion with Him. For it is only through the spiritual apprehension of God's truth that man's ways can be properly directed. Only thus can all his iniquities be shriven so that he can gaze upon the true light of life. Only through the holy spirit can he achieve union with God's truth and be purged of all his iniquities. Only by a spirit of uprightness and humility can his sin be atoned. Only by the submission of his soul to all the ordinances of God can his flesh be made clean. Only thus can it really be sprinkled with waters of ablution. Only thus can it really be sanctified by waters of purification. And only thus can he really direct his steps to walk blamelessly through all the vicissitudes of his destiny in all the ways of God in the manner which He has commanded, without turning either to the right or to the left and without overstepping any of God's words. Then indeed will he be acceptable before God like an atonement-offering which meets with His pleasure, and then indeed will he be admitted to the covenant of the community for ever.

Of the two spirits in man (iii,13-iv,26)

This is for the man who would bring others to the inner vision, so that he may understand and teach to all the children of light the real nature of men, touching the different varieties of their temperaments with the distinguishing traits thereof, touching their actions throughout their generations, and touching the reason why they are now visited with afflictions and now enjoy periods of well-being.

All that is and ever was comes from a God of knowledge. Before things came into existence He determined the plan of them; and when they fill their appointed roles, it is in accordance with His glorious design that they discharge their functions. Nothing can be changed. In His hand lies the government of all things. God it is that sustains them in their needs.

Now, this God created man to rule the world, and appointed for him two spirits after whose direction he was to walk until the final Inquisition.[26] They are the spirits of truth and of perversity.

The origin of truth lies in the Fountain of Light, and that of perversity in the Wellspring of Darkness. All who practice righteousness are under the domination of the Prince of Lights, and walk in ways of light; whereas all who practice perversity are under the domination of the Angel of Darkness and walk in ways of darkness. Through the Angel of Darkness, however, even those who practice righteousness are made liable to error. All their sin and their iniquities, all their guilt and their deeds of transgression are the result of his domination; and this, by God's inscrutable design, will continue until the time appointed by Him. Moreover, all men's afflictions and all their moments of tribulation are due to this being's malevolent sway. All of the spirits that attend upon him are bent on causing the sons of light to stumble. Howbeit, the God of Israel and the Angel of His truth are always there to help the sons of light. It is God that created these spirits of light and darkness and made them the basis of every act, the [instigators] of every deed and the directors of every thought. The one He loves to all eternity, and is ever pleased with its deeds; but any association with the other He abhors, and He hates all its ways to the end of time.

This is the way those spirits operate in the world. The enlightenment of man's heart, the making straight before him all the ways of righteousness and truth, the implanting in his heart of fear for the judgments of God, of a spirit of humility, of patience, of abundant compassion, of perpetual goodness, of insight, of perception, of that sense of the Divine Power that is based at once on an apprehension of God's works and a reliance on His plenteous mercy, of a spirit of knowledge informing every plan of action, of a zeal for righteous government, of a hallowed mind in a controlled nature, of abounding love for all who follow the truth, of a self-respecting purity which abhors all the taint of filth, of a modesty of behavior coupled with a general prudence and an ability to hide within oneself the secrets of what one knows — these are the things that come to men in this world through communion with the spirit of truth. And the guerdon of all that walk in its ways is health and abundant well-being, with long life and fruition of seed along with eternal blessings and everlasting joy in the life everlasting, and a crown of glory and a robe of honor, amid light perpetual.

But to the spirit of perversity belong greed, remissness in right-doing, wickedness and falsehood, pride and presumption, ruthless deception and guile, abundant insolence, shortness of temper and profusion of folly, arrogant passion, abominable acts in a spirit of lewdness, filthy ways in the thralldom of unchastity, a blasphemous tongue, blindness of eyes, dullness of ears, stiffness of neck and hardness of heart, to the end that a man walks entirely in ways of darkness and of evil cunning. The guerdon of all who walk in such ways is multitude of afflictions at the hands of all the angels of destruction, everlasting perdition through the angry wrath of an avenging God, eternal horror and perpetual reproach, the disgrace of final annihilation in the Fire, darkness throughout the vicissitudes of life in every generation, doleful sorrow, bitter misfortune and darkling ruin — ending in extinction without remnant or survival.

It is to these things that all men are born, and it is to these that all the host of them are heirs throughout their generations. It is in these ways that men needs must walk and it is in these two divisions, according as a man inherits something of each, that all human acts are divided throughout all the ages of eternity. For God has appointed these two things to obtain in equal measure until the final age.

Between the two categories He has set an eternal enmity. Deeds of perversity are an abomination to Truth, while all the ways of Truth are an abomination to perversity; and there is a constant jealous rivalry between their two regimes, for they do not march in accord. Howbeit, God in His inscrutable wisdom has appointed a term for the existence of perversity, and when the time of Inquisition comes, He will destroy it for ever. Then truth will emerge triumphant for the world, albeit now and until the time of the final judgment it go sullying itself in the ways of wickedness owing to the domination of perversity. Then, too, God will purge all the acts of man in the crucible of His truth, and refine for Himself all the fabric of man, destroying every spirit of perversity from within his flesh and cleansing him by the holy spirit from all the effects of wickedness. Like waters of purification He will sprinkle upon him the spirit of truth, to cleanse him of all the abominations of falsehood and of all pollution through the spirit of filth; to the end that, being made upright, men may have understanding of transcendental knowledge and of the lore of the sons of heaven, and that, being made blameless in their ways, they may be endowed with inner vision. For them has God chosen to be the partners of His eternal covenant, and theirs shall be all mortal glory. Perversity shall be no more, and all works of deceit shall be put to shame.

Thus far, the spirits of truth and perversity have been struggling in the heart of man. Men have walked both in wisdom and in folly. If a man casts his portion with truth, he does righteously and hates perversity; if he casts it with perversity, he does wickedly and abominates truth. For God has apportioned them in equal measure until the final age, until 'He makes all things new.' He foreknows the effect of their works in every epoch of the world, and He has made men heirs to them that they might know good and evil. But [when the time] of Inquisition [comes], He will determine the fate of every living being in accordance with which of the [two spirits he has chosen to follow].

Of social relations (v, 1-7)

This is the rule for all the members of the community — that is, for such as have declared their readiness to turn away from all evil and to adhere to all that God in His good pleasure has commanded.

They are to keep apart from the company of the froward.

They are to belong to the community in both a doctrinal and an economic sense.

They are to abide by the decisions of the sons of Zadok, the same being priests that still keep the Covenant, and of the majority of the community that stand firm in it. It is by the vote of such that all matters doctrinal, economic and judicial are to be determined.

They are concertedly and in all their pursuits to practise truth, humility, righteousness, justice, charity and decency, with no one walking in the stubbornnes of his own heart or going astray after his heart or his eyes or his fallible human mind.

Furthermore, they are concertedly to remove the impurity of their human mold, and likewise all stiffneckedness.

They are to establish in Israel a solid basis of truth.

They are to unite in a bond indissoluble for ever.

They are to extend forgiveness to all among the priesthood that have freely enlisted in the cause of holiness, and to all among the laity that have done so in the cause of truth, and likewise to all that have associated themselves with them.

They are to make common cause both in the struggle and in the upshot of it.

They are to regard as felons all that transgress the law.

C.

Another account of early Jewish monasticism is to be found in Philo's essay, *On the Contemplative Life*. In this work he describes the therapeutas, a Jewish movement apparently very important in Egypt during the first century. Apparently such Jewish monasticism died out in the ancient world and never appeared again.

But the therapeutic sect of mankind, being continually taught to see without interruption, may well aim at obtaining a sight of the living God, and may pass by the sun, which is visible to the outward sense, and never leave this order which conducts to perfect happiness. But they who apply themselves to this kind of worship, not because they are influenced to do so by custom, nor by the advice or recommendation of any particular persons, but because they are carried away be a certain heavenly love, give way to enthusiasm, behaving like so many revellers in bacchanalian or corybantian mysteries, until they see the object which they have been earnestly desiring.

Then, because of their anxious desire for an immortal and blessed existence, thinking that their mortal life has already come to an end, they leave their possessions to their sons or daughters, or perhaps to other relations, giving them up their inheritance with willing cheerfulness; and those who know no relations give their property to their companions or friends, for it followed of necessity that those who have acquired the wealth which sees, as if ready prepared for them, should be willing to surrender that wealth which is blind to those who themselves also are still blind in their minds.

The Greeks celebrate Anaxagoras and Democritus, because they, being smitten with a desire for philosophy, allowed all their estates to be devoured by cattle. I myself admire the men who thus showed themselves superior to the attractions of money; but how much better were those who have not permitted cattle to devour their possessions, but have supplied the necessities of mankind, of their own relations and friends, and have made them rich though they were poor before? For surely that was inconsiderate conduct (that I may avoid saying that any action of men whom Greece has agreed to admire was a piece of insanity); but this is the act of sober men, and one which has been carefully elaborated by exceeding prudence.

When, therefore, men abandon their property without being influenced by any predominant attraction, they flee without even turning their heads back again, deserting their brethren, their children, their wives, their parents, their numerous families, their affectionate bands of companions, their native lands in which they have been born and brought up, though long familiarity is a most attractive bond, and one very well able to allure any one. And they depart, not to another city as those do who entreat to be purchased from those who at present possess them, being either unfortunate or else worthless servants, and as such seeking a change of masters rather than endeavouring to procure freedom (for every city, even that which is under the happiest laws, is full of indescribable tumults, and disorders, and calamities, which no one would submit to who had been even for a moment under the influence of wisdom), but they take up their abode outside of walls, or gardens, or solitary lands, seeking for a desert place, not because of any ill-natured misanthropy to which they have learnt to devote themselves, but because of the associations with people of wholly dissimilar dispositions to which they would otherwise be compelled, and which they know to be unprofitable and mischievous.

... there is the greatest number of such men in Egypt, in every one of the districts, or nomi as they are called, and especially around Alexandria; and from all quarters those who are the best of these therapeutæ proceed on their pilgrimage to some most suitable place as if it were their country, which is beyond the Mareotic lake, lying in a somewhat level plain a little raised above the rest, being suitable for their purpose by reason of its safety and also of the fine temperature of the air.

For the houses built in the fields and the villages which surround it on all sides give it safety; and the admirable temperature of the air proceeds from the continual breezes which come from the lake which falls into the sea, and also from the sea itself in the neighbourhood, the breezes from the sea being light, and those which proceed from the lake which falls into the sea being heavy, the mixture of which produces a most healthy atmosphere.

But the houses of these men thus congregated together are very plain, just giving shelter in respect of the two things most important to be provided against, the heat of the sun, and the cold from the open air; and they did not live near to one another as men do in cities, for immediate neighbourhood to others would be a troublesome and unpleasant thing to men who have conceived an admiration for, and have determined to devote themselves to, solitude; and, on the other hand, they did not live very far from one another on account of the fellowship which they desire to cultivate, and because of the desirableness of being able to assist one another if they should be attacked by robbers.

And in every house there is a sacred shrine which is called the holy place, and the monastery in which they retire by themselves and perform all the mysteries of a holy life, bringing in nothing, neither meat, nor drink, nor anything else which is indispensable towards supplying the necessities of the body, but studying in that place the laws and the sacred oracles of God enunciated by the holy prophets, and hymns, and psalms, and all kinds of other things by reason of which knowledge and piety are increased and brought to perfection.

Therefore they always retain an imperishable recollection of God, so that not even in their dreams is any other object ever presented to their eyes except the beauty of the divine virtues and of the divine powers. Therefore many persons speak in their sleep, divulging and publishing the celebrated doctrines of the sacred philosophy. And they are accustomed to pray twice every day, at morning and at evening; when the sun is rising entreating God that the happiness of the coming day may be real happiness, so that their minds may be filled with heavenly light, and when the sun is setting they pray that their soul, being entirely lightened and relieved of the burden of the outward senses, and of the appropriate object of these outward senses, may be able to trace out truth existing in its own consistory and council chamber. And the interval between morning and evening is by them devoted wholly to meditation on and to practice of virtue, for they take up the sacred scriptures and philosophise concerning them, investigating the allegories of their national philosophy, since they look upon their literal expressions as symbols of some secret meaning of nature, intended to be conveyed in those figurative expressions.

They have also writings of ancient men, who have been the founders of one sect or another have left behind them many memorials of the allegorical system of writing and explanation, whom they take as a kind of model, and imitate the general fashion of their sect; so that they do not occupy themselves solely in contemplation, but they likewise compose psalms and hymns to God in every kind of metre and melody imaginable, which they of necessity arrange in more dignified rhythm. Therefore, during six days, each of these individuals, retiring into solitude by himself, philosophises by himself in one of the places called monasteries, never going outside the threshold of the outer court, and indeed never even looking out.

But on the seventh day they all come together as if to meet in a sacred assembly, and they sit down in order according to their ages with all becoming gravity, keeping their hands inside their garments, having their right hand between their chest and their dress, and the left hand down by their side, close to their flank; and then the eldest of them who has the most profound learning in their doctrines comes forward and speaks with steadfast look and with steadfast voice, with great powers of reasoning, and great prudence, not making an exhibition of his oratorical powers like the rhetoricians of old, or the sophists of the present day, but investigating with great pains, and explaining with minute accuracy the precise meaning of the laws, which sits, not indeed at the tips of their ears, but penetrates through their hearing into the soul, and remains there lastingly; and all the rest listen in silence to the praises which he bestows upon the law, showing their assent only by nods of the head, or the eager look of the eyes.

And this common holy place to which they all come together on the seventh day is a twofold circuit, being separated partly into the apartment of the men, and partly into a chamber for the women, for women also, in accordance with the usual fashion there, form a part of the audience, having the same feelings of admiration as the men, and having adopted the same sect with equal deliberation and decision; and the wall which is between the houses rises from the ground three or four cubits upwards, like a battlement, and the upper portion rises upwards to the roof without any opening, on two accounts; first of all, in order that the modesty which is so becoming to the female sex may be preserved, and secondly, that the women may be easily able to comprehend what is said being seated within earshot, since there is then nothing which can possibly intercept the voice of him who is speaking.

And these expounders of the law, having first of all laid down temperance as a sort of foundation for the soul to rest upon, proceed to build up other virtues on this foundation, and no one of them may take any meat or drink before the setting of the sun, since the judge that the work of philosophising is one which is worthy of the light, but that the care for the necessities of the body is suitable only to darkness, on which account they appropriate the day to the one occupation, and a brief portion of the night to the other; and some men, in whom there is implanted a more fervent desire of knowledge, can endure to cherish a recollection of their food for three days without even tasting it, and some

men are so delighted, and enjoy themselves so exceedingly
when regaled by wisdom which supplies them with her doctrines in all possible wealth and abundance, that they can
even hold out twice as great a length of time, and will scarcely at the end of six days taste even necessary food, being accustomed, as they say that grasshoppers are, to feed on air,
their song, as I imagine, making their scarcity tolerable to
them.

And they, looking upon the seventh day as one of perfect
holiness and a most complete festival, have thought it worthy of a most especial honour, and on it, after taking due care
of their soul, they tend their bodies also, giving them, just as
they do to their cattle, a complete rest from their continual
labours; and they eat nothing of a costly character, but plain
bread and a seasoning of salt, which the more luxurious of
them do further season with hyssop; and their drink is water
from the spring; for they oppose those feelings which nature
has made mistresses of the human race, namely, hunger and
thirst, giving them nothing to flatter or humour them, but
only such useful things as it is not possible to exist without.
On this account they eat only so far as not to be hungry, and
they drink just enough to escape from thirst, avoiding all
satiety, as an enemy of and a plotter against both soul and
body.

And there are two kinds of covering, one raiment and the
other a house: we have already spoken of their houses, that
they are not decorated with any ornaments, but run up in a
hurry, being only made to answer such purposes as are absolutely necessary; and in like manner their raiment is of the
most ordinary description, just stout enough to ward off cold
and heat, being a cloak of some shaggy hide for winter, and a
thin mantle or linen shawl in the summer; for in short they
practise entire simplicity, looking upon falsehood as the
foundation of pride, but truth as the origin of simplicity, and
upon truth and falsehood as standing in the light of foun-
tains, for from falsehood proceeds every variety of evil and
wickedness, and from truth there flows every imaginable
abundance of good things both human and divine.

D.

The Kairites represent one of the largest and most successful
protest movements against Talmudic authority. This is interesting, for their emphasis was upon a more literal reading of
the Torah and, on the whole, upon a more rigorous obedience to
the Law. Anan ben David (eighth century) was one of the

founders of the movement and represents the Kairite position here on a variety of issues. This is a series of excerpts from his *Book of Precepts.*

BLASPHEMY

He who says that the precepts are as nothing or that the Law is as nothing or he who says, "Who is God?" draws upon himself the punishment of death, and all Israel shall stone him until he is dead, as it is written: *And he who blasphemes the name of the Lord shall surely be put to death, the whole congregation shall surely stone him* (Lev. 24:16). The word *blasphemes* here means "specifies," in which sense it is used also in the verse: *And Moses and Aaron took these men who had been designated by name* (Num. I:17). This word *blasphemes* is here preceded by the conjuction *and* and by the words *Whosoever curses his God shall bear his sin* (Lev. 24:15); this is to teach us that it refers to him who designates the Name of the Merciful One in a light manner, and that he incurs the death penalty. The sixteenth verse then goes on to say: *For his blaspheming of the name he shall be put to death,* indicating thus that also he who speaks lightly of the Law incurs the death penalty, since the Law is sometimes called "the Lord's Name"; e.g., *to bring up from thence the ark of God, upon which was called the name, the name of the Lord of Hosts who dwells over the cherubim* (II Sam. 6:2), meaning that the Name of the Lord was within the Ark. Now there was nothing inside the Ark but the Law, as it is written: *And he took the testimony and put it into the ark* (Exod. 40:20); it follows therefore that the Law is called "the Name of the Lord." And since the precepts and the Law mean the same thing, as it is written: *and I will give thee the stone tablets and the Law and the precepts* (Exod. 24:12), he who speaks lightly of the precepts also incurs the penalty of death.

DIETARY LAW

1. All birds are forbidden to us for use as food, excepting pigeons and turtledoves, since it is written concerning Noah: *And he took of every clean beast and of every clean bird and offered burnt offerings upon the altar* (Gen. 8:20). The clause *and offered burnt offerings upon the altar* indicates that Noah used for burnt offerings only such beasts and fowl as were ritually proper for such a purpose, for if Scripture had merely said "and offered them upon the altar," it would have been sufficient; nevertheless it took pains to make the word

ing precise, by saying *and offered burnt offerings,* to teach us that Noah employed as burnt offerings only that which was ritually suitable.

2. Now we do not find that any birds were used for burnt offerings save turtledoves and pigeons, as it is written: *And if the burnt sacrifice for his offering be of fowls, let him bring his offering of turtledoves or of young pigeons* (Lev. 1:14). The juxtaposition of the words *of every clean bird* and *he offered burnt offerings* thus proves that the only clean birds are turtledoves and pigeons.

SABBATH

1. Carrying a burden, which is forbidden on the Sabbath, signifies only the act of carrying upon one's shoulder, since it is written: *they carried upon their shoulders* (Num. 7:9).

2. [It is forbidden to light fire in Jewish homes on the Sabbath or to permit fire kindled before the arrival of the Sabbath to continue burning into the Sabbath, as it is written: *Ye shall not kindle fire in all your dwellings upon the sabbath day* (Exod. 35:3).

3. One might perhaps say that it is only the kindling of fire on the Sabbath which is forbidden, and that if the fire had been kindled on the preceding weekday it is to be considered lawful to let it remain over the Sabbath. Now the Merciful One has written here: *Ye shall not kindle fire,* and elsewhere: *thou shalt not perform any work* (Exod. 20:10), and both prohibitions begin with the letter *taw.* In the case of labor, of which it is written: *thou shalt not perform any work,* it is evident that even if the work was begun on a weekday, before the arrival of the Sabbath, it is necessary to desist from it with the arrival of the Sabbath. The same rule must therefore apply also to the kindling of fire, of which it is written: *Ye shall not kindle,* meaning that even if the fire has been kindled on a weekday, prior to the arrival of the Sabbath, it must be extinguished.

4. In the case of work, just as one is forbidden to perform it himself, so also is he forbidden to have others perform it for him. [So, too, in the case of fire, one is forbidden to make others kindle it for him on the Sabbath, just as one is forbidden to kindle it himself.] Thus it is clear that we are forbidden to leave either a lamp or any other light burning on the Sabbath in any Jewish home.

E.

In 1700 Israel of Moldavia, better known as Baal Shem Tov (Besht) was born. One could hardly imagine a more humble or less auspicious beginning for a great religious leader, for Israel was poor, uneducated, and seemingly ill-prepared to lead the people of the Law. Nevertheless, from the faith of this obscure lime digger burst forth the Hasidic movement which was to reshape the life of Jewry in Central Europe in the eighteenth and nineteenth centuries and still has not spent its force.

Many stories are told about the Besht. Here are three taken from a famous collection entitled *In Praise of the Baal Shem Tov.*

The Birth of the Besht

While he was on his journey, Elijah the Prophet revealed himself to him and said: "Because of the merit of your behavior a son will be born to you who will bring light to Israel, and in him this saying will be fulfilled: *Israel in whom I will be glorified.*"

He came home and with God's help he found his wife still alive. The Besht was born to them in their old age, when both of them were close to a hundred. (The Besht said that it had been impossible for his father to draw his soul from heaven until he had lost his sexual desire.)

The boy grew up and was weaned. The time came for his father to die, and he took his son in his arms and he said, "I see that you will light my candle, and I will not enjoy the pleasure of raising you. My beloved son, remember this all your days: God is with you. Do not fear anything." (In the name of *Admor,* I heard that it is natural for a son and a father to be closely bound, for as our sages, God bless their memory, have said: "The talk of the child in the market place is either that of his father or of his mother." How much closer then are ties between parents and children who are born to them in their old age. For example, Jacob loved Joseph because he was born to him in his old age, and the ties between them were very great, as it is said in the holy Zohar. And it was true here. Although the Besht was a small child, because of the intensity and sincerity of the tie, the words were fixed in his heart.)

The Besht's Education and Youth

After the death of his father the child grew up. Because the people of the town revered the memory of his father, they favored the child and sent him to study with a melamed. And he succeeded in his studies. But it was his way to study for a few days and then to run away from school. They would search for him and find him sitting alone in the forest. They would attribute this to his being an orphan. There was no one to look after him and he was a footloose child. Though they

brought him again and again to the melamed, he would run
away to the forest to be in solitude. In the course of time they
gave up in despair and no longer returned him to the melamed. He did not grow up in the accustomed way.

He hired himself out as the melamed's assistant, to take
the children to school and to the synagogue, to teach them to
say in a pleasant voice, "Amen, let His great name be blessed
forever and to all eternity, kedushah, and amen." This was
his work — holy work with school children whose conversa-
tions are without sin. While he walked with the children he
would sing with them enthusiastically in a pleasant voice
that could be heard far away. His prayers were elevated
higher and higher, and there was great satisfaction above, as
there was with the songs that the Levites had sung in the
Temple. And it was time of rejoicing in heaven.

And Satan came also among them. Since Satan understood
what must come to pass, he was afraid that the time was approaching when he would disappear from the earth. He
transformed himself into a sorcerer. Once while the Besht
was walking with the children, singing enthusiastically with
pleasure, the sorcerer transformed himself into a beast, a
werewolf. He attacked and frightened them, and they ran
away. Some of them became sick, and, heaven help us, could
not continue their studies.

Afterwards, the Besht recalled the words of his father, God
bless his memory, not to fear anything since God is with him.
He took strength in the Lord, his God, and went to the
householders of the community, the fathers of the children,
and urged them to return the children to his care. He would
fight with the beast and kill it in the name of God.

"Should school children go idle when idleness is a great
sin?" They were convinced by his words. He took a good
sturdy club with him. While he walked with the children,
singing pleasantly, chanting with joy, this beast attacked
them. He ran toward it, hit it on its forehead, and killed it.
The next morning the corpse of the gentile sorcerer was
found lying on the ground.

After that the Besht became the watchman of the beth-
hamidrash. This was his way: while all the people of the
house of study were awake, he slept; and while they slept, he
was awake, doing his pure works of study and prayer until
the time came when people would awaken. Then he would go
back to sleep. They thought that he slept from the beginning
until the end of the night.

The Besht Reveals Himself

After that our master and Rabbi, Rabbi Gershon, rented a

place for the Besht in a certain village where he would be able to earn a living. And there he achieved perfection. He built a house of seclusion in the forest. He prayed and studied there all day and all night every day of the week, and he returned home only on the Sabbath. He also kept there white garments for the Sabbath. He also had a bathhouse and a mikveh. His wife was occupied with earning a living, and God blessed the deeds of her hand and she was successful. They were hospitable to guests: they gave them food and drink with great respect. When a guest came she sent for the Besht and he returned and served him. The guest never knew about the Besht.

It was the Besht's custom when he came to the city for Rosh Hashanah to remain there for the entire month. Once during the intermediate days of Sukkoth, our master and rabbi, Rabbi Gershon, noticed that he was not putting on tefillin. It was his custom to pray by the eastern wall of the synagogue. And he asked him: "Why don't you put on tefillin today?"

He answered: "I saw in the *Taich** books that he who puts on tefillin during the intermediate days is sentenced to death."**

The rabbi became very angry that the Besht followed the customs that are written in the books from Germany. There was no telling what the result would be. He went with him to the rabbi of the community so that the rabbi would admonish him. They considered the Besht to be a pious man, but as the saying goes, "an uncultured person is not sin-fearing."

The rabbi was a very righteous man. When they came to the rabbi's house, Rabbi Gershon kissed the mezuzah, but the Besht put his hand on the mezuzah without kissing it, and our master and rabbi, Rabbi Gershon, became angry with him over this as well.

When they entered the rabbi's house the Besht put aside his mask and the rabbi saw a great light. He rose up before the Besht. Then the Besht resumed the mask and the rabbi

---

*"Deutsch," old Yiddish, the language in which most popular books of exempla were written.

**The Hasidim, following the Kabbalah and in opposition to the custom which prevail among the Jewry of Galicia, did not put on tefillin during the intermediate days of holidays. For a discussion of the dispute concerning this problem see Aaron Wertheim, *Laws and Customs of Chassidism,* Hebrew (Jerusalem, 1960), pp. 79-81.

sat down. And this happened several times. The rabbi was very frightened since he did not know who he was. Sometimes he seemed to be a holy person and at other times he seemed to be a common man. But when our master and rabbi, Rabbi Gershon, complained to him about the tefillin and the mezuzah, the rabbi took the Besht aside privately and said to him: "I command you to reveal the truth to me." And the Besht was forced to reveal himself to him. But the Besht commanded him in turn not to reveal anything that had transpired.

When they came out the rabbi said to our master and rabbi, Rabbi Gershon: "I taught him a lesson, but I think he would not knowingly commit a fault against our customs. He has acted in innocence." Then the rabbi examined the mezuzah and they discovered that it had a defect.

F.

No movement has so changed Judaism in the twentieth century as has Zionism and Zionism has had no greater spokesman than Theodore Herzl. One of his most influential pamphlets was called *The Jewish State*. In the introduction to that work Herzl expresses very clearly his reasons for being a Zionist and his concrete plans for a Jewish homeland.

Chapter I — Introduction

It is astonishing how little insight into the science of economics many of the men who move in the midst of active life possess. Hence it is that even Jews faithfully repeat the cry of the Anti-Semites: "We depend for sustenance on the nations who are our hosts, and if we had no hosts to support us we should die of starvation." This is a point that shows how unjust accusations may weaken our self-knowledge. But what are the true grounds for this statement concerning the nations that act as "hosts"? Where it is not based on limited physiocratic views it is founded on the childish error that commodities pass from hand to hand in continuous rotation. We need not wake from long slumber, like Rip van Winkle, to realize that the world is considerably altered by the production of new commodities. The technical progress made during this wonderful era enables even a man of most limited intelligence to note with his short-sighted eyes the appearance of new commodities all around him. The spirit of enterprise has created them.

Labor without enterprise is the stationary labor of ancient days; and typical of it is the work of the husbandman, who stands now just where his progenitors stood a thousand years ago. All our material welfare has been brought about by men of enterprise. I feel almost ashamed of writing down so trite a remark. Even if we were a nation of entrepreneurs — such as absurdly exaggerated accounts make us out to be — we should not require another nation to live on. We do not depend on the circulation of old commodities, because we produce new ones.

The world possesses slaves of extraordinary capacity for work, whose appearance has been fatal to the production of handmade goods: these slaves are the machines. It is true that workmen are required to set machinery in motion; but for this we have men in plenty, in super-abundance. Only those who are ignorant of the conditions of Jews in many countries of Eastern Europe would venture to assert that Jews are either unfit or unwilling to perform manual labor.

But I do not wish to take up the cudgels for the Jews in this pamphlet. It would be useless. Everything rational and everything sentimental that can possibly be said in their defence has been said already. If one's hearers are incapable of comprehending them, one is a preacher in a desert. And if one's hearers are broad and high-minded enough to have grasped them already, then the sermon is superfluous. I believe in the ascent of man to higher and yet higher grades of civilization; but I consider this ascent to be desperately slow. Were we to wait till average humanity had become as charitably inclined as was Lessing when he wrote "Nathan the Wise," we should wait beyond our day, beyond the days of our children, of our grandchildren, and of our great-grandchildren. But the world's spirit comes to our aid in another way.

This century has given the world a wonderful renaissance by means of its technical achievements; but at the same time its miraculous improvements have not been employed in the service of humanity. Distance has ceased to be an obstacle, yet we complain of insufficient space. Our great steamships carry us swiftly and surely over hitherto unvisited seas. Our railways carry us safely into a mountain-world hitherto tremblingly scaled on foot. Events occurring in countries undiscovered when Europe confined the Jews in Ghettos are known to us in the course of an hour. Hence the misery of the Jews is an anachronism — not because there was a period of enlightenment one hundred years ago, for that enlightenment reached in reality only the choicest spirits.

I believe that electric light was not invented for the purpose of illuminating the drawing-rooms of a few snobs, but rather for the purpose of throwing light on some of the dark problems of humanity. One of these problems, and not the least of them, is the Jewish question. In solving it we are working not only for ourselves, but also for many other overburdened and oppressed beings.

The Jewish question still exists. It would be foolish to deny it. It is a remnant of the Middle Ages, which civilized nations do not even yet seem able to shake off, try as they will. they certainly showed a generous desire to do so when they emancipated us. The Jewish question exists wherever Jews live in perceptible numbers. Where it does not exist, it is carried by Jews in the course of their migrations. We naturally move to those places where we are not persecuted, and there our presence produces persecution. This is the case in every country, and will remain so, even in those highly civilized — for instance, France — until Jewish question finds a solution on a political basis. The unfortunate Jews are now carrying the seeds of Anti-Semitism into England; they have already introduced it into America.

I believe that I understand Anti-Semitism, which is really a highly complex movement. I consider it from a Jewish standpoint, yet without fear or hatred. I believe that I can see what elements there are in it of vulgar sport, of common trade jealousy, of inherited prejudice, of religious intolerance, and also of pretended self-defence. I think the Jewish question is no more a social than a religious one, notwithstanding that it sometimes takes these and other forms. It is a national question, which can only be solved by making it a political world-question to be discussed and settled by the civilized nations of the world in council.

We are a people — one people.

We have honestly endeavored everywhere to merge ourselves in the social life of surrounding communities and to preserve the faith of our fathers. We are not permitted to do so. In vain are we loyal patriots, our loyalty in some places running to extremes; in vain do we make the same sacrifices of life and property as our fellow-citizens; in vain do we strive to increase the fame of our native land in science and art, or her wealth by trade and commerce. In countries where we have lived for centuries we are still cried down as strangers, and often by those whose ancestors were not yet domiciled in the land where Jews had already had experience of suffering. The majority may decide which are the strangers; for this, as indeed every point which arises in the relations between nations, is a question of might. I do not here surrender any portion of our prescriptive right, when I make this statement merely in my own name as an individual. In the world as it now is and for an indefinite period will probably remain, might precedes right. It is useless, therefore, for us to be loyal patriots, as were the Huguenots who were forced to emigrate. If we could only be left in peace . . .

But I think we shall not be left in peace.

Oppression and persecution cannot exterminate us. No nation on earth has survived such struggles and sufferings as we have gone through. Jew-baiting has merely stripped off our weaklings; the strong among us were invariably true to their race when persecution broke out against them. This attitude was most clearly apparent in the period immediately following the emancipation of the Jews. Those Jews who were advanced intellectually and materially entirely lost the feeling of belonging to their race. Wherever our political well-being has lasted for any length of time, we have assimilated with our surroundings. I think this is not discreditable. Hence, the statesman who would wish to see a Jewish strain in his nation would have to provide for the duration of our political well-being; and even a Bismarck could not do that.

For old prejudices against us still lie deep in the hearts of the people. He who would have proofs of this need only listen to the people where they speak with frankness and simplicity: proverb and fairy-tale are both Anti-Semitic. A nation is everywhere a great child, which can certainly be educated; but its education would, even in most favorable circumstances, occupy such a vast amount of time that we could, as already mentioned, remove our own difficulties by other means long before the process was accomplished.

Assimilation, by which I understood not only external conformity in dress, habits, customs, and language, but also identity of feeling and manner — assimilation of Jews could be effected only by intermarriage. But the need for mixed marriages would have to be felt by the majority; their mere recognition by law would certainly not suffice.

The Hungarian Liberals, who have just given legal sanction to mixed marriages, have made a remarkable mistake which one of the earliest cases clearly illustrates: a baptized Jew married a Jewess. At the same time the struggle to obtain the present form of marriage accentuated distinctions between Jews and Christians, thus hindering rather than aiding the fusion of races.

Those who really wished to see the Jews disappear through intermixture with other nations, can only hope to see it come about in one way. The Jews must previously acquire economic power sufficiently great to overcome the old social prejudice against them. The aristocracy may serve as an example of this, for in its ranks occur the proportionately largest numbers of mixed marriages. The Jewish families which regild the old nobility with their money become gradually absorbed. But what form would this phenomenon assume in the middle classes, where (the Jews being a bourgeois people) the Jewish question is mainly concentrated? A previous acquisition of power could be synonymous with that economic supremacy which Jews are already erroneously declared to possess. And if the power they now possess creates rage and indignation among the Anti-Semites, what outbreaks would such an increase of power create? Hence the first step towards absorption will never be taken, because this step would involve the subjection of the majority to a hitherto scorned minority, possessing neither military nor administrative power of its own. I think, therefore, that the absorption of Jews by means of their prosperity is unlikely to occur. In countries which now are Anti-Semitic my view will be approved. In others, where Jews now feel comfortable, it will probably be violently disputed by them. My happier co-religionists will not believe me till Jew-baiting teaches them the truth; for the longer Anti-Semitism lies in abeyance the more fiercely will it break out. The infiltration of immigrating Jews, attracted to a land by apparent security, and the ascent in the social scale of native Jews, combine powerfully to bring about a revolution. Nothing is plainer than this rational conclusion.

Because I have drawn this conclusion with complete indifference to everything but the quest of truth, I shall probably be contradicted and opposed by Jews who are in easy circumstances. Insofar as private interests alone are held by their anxious or timid possessors to be in danger, they can safely be ignored, for the concerns of the poor and oppressed are of greater importance than theirs. But I wish from the outset to prevent any misconception from arising, particularly the mistaken notion that my project, if realized, would in the least degree injure property now held by Jews. I shall therefore explain everything connected with rights of property very fully. Whereas, if my plan never becomes anything more than a piece of literature, things will merely remain as they are. It might more reasonably be objected that I am giving a handle to Anti-Semitism when I say we are a people — one people; that I am hindering the assimilation of Jews where it is about to be consummated, and endangering it where it is an accomplished fact, insofar as it is possible for a solitary writer to hinder or endanger anything.

This objection will be especially brought forward in France. It will probably also be made in other countries, but I shall answer only the French Jews beforehand, because these afford the most striking example of my point.

However much I may worship personality — powerful individual personality in statesmen, inventors, artists, philosophers, or leaders, as well as the collective personality of a historic group of human beings, which we call a nation — however much I may worship personality, I do not regret its disappearance. Whoever can, will, and must perish, let him perish. But the distinctive nationality of Jews neither can, will, nor must be destroyed. It cannot be destroyed, because external enemies consolidate it. It will not be destroyed; this is shown during two thousand years of appalling suffering. It must not be destroyed, and that, as a descendant of numberless Jews who refused to despair, I am trying once more to prove in this pamphlet. Whole branches of Judaism may wither and fall, but the trunk will remain.

Hence, if all or any of the French Jews protest against this scheme on account of their own "assimilation," my answer is simple: The whole thing does not concern them at all. They are Jewish Frenchmen, well and good! This is a private affair for the Jews alone.

The movement towards the organization of the State I am proposing would, of course, harm Jewish Frenchmen no more than it would harm the "assimilated" of other countries. It would, on the contrary, be distinctly to their advantage. For they would no longer be disturbed in their "chromatic function," as Darwin puts it, but would be able to assimilate in peace, because the present Anti-Semitism would have been stopped for ever. They would certainly be credited with being assimilated to the very depths of their souls, if they stayed where they were after the new Jewish State, with its superior institutions, had become a reality.

The "assimilated" would profit even more than Christian citizens by the departure of faithful Jews; for they would be rid of the disquieting, incalculable, and unavoidable rivalry of a Jewish proletariat, driven by poverty and political pressure from place to place, from land to land. This floating proletariat would become stationary. Many Christian citizens — whom we call Anti-Semites — can now offer determined resistance to the immigration of foreign Jews. Jewish citizens cannot do this, although it affects them far more directly; for on them they feel first of all the keen competition of individuals carrying on similar branches of industry, who, in addition, either introduce Anti-Semitism where it does not exist, or intensify it where it does. The "assimilated" give expression to this secret grievance in "philanthropic" undertakings. They organize emigration societies for wandering Jews. There is a reverse to the picture which would be comic, if it did not deal with human beings. For some of these charitable institutions are created not for, but against, persecuted Jews; they are created to despatch these poor creatures just as fast and far as possible. And thus, many an apparent friend of the Jews turns out, on careful inspection, to be nothing more than an Anti-Semite of Jewish origin, disguised as a philanthropist.

But the attempts at colonization made even by really benevolent men, interesting attempts though they were, have so far been unsuccessful. I do not think that this or that man took up the matter merely as an amusement, that they engaged in the emigration of poor Jews as one indulges in the racing of horses. The matter was too grave and tragic for such treatment. These attempts were interesting, in that they represented on a small scale the practical fore-runners of the idea of a Jewish State. They were even useful, for out of their mistakes may be gathered experience for carrying the idea out successfully on a larger scale. They have, of course, done harm also. The transportation of Anti-Semitism to new districts, which is the inevitable consequence of such artificial infiltration, seems to me to be the least of these evils. Far worse is the circumstance that unsatisfactory results tend to cast doubts on intelligent men. What is impractical or impossible to simple argument will remove this doubt from the minds of intelligent men. What is unpractical or impossible to accomplish on a small scale, need not necessarily be so on a larger one. A small enterprise may result in loss under the same conditions which would make a large one pay. A rivulet cannot even be navigated by boats, the river into which it flows carries stately iron vessels.

No human being is wealthy or powerful enough to transplant a nation from one habitation to another. An idea alone can achieve that and this idea of a State may have the requisite power to do so. The Jews have dreamt this kingly dream all through the long nights of their history. "Next year in Jerusalem" is our old phrase. It is now a question of showing that the dream can be converted into a living reality.

For this, many old, outgrown, confused and limited notions must first be entirely erased from the minds of men. Dull brains might, for instance, imagine that this exodus would be from civilized regions into the desert. That is not the case. It will be carried out in the midst of civilization. We shall not revert to a lower stage, we shall rise to a higher one. We shall not dwell in mud huts; we shall build new more beautiful and more modern houses, and possess them in safety. We shall not lose our acquired possessions; we shall realize them. We shall surrender our well earned rights only for better ones. We shall not sacrifice our beloved customs; we shall find them again. We shall not leave our old home before the new one is prepared for us. Those only will depart who are sure thereby to improve their position; those who are now desperate will go first, after them the poor; next the prosperous, and, last of all, the wealthy. Those who go in advance will raise themselves to a higher grade, equal to those whose representatives will shortly follow. [Thus the exodus will be at the same time an ascent of the class.]

The departure of the Jews will involve no economic disturbances, no crises, no persecutions; in fact, the countries they abandon will revive to a new period of prosperity. There will be an inner migration of Christian citizens into the positions evacuated by Jews. The outgoing current will be gradual, without any disturbance, and its initial movement will put an end to Anti-Semitism. The Jews will leave as honored friends, and if some of them return, they will receive the same favorable welcome and treatment at the hands of civilized nations as is accorded to all foreign visitors. Their exodus will have no resemblance to a flight, for it will be a well-regulated movement under control of public opinion. The movement will not only be inaugurated with absolute conformity to law, but it cannot even be carried out without the friendly cooperation of interested Governments, who would derive considerable benefits from it.

Security for the integrity of the idea and the vigor of its execution will be found in the creation of a body corporate, or corporation. This corporation will be called "The Society of Jews." In addition to it there will be a Jewish Company, an economically productive body.

An individual who attempted even to undertake this huge task alone would be either an impostor or a madman. The personal character of the members of the corporation will guarantee its integrity, and the adequate capital of the Company will prove its stability.

PART 5

JUDAISM AND THE WORLD

Much of Jewish life has been profoundly influenced by the attitudes of those non-Jewish peoples among whom Jews have lived. Included in this section are expressions of opinions held about Jews throughout their history. Although several of these excerpts are disquieting in the extreme, it is salutary to remind ourselves repeatedly about the strong strain of anti-Semitism which has characterized Western culture.

A.

Christianity began as a sect within Judaism and as such expressed from the outset ambivalent views toward those Jews who did not accept Jesus as the Messiah. From the many passages in the New Testament which mention Jews two have been chosen as especially significant for inclusion here.

1. In John 8:21-59 the Jews are confronted by the astounding claims of Jesus, i.e. that he existed before Abraham and has come to set them free.

> 21 Again he said to them, "I go away, and you will seek me and die in your sin; where I am going, you cannot come."[22] Then said the Jews, "Will he kill himself, since he says, 'Where I am going, you cannot come'?"[23] He said to them, "You are from below, I am from above; you are of this world,

I am not of this world.[24] I told you that you would die in your sins, for you will die in your sins unless you believe that I am he."[25] They said to him, "Who are you?" Jesus said to them, "Even what I have told you from the beginning.[26] I have much to say about you and much to judge; but he who sent me is true, and I declare to the world what I have heard from him."[27] They did not understand that he spoke to them of the Father.[28] So Jesus said, "When you have lifted up the Son of man, then you will know that I am he, and that I do nothing on my own authority but speak thus as the Father taught me.[29] And he who sent me is with me; he has not left me alone, for I always do what is pleasing to him."[30] As he spoke thus, many believed in him.

31 Jesus then said to the Jews who had believed in him, "If you continue in my word, you are truly my disciples,[32] and you will know the truth, and the truth will make you free."[33] They answered him, "We are descendants of Abraham, and have never been in bondage to any one. How is it that you say, 'You will be made free'?"

34 Jesus answered them, "Truly, truly, I say to you, every one who commits sin is a slave to sin.[35] The slave does not continue in the house for ever; the son continues for ever.[36] So if the Son makes you free, you will be free indeed.[37] I know that you are descendants of Abraham; yet you seek to kill me, because my word finds no place in you.[38] I speak of what I have seen with my Father, and you do what you have heard from your father."

39 They answered him, "Abraham is our father." Jesus said to them, "If you were Abraham's children, you would do what Abraham did,[40] but now you seek to kill me, a man who has told you the truth which I heard from God; this is not what Abraham did.[41] You do what your father did." They said to him, "We were not born of fornication; we have one Father, even God."[42] Jesus said to them, "If God were your Father, you would love me, for I proceeded and came forth from God; I came not of my own accord, but he sent me.[43] Why do you not understand what I say? It is because you cannot bear to hear my word.[44] You are of your father the devil, and your will is to do your father's desires. He was a murderer from the beginning, and has nothing to do with the truth, because there is no truth in him. When he lies, he speaks according to his own nature, for he is a liar and the father of lies.

But, because I tell the truth, you do not believe me.[46] Which of you convicts me of sin? If I tell the truth, why do you not believe me?[47] He who is of God hears the words of God; the reason why you do not hear them is that you are not of God."

48 The Jews answered him, "Are we not right in saying that you are a Samaritan and have a demon?"[49] Jesus answered, "I have not a demon; but I honor my Father, and you dishonor me.[50] Yet I do not seek my own glory; there is One who seeks it and he will be the judge.[51] Truly, truly, I say to you, if any one keeps my word, he will never see death."[52] The Jews said to him, "Now we know that you have a demon. Abraham died, as did the prophets; and you say, 'If any one keeps my word, he will never taste death.'[53] Are you greater than our father Abraham, who died? And the prophets died! Who do you claim to be?"[54] Jesus answered, "If I glorify myself, my glory is nothing; it is my Father who glorifies me, of whom you say that he is your God.[55] But you have not known him; I know him. If I said, I do not know him, I should be a liar like you; but I do know him and I keep his word.[56] Your father Abraham rejoiced that he was to see my day; he saw it and was glad."[57] The Jews then said to him, "You are not yet fifty years old, and have you seen Abraham?"[58] Jesus said to them, "Truly, truly, I say to you, before Abraham was, I am."[59] So they took up stones to throw at him; but Jesus hid himself, and went out of the temple.

2. Romans 9:1-13, 10:1-21, and 11:1-32 contains Paul's classic statement about his own people, the Jews. Much of the later paradoxicality seen in Christian attitudes toward Jews is found here in this passage.

ROMANS 9

I am speaking the truth in Christ, I am not lying; my conscience bears me witness in the Holy Spirit,[2] that I have great sorrow and unceasing anguish in my heart.[3] For I could wish that I myself were accursed and cut off from Christ for the sake of my brethren, my kinsmen by race.[4] They are Israelites, and to them belong the sonship, the glory, the covenants, the giving of the law, the worship, and the promises:[5] to them belong the patriarchs, and of their race, according to the flesh, is the Christ, God who is over all be blessed for ever." Amen.

6 But it is not as though the word of God had failed. For not all who are descended from Israel belong to Israel,[7] and not all are children of Abraham because they are his descendants; but "Through Isaac shall your descendants be named."[8] This means that it is not the children of the flesh who are the children of God, but the children of the promise are reckoned as descendants.[9] For this is what the promise

said, "About this time I will return and Sarah shall have a son."[10] And not only so, but also when Rebecca had conceived children by one man, our forefather Isaac,[11] though they were not yet born and had done nothing either good or bad, in order that God's purpose of election might continue, not because of works but because of his call,[12] she was told, "The elder will serve the younger."[13] As it is written, "Jacob I loved, but Esau I hated."

ROMANS 10

Brethren, my heart's desire and prayer to God for them is that they may be saved.[2] I bear them witness that they have a zeal for God, but it is not enlightened.[3] For, being ignorant of the righteousness that comes from God, and seeking to establish their own, they did not submit to God's righteousness.[4]For Christ is the end of the law, that every one who has faith may be justified.

5 Moses writes that the man who practices the righteousness which is based on the law shall live by it.[6]But the righteousness based on faith says, Do not say in your heart, "Who will ascend into heaven?" (that is, to bring Christ down)[7]or "Who will descend into the abyss?" (that is, to bring Christ up from the dead).[8]But what does it say? The word is near you, on your lips and in your heart (that is, the word of faith which we preach);[9]because, if you confess with your lips that Jesus is Lord and believe in your heart that God raised him from the dead, you will be saved.[10]For man believes with his heart and so is justified, and he confesses with his lips and so is saved.[11]The scripture says, "No one who believes in him will be put to shame."[12]For there is no distinction between Jew and Greek; the same Lord is Lord of all and bestows his riches upon all who call upon him.[13]For, "every one who calls upon the name of the Lord will be saved."

14 But how are men to call upon him in whom they have not believed? And how are they to believe in him of whom they have never heard? And how are they to hear without a preacher?[15]And how can men preach unless they are sent? As it is written, "How beautiful are the feet of those who preach good news!"[16]But they have not all heeded the gospel; for Isaiah says, "Lord, who has believed what he has heard from us?"[17]So faith comes from what is heard, and what is heard comes by the preaching of Christ.

18 But I ask, have they not heard? Indeed they have; for
"Their voice has gone out to all the earth,
and their words to the ends of the world"
19 Again I ask, did Israel not understand? First Moses says,

"I will make you jealous of those who are not a nation;
with a foolish nation I will make you angry."
20 Then Isaiah is so bold as to say,
"I have been found by those who did not seek me;
I have shown myself to those who did not ask for me."
21 But of Israel he says, "All day long I have held out my
hands to a disobedient and contrary people."

ROMANS 11

I ask, then, has God rejected his people? By no means! I
myself am an Israelite, a descendant of Abraham, a member
of the tribe of Benjamin.[2]God has not rejected his people
whom he foreknew. Do you not know what the scripture says
of Elijah, how he pleads with God against Israel?[3]"Lord,
they have killed thy prophets, they have demolished the
altars, and I alone am left, and they seek my life."[4]But what
is God's reply to him? "I have kept for myself seven thousand men who have not bowed the knee to Baal."[5]So too at
the present time there is a remnant, chosen by grace.[6]But if it
is by grace, it is no longer on the basis of works; otherwise
grace would no longer be grace.

7 What then? Israel failed to obtain what it sought. The
elect obtained it, but the rest were hardened,[8]as it is written,
"God gave them a spirit of stupor,
eyes that should not see and ears that should not hear,
down to this very day."
[9]And David says,
"Let their feast become a snare and a trap,
a pitfall and a retribution for them;
[10]let their eyes be darkened so that they cannot see,
and bend their backs for ever."

11 So I ask, have they stumbled so as to fall? By no means!
But through their trespass salvation has come to the Gentiles, so as to make Israel jealous.[12]Now if their trespass
means riches for the world, and if their failure means riches
for the Gentiles, how much more will their full inclusion
mean!

13 Now I am speaking to you Gentiles. Inasmuch then as I
am an apostle to the Gentiles, I magnify my ministry[14]in
order to make my fellow Jews jealous, and thus save some of
them.[15]For if their rejection means the reconciliation of the
world, what will their acceptance mean but life from the
dead?[16]If the dough offered as first fruits is holy, so is the
whole lump; and if the root is holy, so are the branches.

17 But if some of the branches were broken off, and you, a wild olive shoot, were grafted in their place to share the richness of the olive tree,[18]do not boast over the branches. If you do boast, remember it is not you that support the root, but the root that supports you.[19]You will say, "Branches were broken off so that I might be grafted in."[20]That is true. they were broken off because of their unbelief, but you stand fast only through faith. So do not become proud, but stand in awe.[21]For if God did not spare the natural branches, neither will he spare you.[22]Note then the kindness and the severity of God: severity toward those who have fallen, but God's kindness to you, provided you continue in his kindness; otherwise you too will be cut off.[23]And even the others, if they do not persist in their unbelief, will be grafted in, for God has the power to graft them in again.[24]For if you have been cut from what is by nature a wild olive tree, and grafted, contary to nature, into a cultivated olive tree, how much more will these natural branches be grafted back into their own olive tree.

25 Lest you be wise in your own conceits, I want you to understand this mystery, brethren: a hardening has come upon part of Israel, until the full number of Gentiles come in,[26]and so all Israel will be saved; as it is written.

"The Deliverer will come from Zion,
   he will banish ungodliness from Jacob";
[27]"and this will be my covenant with them
   when I take away their sins."
[28]As regards the gospel they are enemies of God, for your sake; but as regards election they are beloved for the sake of their forefathers.[29]For the gifts and the call of God are irrevocable.[30] Just as you were once disobedient to God but now have received mercy because of their disobedience,[31]so they have now been disobedient in order that by the mercy shown to you they also may receive mercy.[32]For God has consigned all men to disobedience, that he may have mercy upon all.

B.

Although the Roman empire was, on the whole, characterized by a broadly tolerant attitude toward all religions, the rise of Christianity to preeminence in the State brought more and more restrictions for the Jews. The Emperor Justinian (527-565) went farther than any of his predecessors when, in

Novella 146, he sought to control what went on within the synagogues of Judaism.

NOVELLA 146 OF JUSTINIAN

8.11.553. Nov. 146. Justinian to Areobindas, P.P.

A Permission granted to the Hebrews to read the Sacred Scriptures according to Tradition, in Greek, Latin or any other Language, and an Order to expel from their community those who do not believe in the Judgment, the Resurrection, and the Creation of Angels.

Preface. Necessity dictates that when the Hebrews listen to their sacred texts they should not confine themselves to the meaning of the letter, but should also devote their attention to those sacred prophecies which are hidden from them, and which announce the mighty Lord and Saviour Jesus Christ. And though, by surrendering themselves to senseless interpretations, they still err from the true doctrine, yet, learning that they disagree among themselves, we have not permitted this disagreement to continue without a ruling on our part. From their own complaints which have been brought to us, we have understood that some only speak Hebrew, and wish to use it for the sacred books, and others think that a Greek translation should be added, and that they have been disputing about this for a long time. Being apprised of the matter at issue, we give judgment in favour of those who wish to use Greek also for the reading of the sacred scriptures, or any other tongue which in any district allows the hearers better to understand the text.

Ch. I. We therefore sanction that, wherever there is a Hebrew congregation, those who wish it may, in their synagogues, read the sacred books to those who are present in Greek, or even Latin, or any other tongue. For the language changes in different places, and the reading changes with it, so that all present may understand, and live and act according to what they hear. Thus there shall be no opportunity for their interpreters, who make use only of the Hebrew, to corrupt it in any way they like, since the ignorance of the public conceals their depravity. We make this proviso that those who use Greek shall use the text of the seventy interpreters, which is the most accurate translation, and the one most highly approved, since it happened that the translators, divided into two groups, and working in different places, all produced exactly the same text.

i. Moreover who can fail to admire those men, who, writing long before the saving revelation of our mighty Lord and Saviour Jesus Christ, yet as though they saw its coming with their eyes completed the translation of the sacred books as if the prophetic grace was illuminating them. This therefore they shall primarily use, but that we may not seem to be forbidding all other texts we allow the use of that of Aquila, though he was not of their people, and his translation differs not slightly from that of the Septuagint.

ii. But the Mishnah, or as they call it the second tradition, we prohibit entirely. For it is not part of the sacred books, nor is it handed down by divine inspiration through the prophets, but the handiwork of man, speaking only of earthly things, and having nothing of the divine in it. But let them read the holy words themselves, rejecting the commentaries, and not concealing what is said in the sacred writings, and disregarding the vain writings which do not form a part of them, which have been devised by them themselves for the destruction of the simple. By these instructions we ensure that no one shall be penalised or prohibited who reads the Greek or any other language. And their elders, Archiphericitae and presbyters, and those called magistrates, shall not by any machinations or anathemas have power to refuse this right, unless by chance they wish to suffer corporal punishment and the confiscation of their goods, before they yield to our will and to the commands which are better and dearer to God which we enjoin.

Ch. II. If any among them seek to introduce impious vanities, denying the resurrection or the judgment, or the work of God, or that angels are part of creation, we require them everywhere to be expelled forthwith; that no backslider raise his impious voice to contradict the evident purpose of God. Those who utter such sentiments shall be put to death, and thereby the Jewish people shall be purged of the errors which they introduced.

Ch. III. We pray that when they hear the reading of the books in one or the other language, they may guard themselves against the depravity of the interpreters, and, not clinging to the literal words, come to the point of the matter, and perceive their diviner meaning, so that they may start afresh to learn the better way, and may cease to stray vainly, and to err in that which is most essential, we mean hope in God. For this reason we have opened the door for the reading of the scriptures in every language, that all may henceforth receive its teaching, and become fitter for learning better things. For it is acknowledged that he, who is nourished upon the sacred scriptures and has little need of direction, is much readier to discern the truth, and to choose the better path, than he who understands nothing of them, but clings to the name of his faith alone, and is held by it as by a sacred anchor, and believes that what can be called heresy in its purest form is divine teaching.

Epilogue. This is our sacred will and pleasure, and your Excellency and your present colleague and your staff shall see that it is carried out, and shall not allow the Hebrews to contravene it. Those who resist it or try to put any obstruction in its way, shall first suffer corporal punishment, and then be compelled to live in exile, forfeiting also their property, that they flaunt not their impudence against God and the empire. You shall also circulate our law to the provincial governors, that they learning its contents may enforce it in their several cities, knowing that it is to be strictly carried out under pain of our displeasure.

C.

In many ways the Quran, a series of revelations delivered to Mohammed by the angel Gabriel, has circumscribed and defined Jewish life in North Africa and Asia since the seventh century A.D. Here are a few of the major references to Jews in the Quran.

Surah II, 61-66

61. And when ye said: O Moses! We are weary of one kind of food; so call upon thy Lord for us that he bring forth for us of that which the earth groweth — of its herbs and its cucumbers and its corn and its lentils and its onions. He said: Would ye exchange that which is higher for that which is lower? Go down to settled country, thus ye shall get that which ye demand. And humiliation and wretchedness were stamped upon them and they were visited with wrath from Allah. That was because they disbelieved in Allah's revelations and slew the prophets wrongfully. That was for their disobedience and transgression.

62. Lo! those who believe (in that which is revealed unto thee, Muhammad), and those who are Jews, and Christians, and Sabaeans — whoever believeth in Allah and the Last

Day and doeth right — surely their reward is with their Lord, and there shall no fear come upon them neither shall they grieve.

63. And (remember, O children of Israel) when We made a covenant with you and caused the Mount to tower above you, (saying): Hold fast that which We have given you, and remember that which is therein, that ye may ward off (evil).

64. Then, even after that, ye turned away, and if it had not been for the grace of Allah and His mercy ye had been among the losers.

65. And ye know of those of you who broke the Sabbath, how We said unto them: Be ye apes, despised and hated!

66. And We made it an example to their own and to succeeding generations, and an admonition to the Godfearing.

Surah IV, 46-47

46. Some of those who are Jews change words from their context and say: "We hear and disobey; hear thou as one who heareth not" and "Listen to us"[1] distorting with their tongues and slandering religion. If they had said:."We hear and we obey; hear thou, and look at us" it had been better for them, and more upright. But Allah hath cursed them for their disbelief, so they believe not, save a few.

47. O ye unto whom the Scripture hath been given! Believe in what We have revealed confirming that which ye possess, before We destroy countenances so as to confound them, or curse them as We cursed the Sabbathbreakers (of old time). The commandment of Allah is always executed.

Surah V, 41-48

41. O Messenger! Let not them grieve thee who vie one with another in the race to disbelief, of such as say with their mouths: "We believe," but their hearts believe not, and of the Jews: listeners for the sake of falsehood, listeners on behalf of other folk who come not unto thee, changing words from their context and saying: If this be given unto you, receive it, but if this be not given unto you, then beware! He whom Allah doometh unto sin, thou (by thine efforts) wilt avail him naught against Allah. Those are they for whom the will of Allah is that He cleanse not their hearts. Theirs in the world will be ignominy, and the Hereafter an awful doom;

42. Listeners for the sake of falsehood! Greedy for illicit gain! If then they have recourse unto thee (Muhammad) judge between them or disclaim jurisdiction. If thou disclaimest jurisdiction, then they cannot harm thee at all. But if thou judgest, judge between them with equity. Lo! Allah lovest the equitable.

43. How come they unto thee for judgement when they have the Torah, wherein Allah hath delivered judgement (for them)? Yet even after that they turn away. Such (folk) are not believers.

44. Lo! We did reveal the Torah, wherein is guidance and a light, by which the Prophets who surrendered (unto Allah) judged the Jews, and the rabbis and the priests (judged) by such of Allah's Scripture as they were bidden to observe, and thereunto were they witnesses. So fear not mankind, but fear Me. And barter not My revelations for a little gain. Whoso judgeth not by that which Allah hath revealed: such are disbelievers.

45. And We prescribed for them therein: The life for the life, and the eye for the eye, and the nose for the nose, and the ear for the ear, and the tooth for the tooth, and for wounds retaliation. But whoso forgoeth it (in the way of charity) it shall be expiation for him. Whoso judgeth not by that which Allah hath revealed: such are wrong-doers.

46. And We caused Jesus, son of Mary, to follow in their footsteps, confirming that which was (revealed) before him, and We bestowed on him the Gospel wherein is guidance and a light, confirming that which was (revealed) before it in the Torah — a guidance and an admonition unto those who ward off (evil).

47. Let the People of the Gospel judge by that which Allah hath revealed therein. Whoso judgeth not by that which Allah hath revealed; such are evil-livers.

48. And unto thee have We revealed the Scripture with the truth, confirming whatever Scripture was before it, and a watcher over it. So judge between them by that which Allah hath revealed, and follow not their desires away from the truth which hath come unto thee. For each We have appointed a divine law and a traced-out way. Had Allah willed He could have made you one community. But that He may try you by that which He hath given you (He hath made you as ye are). So vie one with another in good works. Unto Allah ye will all return, and He will then inform you of that wherein ye differ.

Surah LXII, 5-8

5. The likeness of those who are entrusted with the Law of Moses, yet apply it not, is as the likeness of the ass carrying books. Wretched is the likeness of folk who deny the revelations of Allah. And Allah guideth not wrongdoing folk.

6. Say (O Muhammad): O ye who are Jews! If ye claim that ye are favoured of Allah apart from (all) mankind, then long for death if ye are truthful.

7. But they will never long for it because of all that their own hands have sent before, and Allah is Aware of evil-doers.

8. Say (unto them, O Muhammad): Lo! the death from which ye shrink will surely meet you, and afterward ye will be returned unto the Knower of the invisible and the visible, and He will tell you what ye used to do.

D.

Although there had been many statements made by the Church concerning Jewish-Christian relations, the position taken by the Christian community at the Fourth Lateran Council in 1215 became definitive for the later Middle Ages. Here are the major provisions set forth by that Council:

November 11, 1215

§67. — The more the Christian religion refrains from the exaction of usury, the more does the Jewish perfidy become used to this practice, so that in a short time the Jews exhaust the financial strength of the Christians. Therefore, in our desire to protect the Christians in this matter, that they should not be excessively oppressed by the Jews, we order by a decree of this Synod, that when in the future a Jew, under any pretext, extort heavy and immoderate usury from a Christian, all relationship with Christians shall therefore be denied him until he shall have made sufficient amends for his exorbitant exactions. The Christians, moreover, if need be, shall be compelled by ecclesiastical punishment without appeal, to abstain from such commerce. We also impose this upon the princes, not to be aroused against the Christians because of this, but rather to try to keep the Jews from this practice.

We decree that by means of the same punishment the Jews shall be compelled to offer satisfaction to the churches for the tithes and offerings due them and which these churches were wont to receive from the houses and possessions of Christians before these properties had under some title or other passed into Jewish hands. Thus shall this property be conserved to the Church without any loss.

X.   IV Lateran Council
                                               November 11, 1215

§68. — Whereas in certain provinces of the Church the difference in their clothes sets the Jews and Saracens apart from the Christians, in certain other lands there has arisen such confusion that no differences are noticeable. Thus it sometimes happens that by mistake Christians have intercourse with Jewish or Saracen women, and Jews or Saracens with Christian women. Therefore, lest these people, under the cover of an error, find an excuse for the grave sin of such intercourse, we decree that these people (Jews and Saracens) of either sex, and in all Christian lands, and at all times, shall easily be distinguishable from the rest of the populations by the quality of their clothes; especially since such legislation is imposed upon them also by Moses.

Moreover, they shall not walk out in public on the Days of Lamentation or the Sunday of Easter; for as we have heard, certain ones among them do not blush to go out on such days more than usually ornamented, and do not fear to poke fun at the Christians who display signs of grief at the memory of the most holy Passion.

We most especially forbid anyone to dare to break forth into insults against the Redeemer. Since we cannot shut our eyes to insults heaped upon Him who washed away our sins, we decree that such presumptuous persons shall be duly restrained by fitting punishment meted out by the secular rulers, so that none dare blaspheme against Him Who was crucified for our sake.

§69. — Since it is quite absurd that any who blaspheme against Christ should have power over Christians, we, on account of the boldness of the transgressors, renew what the Council of Toledo[1] already has legislated with regard to this. We forbid that Jews be given preferment in public office since this offers them the pretext to vent their wrath against the Christians. Should anyone entrust them with an office of this kind, he shall be restrained from so doing by the Council of the Province (which we order to be held every year). Due warning having been given him, he shall be restrained (therefrom) by such means as the Council deems fit. These officials themselves, moreover, shall suffer the denial of all intercourse, commercial and otherwise, with Christians until they shall have turned for the use of poor Christians in accordance with the dispositions of the bishop of the diocese, all that they may have earned from the Christians through the office they had undertaken. Disgraced, they shall lose the office which they had so irreverently assumed. This shall apply also to pagans.

---

[1] III Council of Toledo, 589; Hefele, III, 48 ff.

XII.   IV Lateran Council
                                              November 11, 1215

‡70. — We have heard that certain ones who had voluntarily approached the baptismal font, have not completely driven out the old self in order the more perfectly to bring in the new. Since they retain remnants of their former faith, they tarnish the beauty of the Christian Religion by such a mixture. For it is written "Cursed by he who walks the earth in two ways," and even in wearing a garment one may not mix linen and wool. We decree, therefore, that such people shall in every possible manner be restrained by the prelates of the churches, from observing their old rites, so that those whom their free will brought to the Christian religion shall be held to its observance by compulsion, that they may be saved. For there is less evil in not recognizing the way of the Lord than in backsliding after having recognized it.

November 11, 1215

. . . We order that the secular powers shall compel the Jews to remit their usury, and until the Jews have done so they shall be denied commercial intercourse with Christians, the latter being forced to do so under pain of excommunication. Moreoever, for those who are unable at the present time to pay their debts to the Jews, the princes shall procure the needed moratorium, so that, until their death or return be definitely established, they shall not suffer any inconvenience of accruing interest. The Jews shall be compelled to count into the capital, the income from the gage, minus the cost of maintenance, which it will yield in the meantime . . .

E.

Martin Luther (1483-1546) began work on "That Jesus Christ was Born a Jew" in 1512, but it is unclear precisely when it was published. It is noteworthy that although Luther suggests a much more understanding attitude toward the Jews than many of his contemporaries held, his ultimate aim is to convert them. It is also significant — and sad — that later in life Luther was to produce a pamphlet called "On Jews and Their Lies" which was as scurriously anti-Semitic as anything written before or since.

THAT JESUS CHRIST
WAS BORN A JEW

A new lie about me is being circulated. I am supposed to
have preached and written that Mary, the mother of God,
was not a virgin either before or after the birth of Christ, but
that she conceived Christ through Joseph, and had more
children after that. Above and beyond all this, I am supposed
to have preached a new heresy, namely, that Christ was
[through Joseph] the seed of Abraham. How these lies tickle
my good friends, the papists! Indeed, because they condemn
the gospel it serves them right that they should have to
satisfy and feed their heart's delight and joy with lies. I
would venture to wager my neck that none of those very liars
who allege such great things in honor of the mother of God
believes in his heart a single one of these articles. Yet with
their lies they pretend that they are greatly concerned about
the Christian faith.

But after all, it is such a poor miserable lie that I despise it
and would rather not reply to it. In these past three years I
have grown quite accustomed to hearing lies, even from our
nearest neighbors. And they in turn have grown accustomed
to the noble virtue of neither blushing nor feeling ashamed
when they are publicly convicted of lying. They let
themselves be chided as liars, yet continue their lying. Still
they are the best Christians, striving with all that they have
and are to devour the Turk and to extirpate all heresy.

Since for the sake of others, however, I am compelled to
answer these lies, I thought I would also write something
useful in addition, so that I do not vainly steal the reader's
time with such dirty rotten business. Therefore, I will cite
from Scripture the reasons that move me to believe that
Christ was a Jew born of a virgin, that I might perhaps also
win some Jews to the Christian faith. Our fools, the popes,
bishops, sophists, and monks — the crude asses' heads —
have hitherto so treated the Jews that anyone who wished to
be a good Christian would almost have had to become a Jew.
If I had been a Jew and had seen such dolts and blockheads
govern and teach the Christian faith, I would sooner have
become a hog than a Christian.

They have dealt with the Jews as if they were dogs rather
than human beings; they have done little else than deride
them and seize their property. When they baptize them they
show them nothing of Christian doctrine or life, but only subject them to popishness and monkery. When the Jews then
see that Judaism has such strong support in Scripture, and
that Christianity has become a mere babble without reliance
on Scripture, how can they possibly compose themselves and

become right good Christians? I have myself heard from pious baptized Jews that if they had not in our day heard the gospel they would have remained Jews under the cloak of Christianity for the rest of their days. For they acknowledge that they have never yet heard anything about Christ from those who baptized and taught them.

I hope that if one deals in a kindly way with the Jews and instructs them carefully from Holy Scripture, many of them will become genuine Christians and turn again to the faith of their fathers, the prophets and patriarchs. They will only be frightened further away from it if their Judaism is so utterly rejected that nothing is allowed to remain, and they are treated only with arrogance and scorn. If the apostles, who also were Jews, had dealt with us Gentiles as we Gentiles deal with the Jews, there would never have been a Christian among the Gentiles. Since they dealt with us Gentiles in such brotherly fashion, we in our turn ought to treat the Jews in a brotherly manner in order that we might convert some of them. For even we ourselves are not yet all very far along, not to speak of having arrived.

When we are inclined to boast of our position we should remember that we are but Gentiles, while the Jews are of the lineage of Christ. We are aliens and in-laws; they are blood relatives, cousins, and brothers of our Lord. Therefore, if one is to boast of flesh and blood, the Jews are actually nearer to Christ than we are, as St. Paul says in Romans 9 [:5]. God has also demonstrated this by his acts, for to no nation among the Gentiles has he granted so high an honor as he has to the Jews. For from among the Gentiles there have been raised up no patriarchs, no apostles, no prophets, indeed, very few genuine Christians either. And although the gospel has been proclaimed to all the world, yet He committed the Holy Scriptures, that is, the law and the prophets, to no nation except the Jews, as Paul says in Romans 3 [:2] and Psalm 147 [:19-20], "He delares his word to Jacob, his statutes and ordinances to Israel. He has not dealt thus with any other nation; nor revealed his ordinances to them."

This sobering piece of Anti-Semitic writing is drawn from Chapter IX of Hitler's *Mein Kampf* entitled *Nation and Race*. It remains an everlasting monument to prejudice, hate, and the very worst that Western culture can muster.

The Jew has always been a people with definite-racial characteristics and never a religion; only in order to get ahead he early sought for a means which could distract unpleasant attention from his person. And what would have been more expedient and at the same time more innocent than the 'embezzled' concept of a religious community? For here, too, everything is borrowed or rather stolen. Due to his own original special nature, the Jew cannot possess a religious institution, if for no other reason because he lacks idealism in any form, and hence belief in a hereafter is absolutely foreign to him. And a religion in the Aryan sense cannot be imagined which lacks the conviction of survival after death in some form. Indeed, the Talmud is not a book to prepare a man for the hereafter, but only for a practical and profitable life in this world.

The Jewish religious doctrine consists primarily in prescriptions for keeping the blood of Jewry pure and for regulating the relation of Jews among themselves, but even more with the rest of the world; in other words, with non-Jews. But even here it is by no means ethical problems that are involved, but extremely modest economic ones. Concerning the moral value of Jewish religious instruction, there are today and have been at all times rather exhaustive studies (not by Jews; the drivel of the Jews themselves on the subject is, of course, adapted to its purpose) which make this kind of religion seem positively monstrous according to Aryan conceptions. The best characterization is provided by the product of this religious education, the Jew himself. His life is only of this world, and his spirit is inwardly as alien to true Christianity as his nature two thousand years previous was to the great founder of the new doctrine. Of course, the latter made no secret of his attitude toward the Jewish people, and when necessary he even took to the whip to drive from the temple of the Lord this adversary of all humanity, who then as always saw in religion nothing but an instrument for his business existence. In return, Christ was nailed to the cross, while our present-day party Christians debase themselves to begging for Jewish votes at elections and later try to arrange political swindles with atheistic Jewish parties — and this against their own nation.

On this first and greatest lie, that the Jews are not a race but a religion, more and more lies are based in necessary consequence. Among them is the lie with regard to the language of the Jew. For him it is not a means for expressing his thoughts, but a means for concealing them. When he speaks French, he thinks Jewish, and while he turns out German verses, in his life he only expresses the nature of his nationality. As long as the Jew has not become the master of the other peoples, he must speak their languages whether he likes it or not, but as soon as they bacame his slaves, they would all have to learn a universal language (Esperanto, for instance!), so that by this additional means the Jews could more easily dominate them!

To what an extent the whole existence of this people is based on a continuous lie is shown incomparably by the *Protocols of the Wise Men of Zion,* so infinitely hated by the Jews. They are based on a forgery, the *Frankfurter Zeitung* moans and screams once every week: the best proof that they are authentic. What many Jews may do unconsciously is here consciously exposed. And that is what matters. It is completely indifferent from what Jewish brain these disclosures originate; the important thing is that with positively terrifying certainty they reveal the nature and activity of the Jewish people and expose their inner contexts as well as their ultimate final aims. The best criticism applied to them, however, is reality. Anyone who examines the historical development of the last hundred years from the standpoint of this book will at once understand the screaming of the Jewish press. For once this book has become the common property of a people, the Jewish menace may be considered as broken.

G.

The Balfour Declaration was one of the great turning points in the history of the Jewish people. Although the British did not finally wish to honor the terms of this declaration, Balfour so raised the hopes of the Jewish people that not even the British Empire could restrain the force of their movement.

The text of the declaration made in 1917 reads as follows:

His Majesty's Government view with favour the establishment in Palestine of a national home for the Jewish people, and will use their best endeavours to facilitate the achievement of this object, it being clearly understood that nothing shall be done which may prejudice the civil and religious rights of the existing non-Jewish communities in Palestine or the rights and political status enjoyed by Jews in any other country.

H.

The official declaration concerning the Church and its relationship to Non-Christian religions promulgated by the Vatican II

Council in 1965 is of the utmost significance for Jewish-Christian relations. After centuries of hostility, the Church has attempted to right some of those wrongs which have for so long repressed the Jewish people.

4. As this sacred Synod searches into the mystery of the Church, it recalls the spiritual blood linking the people of the New Covenant with Abraham's stock.

For the Church of Christ acknowledges that, according to the mystery of God's saving design the beginnings of her faith and her election are already found among the patriarchs, Moses, and the prophets. She professes that all who believe in Christ, Abraham's sons according to faith (cf. Gal. 3:7), are included in the same patriarch's call, and likewise that the salvation of the Church was mystically foreshadowed by the chosen people's exodus from the land of bondage.

The Church, therefore, cannot forget that she received the revelation of the Old Testament through the people with whom God in his inexpressible mercy deigned to establish the Ancient Covenant. Nor can she forget that she draws sustenance from the root of that good olive tree onto which have been grafted the wild olive branches of the Gentiles (cf. Rom. 11:17-24). Indeed, the Church believes that by His cross Christ, our peace, reconciled Jew and Gentile, making them both one in Himself (cf. Eph. 2:14-16).

Also, the Church ever keeps in mind the words of the Apostle about his kinsmen, "who have the adoption as sons, and the glory and the covenant and the legislation and the worship and the promises; who have the fathers, and from whom is Christ according to the flesh" (Rom. 9:4-5), the son of the Virgin Mary. The Church recalls too that from the Jewish people sprang the apostles, her foundation stones and pillars, as well as most of the early disciples who proclaimed Christ to the world.

As holy Scripture testifies, Jerusalem did not recognize the tine of her visitation (cf. Lk. 19:44), nor did the Jews in large number accept the gospel; indeed, not a few opposed the spreading of it (cf. Rom. 11:28). Nevertheless, according to the Apostle, the Jews still remain most dear to God because of their fathers, for He does not repent of the gifts He makes nor of the calls He issues (cf. Rom. 11:28-29). In company with the prophets and the same Apostle, the Church awaits that day, known to God alone, on which all peoples will address the Lord in a single voice and "serve him with one accord" (Soph. 3:9; cf. Is. 66:23; Ps. 65:4; Rom. 11:11-32).

Since the spiritual patrimony common to Christians and Jews is thus so great, this sacred Synod wishes to foster and recommend that mutual understanding and respect which is the fruit above all of biblical and theological studies, and of brotherly dialogues.

True, authorities of the Jews and those who followed their lead pressed for the death of Christ (cf. Jn. 19:6); still, what happened in His passion cannot be blamed upon all the Jews then living, without distinction, nor upon the Jews of today. Although the Church is the new people of God, the Jews should not be presented as repudiated or cursed by God, as if such views followed from the holy Scriptures. All should take pains, then, lest in catechetical instruction and in the preaching of God's Word they teach anything out of harmony with the truth of the gospel and the spirit of Christ.

The Church repudiates all persecutions against any man. Moreover, mindful of her common patrimony with the Jews, and motivated by the gospel's spiritual love and by no political considerations, she deplores the hatred, persecutions, and displays of anti-Semitism directed against the Jews at any time and from any source.

Besides, as the Church has always held and continues to hold, Christ in His boundless love freely underwent His passion and death because of the sins of all men, so that all might attain salvation. It is, therefore, the duty of the Church's preaching to proclaim the cross of Christ as the sign of God's all-embracing love and as the fountain from which every grace flows.

5. We cannot in truthfulness call upon that God who is the Father of all if we refuse to act in a brotherly way toward certain men, created though they be to God's image. A man's relationship with God the Father and his relationship with his brother men are so linked together that Scripture says: "He who does not love does not know God" (1 Jn. 4:8).

The ground is therefore removed from every theory or practice which leads to a distinction between men or peoples in the matter of human dignity and the rights which flow from it.

As a consequence, the Church rejects, as foreign to the mind of Christ, any discrimination against men or harassment of them because of their race, color, condition of life, or religion.

Accordingly, following in the footsteps of the holy Apostles Peter and Paul, this sacred Synod ardently implores the Christian faithful to "maintain good fellowship among the nations" (1 Pet. 2:12), and, if possible, as far as in them lies, to keep peace with all men (cf. Rom. 12:18), so that they may truly be sons of the Father who is in heaven (cf. Mt. 5:45).

Each and every one of the things set forth in this Declaration has won the consent of the Fathers of this most sacred Council. We too, by the apostolic authority conferred on us by Christ, join with the Venerable Fathers in approving, decreeing, and establishing these things in the Holy Spirit, and we direct that what has thus enacted in synod be published to God's glory.

Rome, at St. Peter's, October 28, 1965

I, Paul, Bishop of the Catholic Church

BIBLIOGRAPHY

General

Baeck, Leo. *Judaism and Christianity.* Translated by W. Kaufmann. Philadelphia: Jewish Publication Society, 1958.

———. *This People Israel.* Translated by Albert H. Friedlander. Philadelphia: Jewish Publication Society, 1965.

Bamberger, Bernard Jacob. *The Story of Judaism.* New York: Schocken Books, 1964.

Baron, Salo W. *A Social and Religious History of the Jews,* rev. ed., 12 vols. New York: Columbia University Press, 1955.

Ben-Sasson, H.H., ed. *A History of the Jewish People.* Cambridge, MA: Harvard University Press, 1976.

Epstein, Isidore. *Judaism: A Historical Presentation.* Baltimore: Penguin Books, 1959.

Finkelstein, Louis, ed. *The Jews, Their History, Culture, and Religion,* 2 vols., 3rd edition. New York: Harper Brothers, 1960.

Ginzberg, Louis. *The Legends of the Jews,* 7 vols. Philadelphia: Jewish Publication Society, 1938.

——— *Students, Scholars, and Saints.* Philadelphia: Jewish Publication Society, 1928.

Graetz, Henrich. *A History of the Jews,* 6 vols. Philadelphia: Jewish Publication Society, 1891-98.

Grayzel, Solomon. *A History of the Jews: From the Babylonian Exile to the Present.* New York: New American Library, 1968.

Parkes, James. *A History of the Jewish People.* Baltimore: Penguin Books, 1964.

——— *The Conflict of the Church and the Synagogue.* London: Soncino Press, 1934.

Roth, Cecil. *A History of the Jews: From Earliest Times Through the Six-Day War,* rev. ed. New York: Schocken Books, 1970.

Sachar, Abram Leon. *A History of the Jews,* 5th ed. New York: Alfred A. Knopf, 1967.

Silver, Abba Hillel. *Where Judaism Differed.* Philadelphia: Jewish Publication Society, 1957.

Silver, Daniel Jeremy and Martin, Bernard. *A History of Judaism,* in two volumes. New York: Basic Books, Inc., 1974.

Ancient Israel Before 587 B.C.

Albright, William Foxwell. *The Biblical Period from Abraham to Ezra.* New York: Harper and Row, 1963.

Bright, John. *A History of Israel.* Philadelphia: Westminster Press, 1959.

Buber, Martin. *The Prophetic Faith.* Translated by Carlyle Witton-Davies. New York: Macmillan Co., 1949.

Heschel, Abraham J. *The Prophets.* New York: Harper and Row, 1962.

Kaufmann, Yehezkel. *The Religion of Israel: From its Beginnings to the Babylonian Exile.* Translated and abridged by Moshe Breenberg. New York: Schocken Books, 1972.

Noth, Martin. *The History of Israel,* rev. ed. New York: Harper and Brothers, 1960.

Vaux, Roland, ed. *Ancient Israel,* 2 vols. New York: McGraw-Hill, 1965.

Williams, Jay G. *Ten Words of Freedom: An Introduction to the Faith of Israel.* Philadelphia: Fortress Press, 1971.

—— *Understanding the Old Testament.* New York: Barron's Educational Series, 1972.

Chapter I: From Cyrus to the Last of the Hasmoneans

Primary Sources

Box, G.H., trans. *The Apocalypse of Ezra.* London: S.P.C.K., 1917.

Charles, R.H., ed. *The Apocrypha and Pseudepigrapha of the Old Testament,* 2 vols., ed. Oxford: 1913.

——., ed. and trans. *The Book of Enoch.* Naperville, IL: Alec R. Alleson, 1917.

——. *The Testaments of the Twelve Patriarchs.* London: A. & C. Black, 1908.

——. *The Book of Jubilees; or the Little Genesis.* London: A. & C. Black, 1902.

Morfill, W.R., trans. *The Book of the Secrets of Enoch.* Clarendon Press, 1896.

The New English Bible; the Acocrypha. London: Oxford University Press and Cambridge University Press, 1970.

Secondary Sources

Ackroyd, Peter R. *Exile and Restoration.* Philadelphia: Westminster Press, 1968.

Bickermann, Elias. *From Ezra to the Last of the Maccabees.* New York: Schocken Books, 1962.

Box, George Herbert. *Judaism in the Greek Period, from the Rise of Alexander the Great to the Intervention of Rome (333-63 B.C.).* Oxford: Clarendon Press, 1932.

Russell, D. S. *The Method and Message of Jewish Apocalyptic.* Philadelphia: Westminster Press, 1964.

Snaith, Norman. *The Jews from Cyrus to Herod.* New York: Abingdon Press, 1956.

Tcherikover, Victor. *Hellenistic Civilization and the Jews.* Translated by S. Applebaum. Philadelphia: Jewish Publication Society, 1959.

Chapter II: From Pompey to the Close of the Talmud (63 B.C.-500 C.E.)

Primary Sources

Epstein, Isidore, ed. *The Babylonian Talmud in English,* with introductions, translation and commentary, 36 vols. London: Soncino Press, 1935-53.

Freedman, H. and Simon, M., eds. *Midrash Rabbah,* translation with brief notes, 10 vols. London: Soncino Press, 1939.

Gaster, Theodor H. *The Scriptures of the Dead Sea Sect in English Translation,* rev. ed. Garden City, N.Y.: Doubleday and Co., 1964.

Joseph, Rabbi Akiba ben. *The Book of Formation (Sepher Yetzirah).* Translated and edited by Knut Stenring. New York: Ktav Publishing House, 1970.

Josephus, Flavius. *The Complete Works of Flavius Josephus.* Translated by William Whiston. Grand Rapids, Michigan: Kregel, 1970.

Lipman, Eugene J., ed. and trans. *The Mishnah, Oral Teachings of Judaism.* New York: Norton, 1970.

Philo, Judaeus. *Philo.* 10 vols. Translated by F. H. Colson and G. H. Whitaker. Cambridge, Mass.: Harvard University Press, 1961.

"The New Testament." In *The New English Bible.* London: Oxford University Press/Cambridge University Press, 1970.

Secondary Sources

Adler, Morris. *The World of the Talmud,* 2nd ed. New York: Schocken Books, 1963.

Bultmann, Rudolf. *Jesus and the Word.* Translated by L. P. Smith and E. H. Lantero. London: Collins, 1958.

Cross, Frank Moore. *The Ancient Library of Qumran,* rev. ed. Garden City, N.Y.: Doubleday and Co., 1961.

Davies, W. D. *Christian Origins and Judaism.* Philadelphia Westminster Press, 1962.

Finkelstein, Louis. *Akiba: Scholar, Saint, and Martyr.* New York: Covici, Friede, 1936.

———. *The Pharisees,* 2 vols. Philadelphia: Jewish Publication Society, 1938.

Glatzer, Nahum. *Hillel the Elder: The Emergence of Classical Judaism,* rev. ed. New York: Schocken Books, 1966.

Goodenough, Erwin R. *Jewish Symbols in the Greco-Roman Period,* 13 vols. Princeton: Princeton University Press, 1953-1969.

Guttmann, Alexander. *Rabbinic Judaism in the Making: The Halakhah from Ezra to Judah I.* Detroit: Wayne State University Press, 1970.

Herford, R. T. *The Pharisees.* London: G. Allen and Unwin, 1924.

Hoskyns, Sir Edwyn and Davey, Noel. *The Riddle of the New Testament.* London: Faber and Faber, 1931.

Kee, Howard Clark. *Jesus in History.* New York: Harcourt, Brace, and World, 1970.

Klausner, Joseph. *Jesus of Nazareth.* New York: Macmillan Co., 1925.

Moore, George Foot. *Judaism in the First Centuries of the Christian Era,* 3 vols. Cambridge, MA: Harvard University Press, 1930-32.

Neusner, Jacob. *A History of the Jews in Babylonia,* 5 Pts. New York: Humanities Press, 1969-70.

————. *There We Sat Down: Talmudic Judaism in the Making.* New York: Abingdon Press, 1972.

Schechter, Solomon. *Aspects of Rabbinic Theology: Major Concepts of the Talmud.* New York: Schocken Books, 1961.

Scholem, Gershom. *Jewish Gnosticism, Merkabah Mysticism, and Talmudic Tradition.* New York: The Jewish Theological Seminary of America, 1965.

Schurer, Emil. *The History of the Jewish People in the Time of Jesus.* Edited and introduced by Nahum N. Glatzer. New York: Schocken Books, 1961.

Schweitzer, Albert. *The Quest of the Historical Jesus.* Translated by W. Montgomery. New York: Macmillan Co., 1964.

Simon, Marcel. *Jewish Sects at the Time of Jesus.* Philadelphia: Fortress Press, 1967.

Strack, H. L. *Introduction to Talmud and Midrash.* Philadelphia: Jewish Publication Society, 1931.

Yadin, Yigael. *Bar-Kokhba.* New York: Random House, 1971.

————. *Masada, Herod's Fortress, and the Zealots' Last Stand.* New York: Random House, 1966.

————. *Message of the Dead Sea Scrolls.* New York: Simon and Schuster, 1957.

Zeitlin, Solomon. *Rise and Fall of the Judean State,* 2 vols. Philadelphia: Jewish Publication Society, 1967.

Chapter II: From Mohammed to the Expulsion from Spain (570-1492)

Primary Sources

Albo, Joseph. *Sefer ha-Ikkarin,* 5 vols. Edited and translated by I. Husik. Philadelphia: Jewish Publication Society, 1929-1935.

Bachya, ibn Pakuda. *Duties of the Heart,* 5 vols. Translated by M. Hyamson. New York: Bloch, 1925-45.

Ben Isaac, Solomon (Rashil). *Pentateuch with Targum Onkelos, Haphtaroth, and Prayers for the Sabbath and Rashi's commentary.* Edited and translated by M. Rosenbaum and A. M. Silbermann. London: Shapiro, Vallentine, 1946.

Freehof, Solomon B. *A Treasury of Responsa.* Philadelphia: Jewish Publication Society, 1962.

Ha-Levi, Yehudah. *Kitab al Khazari (Kuzari).* Translated by H. Hirschfeld. Cailingold, 1931.

Ibn Gabirol, Solomon B. *Improvement of the Moral Qualities: An Ethical Treatise of the Eleventh Century.* Edited by Stephen S. Wise. New York: A.M.S. Press, 1902.

Three Jewish Philosophers. Lewy, Hans et al., ed. New York: Harper and Row, 1965.

Maimonides, Moses. *The Code of Maimonides.* New Haven: Yale University Press, 1949-.

―――. *The Commandments, Sefer Ha-Mitzvoth of Maimonides,* 2 vols., Translated by Charles B. Chavel. London: Soncino Press, 1967.

―――. *The Guide of the Perplexed.* Translated and introduced by Shlomo Pines. Chicago University Press, 1963.

Gaon, Saadya. *The Book of Doctrines and Opinions.* Translated by S. Rosenblatt. New Haven: Yale University Press, 1948.

The Zohar. Sperling, H. et al, trans. London: Soncino Press, 1931-34.

Secondary Sources

Abrahams, Israel. *Jewish Life in the Middle Ages.* Philadelphia: Jewish Publication Society, 1911.

Guttmann, Julius. *Philosophies of Judaism: The History of Jewish Philosophy from Biblical Times to Franz Rosenweig.* Translated by David W. Silverman, and introduced by R. J. Werblowsky and Co., 1966.

Finkelstein, Louis, ed. *Rab Saadia Gaon: Studies in His Honor.* New York: Jewish Theological Seminary, 1944.

Husik, Isaac. *A History of Medieval Jewish Philosophy.* New York: Meridian Books, 1958.

Marcus, John R. *The Jew in the Medieval World.* Cincinnati: Union of American Hebrew Congregations, 1938.

Roth, Cecil. *A History of the Jews in England.* Oxford: Oxford University Press, 1941.

———. *The History of the Jews in Italy.* Philadelphia: Jewish Publication Society, 1946.

———. *A History of the Marranos.* Philadelphia: Jewish Publication Society, 1932.

Scholem, Gershom. *Major Trends in Jewish Mysticism,* 3rd rev. ed. New York: Schocken Books, 1954.

———. *On the Kabbalah and Its Symbolism.* Translated by Ralph Manheim. New York: Schocken Books, 1969.

Watt, W. Montgomery. *Muhammed: Prophet and Statesman.* London: Oxford University Press, 1961.

Chapter IV: Judaism in the Modern World

Agus, Jacob. *Modern Philosophies of Judaism.* New York: Behrman, 1971.

Bein, Alex. *Theodore Herzl.* Philadelphia: Jewish Publication Society, 1940.

Bergman, Samuel Hugo. *Faith and Reason: An Introduction to Modern Jewish Thought.* Translated and edited by Alfred Jospe. New York: Schocken Books, 1963.

Buber, Martin. *I and Thou.* Translated by Walter Kaufmann. New York: Charles Scribner's Sons, 1970.

———. *Jewish Mysticism and the Legends of Ba'al Shem.* Translated by Lucy Cohen. London: Dent, 1931.

———. *Tales of Hasidim,* 2 vols. New York: Schocken Books, 947.

———. *Ten Rungs: Hasidic Sayings.* New York: Schocken Books, 1962.

Cohen, I. *The Rebirth of Israel.* London: Goldston, 1952.

Diamond, Malcolm M. *Martin Buber, Jewish Existentialist.* New York: 1960.

Friedman, Maurice. *Martin Buber: The Life of Dialogue.* London: Routledge, 1955.

Glatzer, Nahum N. *Franz Rosenzweig: His Life and thought.* New York: Schocken Books, 1953.

Glazer, Nathan. *American Judaism.* Chicago: University of Chicago Press, 1957.

Grayzel, Solomon. *History of the Contemporary Jews from 1900 to the Present.* New York: Atheneum, 1969.

Harshberger, Luther H. and Mourant, John N. *Judaism and Christianity: Perspectives and Traditions,* with a forward by Rabbi Benjamin Kahn. Boston: Allyn and Bacon, 1968.

Hertzberg, Arthur. *The French Elightenment and the Jews.* Philadelphia: Jewish Publication Society, 1968.

——. *The Zionist Idea.* Garden City, N.Y.: Doubleday and Co., 1959.

Herzl, Theodore. *The Complete Diaries of Theodore Herzl,* 5 vols. Edited by R. Patai, Cranbury, N.J.: A. S. Barnes, n.d.

Heschel, Abraham. *God in Search of Man.* New York: Farrar, Straus & Cudahy, 1955.

Janowsky, Oscar I., ed. *The American Jew: A Reappraisal.* Philadelphia: Jewish Publication Society, 1965.

Kaplan, Mordecai. *Judaism as a Civilization: Toward a Reconstruction of American Jewish Life.* New York: Schocken Books. 1967.

Luzzatto, Moses. *Mesillat Yesharim: The Path of the Upright.* Translated by Mordecai M. Kaplan. Philadelphia: Jewish Publication Society, 1966.

Mendelssohn, Moses. *Jerusalem: And Other Jewish Writings.* Edited by Alfred Jospe. New York: Schocken Books, 1959.

Meyer, Michael A. *Origins of the Modern Jew.* Detroit: Wayne State University Press, 1967.

Newman, Louis I. *The Hasidic Anthology.* New York: Scribner's 1938.

Patai, R. *Israel Between East and West.* Philadelphia: Jewish Publication Society, 1953.

Raisin, M. *The Haskalah Movement in Russia.* Philadelphia: Jewish Publication Society, 1913.

Rotenstreich, Nathan *Jewish Philosophy in Modern Times.* New York: Holt, Rinehart, and Winston, 1968.

Schecter, Solomon. "The Chassidim." In *Studies in Judaism,* First Series. Philadelphia: Jewish Publication Society, 1915, pp. 1-45.

——. "Rabbi Elijah Wilna Gaon." In *Studies in Judaism,* First Series. Philadelphia: Jewish Publication Society, 1915, p. 73-98.

——. "Safed in the Sixteenth Century." In *Studies in Judaism,* Second Series. Philadelphia: Jewish Publication Society, 1908, pp. 202-285.

Simon, L. *Ahad Ha-Am: Essays, Letters and Memoirs.* London: East and West Library, 1946.

Stern, Selma. *The Court Jew.* Philadelphia: Jewish Publication Society, 1950.

Walter, H. *Moses Mendelssohn.* New York: Block, 1930.

Werblowsky, R. J. Z. *Joseph Karo, Lawyer and Mystic.* London: Oxford University Press, 1962.

QUEST BOOKS

are published by
The Theosophical Society in America,
a branch of a world organization
dedicated to the promotion of brotherhood and
the encouragement of the study of religion,
philosophy, and science, to the end that man may
better understand himself and his place in
the universe. The Society stands for complete
freedom of individual search and belief.
In the Theosophical Classics Series
well-known occult works are made
available in popular editions.

Zen and ᕼasidism

Student of Jewish culture, novelist and
playwright, Harold Heifetz suggests that
there are strong parallels between the two
spiritual disciplines of *Zen* and *Hasidism*. He
has compiled a book of essays featuring
distinguished scholars of each of these
systems of thought.

Available from.
QUEST BOOKS
306 West Geneva Road
Wheaton, Illinois 60187